Reviews

"Bart practices what he preaches. Throu[...]
he generously shares his eclectic profes[...]
ences to provide valuable stepping ston[...]
writers."

*--Darlene Cavalier, Founder, Science Cheerleader and SciStarter;
Professor of Practice, School for the Future of Innovation in Society,
Arizona State University*

"Are you looking to understand the world of technical communication and find your place in it? If so, *Heroic Technical Writing* is your trusted guide. Bart Leahy draws on his years of experience to provide insight into the profession and help you land your ideal job. Clear a space on your primary bookshelf: after you've read this book, you'll want to keep it handy for future reference."

--Larry Kunz, Fellow, Society for Technical Communication (STC)

"Bart Leahy provides entertaining, insightful, and rubber-meets-the-road advice for technical communicators at all levels, novice to professional. The author takes the reader on a journey through the practical side of technical communications and fills in the details of how to understand various customers' needs and how to effectively meet them. When reading the book, I felt like I was at the table with the author receiving hard-learned sage advice from a master – sometimes commiserating with him as the more difficult tasks presented themselves and were tackled, sometimes chuckling at the vagaries of the human condition, but mostly trying to take it all in."

--Les Johnson, Author and Space Technologist

Heroic Technical Writing

Making a Difference in the Workplace and Your Life

By Bart Leahy

ISBN 13: 978-0-578-72819-3

Cover art by Mars Dorian

TABLE OF CONTENTS

Acknowledgments

This book probably would not have happened without the instigation and encouragement (pushing) of multiple people because I'm lazy about publishing my own work. That said, my thanks go out to Hugh Stanley, who suggested I write a blog about "something you know a lot about"; Kate Miller, who suggested writing a book; Karla Kitalong, my former master's thesis advisor, who assigned my blog as required reading to her tech writing classrooms; and my advisors and "cheerleaders" who kept me going: Kathy Leahy (Mom), Colleen Otto (Sister), Dan Leahy (Padre), Marilyn Leahy (Bonus Mom), Darlene Cavalier, Karl Fry, Melinda Hough, Ciara Knight, Tara Maynard, Katrina van Oudheusden, Dede (D2) Rector, Laura Seward, and Tim & Gwen Van Voorhis.

All stock images were acquired through Pexels.com, a public-domain image-sharing site.

A huge dose of thanks must be reserved for my editor Betty Bolté, who graciously took time away from her own projects to apply some literary law and order to this text. ¡Mucho apreciado!

Introduction: The Mentor in the Hawaiian Shirt

I can see you now: you're in your early or mid-twenties. A little too free-thinking to be a business major, a little too practical to be a fine arts major. School's over, and you've got that deer-in-the-headlights expression that creeps up on liberal arts students who realize they have no idea what they're going to do with their lives. And worse, you don't even know what to do about it.

Whom do you ask?

Your family? They all took practical jobs: accountant, doctor, or lawyer. They didn't like your choice of major and thought it impractical in the first place.

You turn to your professors and discover that a lot of them have spent most of their time in academia. They suggest you pursue a master's degree until you figure out what you want to do. Another one suggests you consider teaching. Maybe one of them knows a friend who might be hiring a junior assistant editor on a nonprofit literary magazine. That all sounds well-meaning, but not quite what you had in mind.

This is getting you nowhere.

You've got a pragmatic bent to your thinking. You want a life: one that pays the bills, lets you buy a car that's less than ten years old, and afford a home that you wouldn't be embarrassed to show to a prospective significant other. There is another option, of course.

Friends compliment you on your writing. Perhaps you took a technical writing elective and realized some people actually pay their bills writing things like proposals, reports, training manuals, product sheets, or online help. You probably could do that. But what is the job really like? What sort of life would you be getting into?

Your technical writing prof tells you that there's a technical writer who hangs out at Walt Disney World. "He's easy to spot: gray hair, Van Dyke beard, and garish Hawaiian shirts. He's usually walking around the resorts between Epcot and Hollywood Studios after 4 p.m. He gives advice pretty regularly. He can answer the sorts of questions you're asking."

So you head for the walkway that connects the two theme parks, deciding to dress in tourist attire so your university t-shirt doesn't stand out too much. And there he is, as advertised: wearing an orange-and-yellow Star Wars shirt so loud your ears hurt to look at it. He's standing in line in one of the hotel stores, buying a bottle of water and a chocolate chip cookie.

You take a breath and take the plunge: "Are you Bart Leahy?"

You hear the flat tones of a Midwestern American accent. "Most days. How can I help you?"

"I want to be a technical writer. I want to know what the life is really like—the business world, the job, the people, networking—well, everything!"

The man's square, florid face breaks into a wide grin and he finishes buying his snack. "Sure, follow me."

In reality, I'm not this easy to find. However, I have spent over 20 years paying my bills as a business and technical writer. I can give you first-hand accounts of what the day-to-day life of a professional technical writer is like—the awesome stuff you can look forward to and the stuff that sucks that English professors won't tell you about. This book offers a writer's-eye-view of jobs ranging from Walt Disney World Resort to the National Aeronautics and Space Administration (NASA) to the Science Cheerleaders. I've been blogging for years to help students and young professionals get a feel for what daily life is like in the business world.

So, you want to know what the tech writer's life is really like? Great! Let's take a walk.

Chapter 1: So You Want to Be a Technical Writer...

Hi! I'm Bart Leahy, and I'd like to welcome you to my book. Grab a chair, sit back, relax, and make yourself comfortable. I'm here to help. I thought I'd take this first chapter to introduce myself, explain why I wrote this book, and let you know what you can expect to get out of it.

Why Should You Read This Book?

I'm what some folks call a "late bloomer." I was ten years old when I declared that I wanted to move to Florida, work for NASA, and be a writer. I managed to accomplish that ten-year-old's dream plus a few others. However, it took me much longer to "live the dream" than it should have. I didn't move to Florida until I was 22. I didn't get paid to write until I was 27. I didn't get a job with "technical writer" in the title until I was 32. I didn't get a job writing for NASA until I was 36. If this book accomplishes anything, I hope it will help you get your career moving in the right direction faster than mine did.

That long gap between imagining and living resulted, partly, from not getting (or taking) good advice. That need not be the case for you! As I walk you through the mysteries of being a technical writer, I'll throw in pointers to help you understand:

1. Products or services you're writing about.
2. Processes used in businesses and other organizations.
3. The people and politics that surround seemingly mundane work activities.
4. The things you can and should do to create and maintain your reputation—the most important asset you possess.
5. How to take care of yourself personally and professionally because, sadly, others likely won't.
6. How to make a positive, active—dare I say heroic?—contribution to your workplace.

This is a book about operating as a professional tech writer in the white-collar world.

What Are My Credentials and Why Should You Care What I Have to Say?

This is a fair question. I don't want to waste your time with a too-long biography, but I would like to share some of the highlights so you feel confident that I know what I'm doing.

I have a B.A. in English Literature from Northern Illinois University and an M.A. in Technical Writing from the University of Central Florida. That makes me an English major through and through.

I've written for three of the most demanding, image-conscious organizations in these United States: The Walt Disney Co., the U.S. Department of Defense (DoD), and NASA. At Disney I answered complaint letters; wrote management training classes at the in-house Disney University; developed documentation for the Information Technology department; and wrote training classes for the Disney Reservation Center. In my DoD guise, I wrote hardware proposals and technical documents for water, petroleum, and electrical logistics systems. At NASA, I wrote technical papers, education and outreach materials, and speeches for program managers based at Marshall Space Flight Center.

As a space reporter, I've written for Ad Astra, Space.com, The Space Review, and SpaceflightInsider.com.

I'm a member in good standing (most of the time) of the American Institute of Aeronautics and Astronautics (AIAA) and the Society for Technical Communication (STC). (Yes, I am a space geek, so you'll be reading about more than a few examples of life in the aerospace business. There are other lines of work.)

As a freelance technical writer, I've worked for Nissan USA; a couple of aerospace firms; and a bestselling business consultant.

I taught a semester of business writing at the University of Alabama in Huntsville.

In my free time, I've done volunteer work for the National Space Society, Space Frontier Foundation, Mars Foundation, Mars Society, Space Exploration Alliance, Tennessee Valley Interstellar Workshop, SciStarter, and the Science Cheerleaders, a group of NFL and NBA cheerleaders who have day jobs as scientists and engineers.

I've been writing a blog about the business of technical writing, which gave this book its name—Heroic Technical Writing—since 2011. I finished 2019 with just over 18,000 visitors and 32,000 views. Those are not Kardashian-level numbers, certainly, but respectable enough for such a niche subject.

The point is that yes, I know what I'm talking about.

You're a Member of Generation X. What Does Your Experience Have to Do with Mine?

You might still be questioning the value of my advice. I'm writing at a time where "OK, Boomer" is considered a great way for younger people to dismiss things said by the generation preceding mine because what they say sounds clueless or irrelevant.

You might be thinking, "It's easy for you to suggest X. You're a single, 50-something, middle-class, heterosexual white male with no kids!" Or: "It's easy for you to suggest that I do X. You've worked at Disney, Department of Defense, and NASA. You've got an extensive network. You worked in the corporate world before you became a freelancer. You grew up in a different economy from me." Et cetera.

I beg to differ. The advice I'm dispensing in 2020 is still relevant to technical writing students or professionals because I'm still working in the field, and the corporate, white-collar environment hasn't changed that much. I've stayed employed during recessions. The tools I use to ply my trade are the same ones you will be using. I'm facing the same job market you are—though I hasten to add that I see you as a colleague, not competition—and if I'm ever in a position to hire or work with you, I'd hope that you know how to function in a professional setting. If anything, I'm offering advice to give you a head start, so you don't have to be over 35 before you get your dream job.

That's part of what this book is about. Many of the following actions and behaviors[1] I advocate will serve you well in your career, regardless of where you work, even if you choose a career other than technical communication. This includes things such as producing the best

---

[1] "Summarizing My Career Advice," HeroicTechWriting.com 7 August 2017
https://heroictechwriting.com/2017/08/07/summarizing-my-career-advice/

work you can, getting along with your professional colleagues, building your professional network, and learning what you need to learn to get the career you want.

Does that sound relevant enough?

What Is This Book About?

Like my Heroic Technical Writing blog, this book is being written to help you, the aspiring technical writer, get better acquainted with the world of work. I will walk you through my personal approach to my career:

1. Product
2. Process
3. People and Politics
4. Professionalism
5. Pursuing Work
6. Protecting Yourself

Product

Product refers to the product (or service) your employer or customer is creating—in other words, the content about which you are writing. Some English majors get intimidated by the notion of having to learn science, technology, engineering, or math (STEM). After all, if we wanted to know or do math or those other things, we wouldn't have gotten a liberal arts degree, right? Some of you might work in one industry but hope to make the transition to another.

Regardless of your point of origin, I will spend some time helping you adjust your thinking so that you can write for number- or symbol-based disciplines. (Hint: You don't always have to know the math).

Process

You might have your own idea of how a proposal, paper, or marketing brochure should be done. However, if you're going to work for someone else, you will quickly learn that each business has their process for getting things done. The tasks that need to be done don't differ greatly by industry or company, but each will have its own little rules and procedures. This will be the "how to" section, explaining those tasks from the perspective of someone who's been there.

In addition, how organizations run their operations is something you learn on the job, not something they teach in colleges or vocational training centers. I'll share my varied experiences with doing tasks in the tech writing world.

People and Politics

No one writes in a vacuum. You have people on both ends of your products: customers, subject matter experts (SMEs), and your employer on one end of the action, and the intended audience on the other. In addition to those individuals, you also interact with other people on the job. When you get to your work location, you'll have to learn: who works with you? What do they do? Who does everyone report to? Who are your subject matter experts? What are the operational relationships? What's the internal history of the organization?

And of course whenever you work in groups of human beings, politics inevitably intrude. Who's in charge? Whose voice carries the most weight? How much authority do you have to do your work as you please? And what about the broader politics of our society—how do you handle those sensitivities on the job? These are realities that are not covered in most university classrooms, yet they affect almost every part of how you do your work.

Professionalism

Most of the topics in the first three sections of this book are beyond your control to some extent. The rest is up to you: how hard you work, how well you work with others, and how well you respond when the work hits your desk—or doesn't. You need to be conscious of the fact that your personal and professional reputations affect how much work you get.

This section addresses issues of personal behavior and responsibility. Call it the literary version of "charm school." I've made mistakes that you don't need to repeat. I'm Gen Xer—how many times do you think my big, snarky mouth got me in trouble? I see people younger than me making mistakes now that I didn't back in the day only because new technologies have created whole new ways to irritate bosses, clients, and coworkers. Your future success often depends on how you present yourself. A lot of it comes down to good manners, good behavior, and good sense.

Pursuing Work

So you want to be a technical writer…great! How do you actually get a tech writing job? How do you format your resume to best showcase your skills and background? If you're an introvert, do you still need to network? (Hint: yes!) If you take a business writing class, they might walk you through "the basics" of the business world: the cover letter, the resume, the portfolio, et cetera. Then again, they might not.

This book is not solely about the job-hunt. However, this section does offer some hints for the fresh-out (of college) job seeker as well as the mid-career job-hunter. I'm not talking only about the mechanics of interviews and resumes, but also how to truly think about pursuing a career you want. You want to be happy on the job, yes?

Protecting Yourself

There are things you need to do in a workplace to ensure your needs are being met as a professional: are you getting the information you need? Are you being respected? Are you informed about matters that affect your job security? Are you getting your bills paid? Are you getting benefits? More importantly, are you getting the results you want? Are you (dare I say it) happy?

This last section talks about the importance of looking after the physical, mental, emotional, and financial health of You, Inc. I'll touch on life in the corporate environment but also operating as a freelancer.

How to Read This Book

What does he mean, "How to Read This Book?" I know how to read! Okay, sure. However, it might help you a bit to know that this is written primarily as a reference text. This might be helpful if you're taking (or teaching) a technical writing class and want to include the practicing professional's perspective along with a more academic textbook. You can read Heroic Technical Writing cover to cover if you like to get the whole story of the technical writing life; however, it's broken up into specific topics so you can focus on one item or area if you choose. If there is relevant content to be found in previous chapters, I've done my best to refer to them.

So, reading all that, are you ready to dive in? As I've said before, I'm here to help. No, really…

Part I: Product

Chapter 2: What Is Technical Writing?

My joking shorthand for technical writing is "translating Engineerish into English." More seriously, the dictionary definition of technical writing is writing and organizing specialized or complex content into a format that allows the reader to take constructive action in the real world.

Learning technical content can be one of the biggest barriers to liberal arts majors considering a career in technical writing. It's understandable, to some extent: science and technology both have plenty of equations. However, most of the writing that needs to be done does not require equations because you're translating science and engineering writing into information that non-scientists or non-engineers can use to do something important to them.

So how much science or engineering do you really need to know to work as a technical writer? As with many things, the answer is, it depends.

What follows are some discussions about how aspiring technical writers can learn and make themselves useful in different types of writing. These areas include:

- Business and marketing
  - Journalism
  - Proposals
  - Technical/white papers
  - Education and outreach
  - Other business
- Engineering and science processes
- Science, engineering, and business—differences and similarities
- Writing for the military-industrial complex
- Advocacy

Business and Marketing
Writing for a scientific or engineering company can pay the bills, even if you aren't writing for engineers directly. Among these business-side jobs are: journalists, proposal writers, technical or white paper writers, education and outreach writers, and other business writers.

Science- and engineering-related organizations generate a lot of content, which must be "translated" to make it interesting or useful to the general public, so there is a demand for these types of writers. The Department of Labor's Bureau of Labor Statistics states that the likely job growth for the profession is 8 percent between 2018 and 2028, which is better than the national average.[2]

Journalism

I once worked a side gig as a journalist for a space news website (SpaceflightInsider.com). Space journalists do not work directly for an aerospace company but a news media organization, sharing information about space activities for the general public and providing an assessment or explanation of what's going on. These assessments are not completely unbiased, but the level of bias will vary with the writer and their publication's editorial preferences. Some media outlets, for example, think the private sector can do no wrong and that NASA can do no right. Others have the opposite view. Some publications—and I think Spaceflight Insider is one of them—try to report the news as it is in a relatively unbiased (albeit pro-space) fashion. Aerospace or other science and technology writers enjoy an advantage if they have a technical background, but such is not always required. If you're interested in other topics, the odds are good that there are similar roles available in those industries as well.

Proposals

Proposal writers work for technology companies hoping to sell a product or service to the government or another company. Intra-government and intra-business proposals also exist. For example, different offices within NASA or a private-sector company compete for internal research and development (IRAD) money. This type of writing is a lot more technical than feature-story article writing, as you're getting into the nuts and bolts of how some new widget functions. Some of that information can be highly technical, export-controlled, or proprietary.

---

[2] Bureau of Labor Statistics, U.S. Department of Labor, Occupational Outlook Handbook, Technical Writers,
on the Internet at https://www.bls.gov/ooh/media-and-communication/technical-writers.htm (visited January 4, 2020).

Proposal writing is also marketing writing, because you are using your words to sell your company's or team's product. As such, it differs from journalism in that it has no pretensions about being unbiased: you want your product to get funded. Technical proposal writers develop their content in several ways, including conducting internal and external research; editing content written by subject matter experts (SMEs); or interviewing SMEs and writing content based on those discussions. Proposal teams can be distributed across the country or all crowded together into a single room. The bottom line for proposal writers is to get the proposal out the door in the proper format, on time, and sell the program.

Technical/White Papers

My first job at NASA's Marshall Space Flight Center was ghost writing technical papers for managers of the Ares Launch Vehicles. These papers were presented to other engineers at technical conferences for groups such as the American Institute of Aeronautics and Astronautics (AIAA), Institute of Electrical and Electronic Engineers (IEEE), and the Joint Army-Navy-NASA-Air Force (JANNAF) Conference. Depending on the type of technology you're writing about and the interests of your audience, you might be required to write about the same content for multiple conferences, just from slightly different angles.

This type of writing can be more technical than the proposal writing described above, as the author is generally less interested in "selling" a program and more interested in demonstrating capabilities and progress. White papers are a variation of technical or conference papers. They describe existing or nearly existing technology that could be used to solve another problem, not directly related to its original mission.

Education and Outreach

While conference papers are focused on reaching the technical community, education and outreach writing usually is geared toward a more general audience: the STEM[3]-interested public, visitors to science centers or booths, elected officials, or educators hoping to get students interested in STEM through science- or technology-related content. The content is still technical, albeit simplified to match the

---

[3] STEM = Science, Technology, Engineering, and Math

educational level of the audience. This could include explaining why space activities add value to life on Earth or relating space technology to more familiar Earth analogues for comparison. I once worked with the education and outreach team to create a fact sheet that was distributed at NASCAR races. As part of this work, I dug up facts such as comparisons between the Ares I rocket and the horsepower of your standard race car. The graphic designers developed a simulated image of an Ares rocket flying down a racetrack straightaway.

Some engineers I know call this type of writing "dumbing down," forgetting that they, too, were once in fourth grade and unable to do calculus or describe how turbopumps work. I don't mind outreach writing at all, though I confess to being more effective with audiences age 18+. If what I write gets students interested in space or wanting to pursue science or engineering as a career, then I've done my job.

Other Business

Into the "other business writer" category I would lump folks who write marketing brochures, training materials, web content, press releases, executive sales correspondence, and other internal publications necessary to keep a business running. Some of these tasks require teaming up with a graphic designer, engineering expert, or an instructional designer; others require a frank discussion with a chief executive officer (CEO) asking for something very specific.

Engineering and Science Processes

Engineering and scientific writers are, for the most part, actual engineers or scientists who are designing or building equipment, or are sufficiently familiar with the technology that scientists/engineers trust them to write down procedures for how the actual work gets done: exploring the universe, designing a telescope, developing a piece of guidance software, building a rocket, or launching a spacecraft.

At NASA, I helped write or (usually) edit several dozen internal operational plans that the agency used to describe how they planned to design, develop, test, fly, and evaluate their launch vehicle. This could include the Systems Engineering Management Plan (SEMP), Concept of Operations (CONOPS), Payload User Guide (PUG), or other internal documents. Information technology documents, such as the ones I wrote for Disney, included design documents along with functional or interface descriptions.

11

This is as close to working on the hardware as an English major is likely to get. Much of this work can be described as process or technical documentation. If a SME is providing the content, your goal is to make the science or technology understandable to an external audience, usually someone without the same level of expertise. That's good because that includes you. If you don't understand something, you can ask for clarification; if you understand something better, you can explain it better to someone else and use words that make sense to you.

Science writing is a slightly different category from writing engineering papers or documents. Most of the engineering journals I've written for—aside from IEEE—are not peer-reviewed. Science paper writing (such as for Nature, which is perhaps the premier outlet for sharing scientific knowledge) is written by scientists for scientists, with the expectation that it will be reviewed, picked apart, and eventually replicated to confirm the results. I suppose the reason I put science writing in such a different category is because the engineering author knows what he or she is trying to accomplish at the outset of a project. Scientists go into their work seeking and expecting the unknown. They have to provide a precise description of their experimental methodology; data to back up their assertions about their discovery; and a lot of background research to encompass every study that came before.

Science writing—whether you're talking about life on Earth, conditions on Mars, or the potential existence of "dark matter" in deep space—is simultaneously more detailed and less certain than engineering paper writing. The authors are expected to use all of the proper terminology and the approved, scientific passive-voice style to demonstrate that they are, in fact, real scientists and know what they're talking about. For me, science writing is the most challenging type of space writing because it requires that you speak the language of science, which includes statistics (at a minimum) and often calculus and a few other forms of math. Your experience could vary.

Science, Engineering, and Business—Differences and Similarities
As noted previously, there are three broad categories of "technical" writing: science, engineering, and business. Scientists, engineers, and businesspeople often are not the same kinds of people, nor are their content needs the same.

Rather than generalize overmuch and get myself into a heap of trouble, I'll share some measured observations of my experiences with these three groups.

Writing for Engineers

I spent most of my six years at Marshall Space Flight Center writing for engineers. These are the folks who are trying to apply physical laws to human problems. They design hardware or software in what appears to be a linear process (design, develop, test, evaluate, repeat until suitable for operations), but which is in fact rather chaotic and creative. Engineers are often a conservative lot. I don't mean they're all Republicans or Tories. I mean that they tend to operate very empirically, are distrustful of wild claims ("marketing"), and have a healthy appreciation for Murphy's Law.[4]

One example of this conservatism appears in the designs they create: they add something called "margin" to everything. For example (this is not relating to any particular product, I hasten to add), the combustion chamber of a rocket—where the fire and smoke occur before shooting out the nozzle—might create an internal pressure of X pounds per square inch. While X might be the theoretical maximum or "nominal" expected pressure, the engineer(s) designing the combustion chamber will add a margin of strength—what I call a fudge factor—on top of that to make sure the chamber doesn't over-pressurize and explode.

All well and good, right?

Well, that would be fine if it was only the combustion chamber engineers doing that. However, down the hall the avionics people are looking at the temperatures this rocket engine will produce, and they're thinking, "Our cables are going to melt!" so they add more insulation to the cables to prevent them melting. Meanwhile, on the other end of the engine, the folks designing the nozzle—the bell-shaped portion of the engine that points the fire and smoke in a useful direction—are also concerned by the heat of the propellants coming out of the combustion chamber, so they thicken up the walls of their nozzle so it doesn't crack or melt.

---

[4] "Anything that can go wrong will go wrong."

At the end of this process, the chief engineer (CE) or project manager (PM) looks at the overall design of the rocket engine, sees the weight, and loses her temper because the bloody thing is now X pounds over the design specification. So the CE or PM tells the subsystems engineers to go back, "sharpen their pencils," and reduce the amount of extra mass so the engine still performs its designed function, but isn't as heavy. The creative part comes in "trades" (tradeoffs) between margins of safety on this part versus that, and then making sure everything fits within the allotted mass, performance, and cost budget.

So how does the technical writer fit into this sort of culture? When I worked for the Ares Projects, the technical papers were usually written for an audience interested in what progress was being made, what sorts of technologies were being used, and how technical challenges were being addressed. The most important things the writer has to do are:

- Learn quickly.
- Get the terminology and acronyms right.
- Understand how the overall system works (what it's supposed to do).
- Understand what the individual parts of the system are and how they work.

In a sense, the Ares technical writers became system engineers or project managers without the engineering work or responsibility, which is a pretty sweet gig if you're a space geek but lack the skills or temperament to be an actual engineer. However, perhaps what I like best about writing for engineers is that there's a definite logic to their work: every part is designed by human beings with a human purpose in mind. You know why things are there and what they're supposed to do.

Writing for Scientists

As with engineers, so it is with scientists: no two are exactly alike. They are there to observe the known universe, anything from bacteria to black holes, and figure out how they work. They require precision of a different sort from engineers and have a different understanding of, and tolerance for, vagueness or unknown-unknowns (things we don't know we don't know). The precision that scientists seek revolves around data: how it is captured and how it is characterized.

They want to know: what equipment was used, how it was calibrated, to what degree of precision, and with what margin for error.

Where things get creative for the scientists is when they formulate theories to account for data that doesn't fit an existing theory or for which a theory hasn't been developed yet. To take a space-age example, galactic cosmic rays (GCRs) are a type of highly charged particle that had never been detected until we sent satellites into orbit because we are protected from them by the Earth's atmosphere. GCRs originate from outside our solar system—we know this because they're not coming from the direction of the Sun or the other planets—but the question remains: where did they come from? What creates them? Where are these GCR-generators, and how can they launch particles through space with such energy that they strike our upper atmosphere at nearly the speed of light? For scientists, the creative part comes from trying to develop theories that would account for all these questions and then from developing a repeatable experiment that backs up the theory.

Scientists are inordinately fond of the question "Why?" If you have kids who ask that a lot, give them a science textbook. If they start wanting to do science experiments, you might have a budding scientist on your hands. If they start asking, "How does that work?" or "What is that good for?" or saying, "I can make a cool machine with that," you've probably got an engineer. If they say, "I know how you can make money from that," you might have a potential businessperson in your family. And if they keep trying to write down or explain what they learned to you, you might have a technical writer on your hands.

As a technical writer in the scientific environment, I've noticed more emphasis on math than in the engineering world. It's not that engineers don't require math, but rather that math isn't always necessary to explain what a machine or program is doing. By contrast, when writing a technical paper or proposal, scientists seem to require more math to explain or justify their approaches to particular problems.

Another challenge when writing for scientists is that sometimes they don't understand what's going on, either—note the creative part above. I believe Arthur C. Clarke stated that "Eureka!" isn't the sound of progress about to happen, but rather, "That's strange…" In situations where the origins of a puzzle or outcomes of an experiment are not known, scientists are much more forgiving about the uncertainty factor. Often they just don't know what's happening, which is why they're doing an experiment in the first place: to see if they can figure it out. Engineers want to know, with as much certainty as possible, how a test is going to come out, or they won't proceed.

Lastly, scientists demonstrate their own form of caution when it comes to publishing results. They are more hesitant to propose a theory for the heretofore unexplained because they might be wrong. In this case, scientists and engineers (usually) share a common skepticism for "marketing" or hype. More often than not, they'll say, "Let me see your data."

Writing for Businesspeople

Technical writers writing for businesspeople are supporting individuals whose primary function is to advance or maintain the effective day-to-day functioning of a business, government agency, nonprofit, or other organization. Their work is practical and grounded in everyday needs: how do we get our product/service out to more customers? How do we make sure our people deliver the product/service effectively? How do we recover if things go awry?

Businesspeople—another, less respected word might be bureaucrats—are concerned with keeping an operation going, whether it be a scientific, engineering, technical, service, governmental, or other type of firm. They operate at the intersection between people and business: how the money is handled, how products or services are delivered, or how operations can be made better. There are businesspeople inside of NASA who have little to do with building rockets or studying the stars but are nevertheless needed to keep the agency functioning. Someone has to make certain that the engineers and scientists have the funding, materials, and facilities they need. Someone has to make certain enough good scientists and engineers are hired and trained. Someone has to keep Congress informed of what and how the agency is doing: operationally, scientifically, and technically.

Many of these activities have concrete outcomes, though admittedly some are harder to quantify (how do you measure how well your organization's "message" got out?). You can argue about how many businesspeople or bureaucrats an organization really needs—and they do get downsized occasionally—but without them, the people doing "the actual work" (producing goods and services, studying the universe, building the next cool gadget) would have to take time out of their creative work to handle marketing, accounting, hiring and firing, or cleaning the meeting rooms. Think of bureaucracy as a necessary evil.

Good, Bad, or Indifferent?

Human beings were doing business and performing engineering thousands of years before we had science. Science, as currently understood using the scientific method, has only been around for a couple of centuries. The rapid technological advances our civilization has seen since 1800 have been fed by our vastly broadened understanding of the universe and its physical laws. Both scientists and engineers need to make new discoveries or practices understandable to the taxpaying public or skeptical investor. Sometimes that means hiring a professional communicator.

The writing needs for each field vary, so where you choose to hang your writing hat will often depend on what kinds of questions you like to answer ("Why does it do that?" vs. "What's it good for?" vs. "How can we make or save money from that?"). I confess to an affinity for engineering. I have other friends who are more inclined to the science or business side of things. Regardless of your "favorite," science and engineering are complementary, with each providing a unique perspective on the other, and the businesspeople keep the bills paid and the operation humming along smoothly. For the foreseeable future, these professions will continue to lead the nation and the world in creating the future. It's fun to have a front-row seat.

Writing for the Military-Industrial Complex

The Department of Defense (DoD) is its own special animal within the technical writing world. It's worth taking the time to understand how they operate because the military has a unique culture, and not everyone is suited to it. I have a good friend, for example, who absolutely refuses to work for DoD on moral grounds. I don't begrudge her position, I'm a rather nonviolent person myself. However, I've also grown up with family members who served in the armed forces for a different set of moral reasons. If writing about hardware (or software) that could be used to destroy people and property bothers your conscience, don't work for them.

As it happens, I worked for a company that handled petroleum and water logistics, power systems, transport (truck) maintenance, and security systems, practically everything except the stuff that kills people and breaks things on purpose.

The Work

Before being hired for a U.S. defense company, you will have to meet certain minimum requirements:

- Are you a U.S. citizen? In some cases, citizens of closely allied countries (Canada, UK, Australia, and New Zealand) who already hold a clearance with their country can get a clearance here as well.
- Can you obtain some form of security clearance by passing a background check? For the lowest-level clearance, this involves a criminal records check and a credit check, nothing more. If you want to handle the really secret stuff, the background checks can be exhaustive, taking months to complete, as they will include the FBI interviewing your friends, coworkers, and neighbors.

Once you get your clearance—whatever is required based on the sensitivity of the information you're handling—you'll find yourself taking extra precautions not to talk about your work with outsiders, which could mean friends and family, other companies, or even other people within your company. The "need to know" is very much a guideline for handling your communications. You likely will have to encrypt some of your physical files, your computer, or your emails.

Along with the clearance will come a non-disclosure agreement (NDA), which is your signed, legally binding promise not to disclose the information in your head or files during or after your employment. Failure to do so carries with it a lot of potential consequences, including being fired or sued by your employer as well as being charged with and being imprisoned for espionage by the government.

If you are hired as a technical writer in the DoD environment and have no military background, odds are that you're being hired to write proposals, marketing materials, websites, or other outreach content. While I've edited technical manuals for some of the hardware, most often a former operator of the hardware will be hired to write them. The logic of that is simple: if you've handled the equipment before, you know what the reader's needs are, what their skill levels are, and what they need to know to operate the hardware safely. If you're not a technical person, however, you might still be tasked to assist the expert, especially if a project has a short deadline. Often you'll get to study some really cool toys (tools—these folks don't like it when you call their technology "toys") in person.

As a contractor supporting one or more units within the Armed Forces, you'll come to learn the needs, constraints, and politics of your customers. There are a lot of rules and regulations governing how DoD interacts with civilian contractors to prevent things like fraud or corruption, and those rules are—so far as I observed (and a 2018 Pentagon audit showed[5])—effective.

The Workplace Culture
Many defense contractors—called "Beltway Bandits" or "Highway Helpers" in the Washington, DC, area—often are staffed with retired military personnel. That means they are predominantly male, if only because up until recently, the U.S. Armed Forces were a male-heavy enterprise. Carrying over habits from their former military careers, these people maintain hierarchical (top-down) organizations that can still sometimes be sexist and prone to male humor. Given the higher percentage of women in the armed forces now, and the federal laws prohibiting this sort of behavior, NSFW (not safe for work) comments have all but disappeared. There are also individuals who are just politer than others. In any case, the environment can require a little skin thickening.

Military retirees come in from all ranks, from sergeants and Navy chief petty officers all the way up to generals and admirals. They tend to carry their military behaviors over into the civilian world as well.

---

[5] Mehta, Aaron. "Here's what the Pentagon's first-ever audit revealed." Defense News. 16 November, 2018 https://www.defensenews.com/pentagon/2018/11/15/heres-what-the-pentagons-first-ever-audit-found/.

(A military friend who reviewed this section noted that a retired general we worked with didn't expect you to call him "sir," but then he wouldn't correct you when you did, either.)

I recall a manager asking me soon after I moved over to NASA what the biggest difference was between DoD and the space agency. I said, "People talk to you in the men's room [at NASA]." In general, you'll find the higher the need for secrecy, the less extraneous chat you'll hear.

All this snark aside, you can get a better understanding of how these retired military personnel think by how they approach their work. They might throw around a lot of harsh language and joke around, but when it comes to the work, they are deadly serious. This is often because in their previous lives, they had been the soldiers, sailors, airmen, or marines using the equipment they are now supporting as the contractor. Their lives and careers depended on that equipment functioning well in the field; they know what can go wrong; and they apply this knowledge to making the equipment as good as possible. This is one advantage of the "revolving door" between the government and contractor worlds.

As a civilian in this mix, I had to learn some of the conventions the hard way. One of the more useful lessons I learned was from the aforementioned former general. That lesson being: when a problem occurs, whether it's my fault or not, do not try to explain ("No excuses, sir"); just snap to it and fix the issue. One can also find oneself the target of good-natured ribbing, much like a new recruit. If you're told to go hunt for a snipe, a gallon of prop wash, or ten feet of flight line, odds are, someone is pulling your leg.

Another thing I picked up from listening to the banter among "the boys" is that you can joke about the mission, the hardware, or the situation; however, you *don't* joke about the service (Army, Navy, Air Force, Marines, or Coast Guard) unless you've been in that service. You also don't joke about your leadership or the people being sent to *do* a mission. Mind you, that might be what I internalized from that particular company. I worked for a much larger defense contractor years later and the level of humor was practically nil. Just as in any other new job, start your first few months listening before contributing to the merriment.

Lastly, having interacted with U.S. veterans ranging from Vietnam to the 9/11 era, I acquired even more respect for the men and women serving in our armed forces. They volunteered and are well trained to go into dangerous situations or lead other soldiers/sailors/airmen/marines in those situations. They take their responsibilities very seriously; are fiercely loyal to their peers and these United States; and while often smart-alecks as only Americans can be, they are nowhere *near* the sociopathic stereotypes portrayed in the media, TV or movies. Their attitude can be contagious, and that's a good thing. At least it was for me.

Advocacy

Advocacy is usually a nonprofit activity designed to change the public's mind about a particular issue. I've defined technical advocacy as a combination of marketing, technical writing, and politics because what you're doing is selling voters or elected officials on specific policies that affect science or technology.

Your hot-topic interest might be nuclear power, the environment, animal rights, genetically modified organisms (GMOs), or (like me) space exploration. Regardless of the topic, you need to write accurately while also engaging with politicians and members of the general public in a way that helps your cause win the day. To write effectively in technical advocacy, you need to be willing to read public laws, government regulations, and sometimes technical specifications to acquire critical factual information. The critical aspects of advocacy will be familiar to rhetoric students: ethos (credibility), pathos (emotion), and logos (logic). You might be able to draw upon in-house experts who understand the science or technology, but the writer must present information to multiple audiences credibly, emotionally, and logically to win the day…write heroically, as it were.

Now that you know the types of environments and jobs out there, let's talk about actually writing!

Chapter 3: How to Get Smart on Your Subject Matter

Writers spend a remarkable amount of time sitting (or walking) around just thinking. In Chapter 3, we'll review the various types of thinking required to get your content right for your audience, situation, and intended outcome. You might, for example, learn to think like a science fiction writer. Additionally, I'll touch on research methods and how to organize the content you assemble along the way. The more work you do up front, the easier you make your audience's reading experience.

The Keys to Technical Writing: Audience, Situation, and Outcome
Before you start writing any product, it is best to know your Audience, Situation, and Outcome. If you learn nothing else from this book, at least remember them. They'll help you ask the right questions and think clearly whenever you get a new assignment.

Audience
Ideally, you should identify at least one person in your target audience. That individual will have a specific background, education, understanding of the world (or your organiza-

Who's Reading?

tion), and other factors that determine how they will receive your message. You need to get educated about who your audience is, regardless of whom you are writing for, and make certain the content and tone you're using meets that audience's needs or expectations.

Situation
Why is this particular document, tweet, or message being written now? What is the social or political environment into which it is being placed? Is the content good news, bad news, or relatively neutral? How much connection does your audience have to the content? What is their relationship to you or the organization you're writing for? How are people likely to feel or react upon reading or hearing the content? Is there a time sensitivity to the information? Does the time your audience receives the message make a difference in how they'll receive it (first thing Monday morning vs. 3 p.m. on a Friday afternoon)? All of these factors affect how you phrase your content.

Outcome

You cannot control your audience's reaction, but you can at least hope to direct it. Regardless of the circumstances, your content should be written with a specific outcome in mind. Usually you want your audience to just be

> How Do You
> WANT Them to
> React?

aware of the content, comply with it, make a decision after reading it, feel a specific emotion from reading it, or change their mind and agree with it.

In the end, business and technical writing are what might be called instrumental writing in that you expect the audience to take some specific action based on the content. It's a simple notion—audience, situation, outcome—but it can also become complex, as you'll see in subsequent chapters. However, it's also a form of creative wordsmithing that has an impact in the real world.

Everything I Needed to Know about Tech Writing I Learned from Reading Science Fiction

Writing about technology can be disorienting. My first tech-focused technical writing job was in Disney's Information Technology (IT) department. In IT, I faced a mysterious world. I faced unfamiliar concepts, unfamiliar terminology, and an alphabet soup of acronyms to memorize. It was difficult to know how to decipher what was going on or where to start. Then I realized that this feeling was familiar: Of course: it was like reading science fiction!

The tasks of the science fiction (also called speculative fiction or SF) writer and the technical communicator are in fact similar. The SF writer places a character, the reader, or both into an unfamiliar environment; creates challenges for the character (reader) resulting from real or imagined aspects of science; and provides solutions to those challenges based on situated knowledge. A technical communicator seeks to help the user understand an unfamiliar technology and solve certain problems based on the communicator's description of that technology.

If you've never been a SF reader, the genre can give you a new window into your work.

Science Fiction Defined

A prominent critic in the field, Brian Aldiss, described science fiction (SF) as

> The search for a definition of mankind and his status in the universe which will stand in our advanced but confused state of knowledge (science), and is characteristically cast in the Gothic or post-Gothic mode.[6]

Gothic fiction, of course, is "a type of romance developed in the late eighteenth century, relying on suspense and mystery and containing a number—a limited number—of startling props."[7] The most famous Gothic novels are Frankenstein and Dracula.

SF deals with mysteries of science, some known, some invented. Technical communication deals with science and technology, some of which might be mysterious to the neophyte technical writer or reader. However, by reading SF stories, you can find clues to making the unknown known.

The field of SF is as broad and varied as other forms of fiction, like westerns or crime dramas. However, three subgenres of SF best demonstrate the connection between the fictional and nonfictional worlds: "enormous big thing" stories, time travel stories, and sociological stories.

"Enormous Big Thing" Stories

These are stories where characters explore massive, unknown alien artifacts. Much like the protagonists in these types of stories, technical communicators must constantly reevaluate their preconceptions, experimenting with new ideas until they finally "get it" (the central mystery of the environment).

Examples:
Ringworld by Larry Niven
Rendezvous with Rama by Arthur C. Clarke
Orbitsville by Bob Shaw

Lesson Learned: Don't be afraid of metaphor and simile when constructing your mental model of a process.

---

[6] Aldiss, Brian, Trillion Year Spree, pg. 25
[7] Ibid., pg. 16

To reach non-technical readers, the SF writer uses vivid, descriptive language relatable to the non-scientific reader. Otherwise, most likely only people with science degrees would read SF. The SF writer must rely on a variety of similes and metaphors to convey their "vision," either through exposition or dialogue, as characters voice their reactions to the unknown.

This metaphorical thinking can apply to the daily work of a technical communicator, especially when brainstorming about a new topic. By playing with metaphors, the technical communicator can find a common frame of a reference for the potential reader. The writer can also use the power of words to describe a scientific theory that changes our view of reality or to introduce potential customers to a new product with little or no precedent in the market.

Time Travel Stories

In typical time-travel stories, protagonists face the possibility of altering the known order of history; in "alternate history" stories, protagonists live in worlds where history has already taken a different turn. In both cases, technical communicators can learn lessons in ordering operations—how processes "should" happen and how to avoid "paradoxes."

Examples:
"All You Zombies–" by Robert A. Heinlein (short story)
Time Patrol by Poul Anderson
Terminator, Terminator 2, 12 Monkeys (motion pictures)

Lesson Learned: Like SF writers, technical communicators must ensure that complex information flows in a logical order.

Technical manuals can be written for technologies with multiple, concurrent, or "dependent" operations. Written content must be clear to the user so that operations occur in the proper order to prevent incorrect assembly, damage to hardware, or harm to people.

As technology gets more and more complex, it becomes more and more important that the documents supporting the technologies are written clearly, in a useful, logical, and functionally correct order. Otherwise, a minor error in the document could result in large user errors further down the line. This is sometimes called a "cascade effect," where one minor change can have large unintended consequences. Alternate history SF teaches us that sometimes small events or changes can have a major impact down the road. If a process goes wrong, engineers (like readers of alternate history) will try to trace back through a process until they discover where the correct version of events diverged from what was "supposed" to happen.

The SF-reading technical communicator, acting as a project's institutional memory, can help guard against errors and unintended consequences. By becoming familiar with fictional opportunities and problems, the technical communicator can better anticipate them in the real world.

Sociological SF Stories

A protagonist is placed into an unusual social environment and must learn to act appropriately based on new social, legal, political, or other mores. Such situations often occur in our work lives, especially when new technologies affect the way people interact with each other. Sociological SF enables readers to think about the social and ethical implications of the technologies they describe.

Examples:
The Left Hand of Darkness by Ursula K. LeGuin
The Caves of Steel, The Naked Sun, and I, Robot by Isaac Asimov
Red Mars, Green Mars by Kim Stanley Robinson
Cat's Cradle by Kurt Vonnegut

Lesson Learned: Science fiction is about human beings and human concerns.

One of the best ways I've found SF to translate into technical communication is by its focus on the end user. It's easy to get lost in the complexity or wonder of technology, but science fiction stories truly excel when they give us a relatable protagonist to focus on and a direction for that character to follow. In SF, a protagonist uses what he or she knows about an unfamiliar environment to solve a particular problem.

The ambassador and "police officer" characters in SF can teach technical communicators lessons about how to approach their work. You have to love the work, have an inquisitive mind, and have a strong willingness to ask questions, even in the face of possible rejection or obstruction.

For instance, when a project team I was on started collecting requirements for software to be used at Disney's Animal Kingdom, we had to understand not only the veterinarians' technical needs but also their internal culture: how did they run their daily operations? How did they interact with the animals? Who decided who performed which treatments? Who was allowed access to what?

Interacting with subject matter experts (SMEs) and end users, the technical communicator must act as an ambassador of sorts between SMEs and those who operate in the unfamiliar environment created by those SMEs. In addition, the technical communicator can bridge gulfs of understanding between SMEs, engineers, and end users, all of whom might operate in separate, distinct, and potentially hostile "alien" worlds.

As an investigator, a technical communicator must identify the means, motives, and opportunities that drive end users to employ specific technologies. Technical communicators can draw upon the experiences of science fictional police officers in jobs where a mystery must be solved, whether they're experiments or accident investigations. As an investigator, the communicator must gather evidence, assemble the parts that fit together, and arrive at a suitable answer.

In short, science fiction can open one's eyes to the possibilities of technology. Therefore, by reading SF, the wise technical communicator can learn to ask the appropriate "What if" questions, and become an integral part of any project team.

Why I Study Philosophy

In addition to science fiction I read a great deal of philosophy. As a result, I was surprised and pleased by how much instruction in philosophy was provided in the graduate program\ in tech writing at the University of Central Florida.

Philosophy Helps You Set Priorities

As you've no doubt noticed, different philosophers have different perspectives on what constitutes the best approach to metaphysics, ethics, politics, epistemology, or aesthetics. Those perspectives can be instructive as well, even if you disagree with them. But what does all that have to do with technical communication?

Aside from learning and general mind-expanding, philosophy provides technical communicators with insights that help them identify what's important to different customers or audiences within a specific document. Are facts or ideas more important? The physical or the intellectual? The spiritual or the logical? The facts or opinions? The parts or the whole? The individuals or the team?

You probably have (or at least should have) your own convictions about which ideas should take priority. Those are the convictions that drive you toward your personal goals and ensure that you behave in an ethical or responsible manner. However, it's important that you have some notion of other interpretations of reality, not because other perspectives are more or less ethical, but simply because different customers or tasks will require different priorities. The more different perspectives you encounter, the better you are able to understand other people's priorities, how they think, and how best to communicate in ways that will persuade or make sense to them. (Science fiction can do this, too, by the way.)

Philosophy Helps You Better Reach Your Audience

Another aspect of philosophy emphasized in formal technical writing classes is ancient Greek (Aristotelian) forms of argument: ethos, pathos, and logos.

Ethos is, essentially, writing with authority. It's not just writing ethically (though that's the same root word); you write with ethos when you back up your work with solid knowledge or speak in "the company voice." Writing with ethos is a way to show that you know what you're talking about.

Pathos is emotion—the same root word from which we get sympathy and empathy. It's writing with feeling. Depending on what you're writing, you might or might not use pathos. If you're writing technical instructions for something that could go boom, you probably want to focus on "just the facts, ma'am." However, you might have a situation where you're trying to keep things light, in which case some added humor might be of use. Or let's say you're writing a persuasive speech about a particular technology—for or against. You can cite fact and

28

statistics all day, but occasionally you might need to move your audience, and emotional appeals do that more quickly and effectively than recitations of the facts. Of course, even a recitation of the facts can have an effective **emotional** appeal.

Logos is logic—your reasoning. What facts or arguments do you use to make your case? How do you arrange them? What train of thought do you use to ensure that your audience reaches the same conclusion?

Truly effective technical communication draws upon ethos, pathos, and logos. You must communicate ethically and with authority, you must touch the right emotional chord with your audience, and you must reason clearly so that your audience is persuaded of your point of view.

Philosophy Informs Your Views of the World
I had a friend who insisted that "politics has nothing to do with philosophy." I most respectfully and vehemently disagree. As I noted above, philosophy is the personal framework we use for determining what our priorities are. If politicians champion particular public priorities, they are taking a philosophical stance, and they must use ethos, pathos, and logos to convince us of the rightness of their position(s).

In a similar way, effective technical communicators must set priorities in their work to determine the most important ideas in a document and make those ideas accessible to their audiences. So if someone tells you that philosophy has nothing to do with technical communication, you now have a bit of logos to refute their argument. How much ethos and pathos you use is up to you.

The Information-Gathering Process
So now that you know your audience, situation, and outcome, and you have a mental model for how to approach your subject matter, you're reading to start gathering sources to inform your document or other deliverable.

1. As discussed previously, you need to know your audience, situation, and expected outcome so that you understand how much content you need to fulfill the assignment.
   a. Is the topic new to your audience?

  b. Are you providing a brief memo or a full, multi-page report?

  c. Do you expect a simple acknowledgment, emotional reaction, or a concrete decision?

2. Determine what materials are already on hand.

3. Ask which subject matter point(s) of contact will have the answers if you have questions.

4. Read the existing materials first. Look up any terms, acronyms, or factual questions that came up during your reading.[8]

  a. This includes all "What is…?" questions.

  b. This research could include the internet, company intranet
folders, marketing materials, or (yes, this still happens)
textbooks.

  c. Note any procedural, contextual, or situational questions
about the tech that you couldn't find during your research.

5. Attend the meetings where SMEs are discussing the tech. Take
notes during the meetings and see which questions are answered before you raise your hand.

6. Arrange time with one or more SMEs to ask the questions that
couldn't be answered by the materials you've read. Ask follow-up questions if something they say sparks another idea.
(Note: If you're working for a small start-up company and
there are no pre-existing materials because you were hired to
create them, this step will have to move further up in the process!)

Getting Started by Reading

It's not surprising or a sin that you spend the first week or even month
on a new job reading. This isn't shameful, and it isn't wasting time,
it's ensuring your survival! You need to get used to the subject matter,
the company nomenclature (product/service names), and the acronyms to do your job well[9].

---

[8] I'll discuss this in more detail in Part III: People and Politics, but the reasons you
should read first are twofold: it saves your SMEs' time and it helps build your
credibility by taking the time to familiarize yourself with the material before asking questions.

[9] Oh my, yes, the acronyms. I spent my first six months at NASA writing down
acronyms just so I could understand what people were saying in meetings. The
Ares Projects acronym document I pieced together ran more than 48 pages!

Once you've started absorbing the content, you'll eventually be called upon to produce something: a software design document, a user manual, or a technical paper for an upcoming engineering conference. The process should be similar, regardless of the topic or how long you've been on the job.

Finding the Information You Need: The Magic of Keywords

Whether you're doing general or very specific research about your topic, the internet has become an indispensable tool for finding information or even specific reports you need.

I have a friend at NASA who is terrified of the way I use a computer. He's convinced I'm a member of the Borg collective from the Star Trek universe because of the speed with which I find information on the internet. And while I like to tell him, "Resistance is futile," there's really no big secret to finding things on Google or any other search engine.

It all comes down to keywords.

Life Before Google

In the dark ages before Google (that'd be pre-1998), a lot of research was still done in card catalogs or "the stacks," those long, quiet, dusty rows of library shelves filled with dead-tree things called books.

Why on Earth would anyone subject themselves to the Reader's Guide to Periodical Literature? To write papers, of course. You might get a notion for providing a new insight into, say, J.R.R. Tolkien's The Silmarillion. You read some passages that reminded you a great deal of John Milton's Paradise Lost. You want to write a paper to prove that Milton served as one of the sources of Tolkien's back story to The Lord of the Rings.[10] How do you go about such a preposterous quest? Aside from the usual reading of the two works themselves, you have to look for what critics might have said about the two works. Does anyone else have the same theory you did, like some Ph.D. who's already published? Maybe. But how do you prove it?

You look for keywords. You're not going to find full-sentence references in the index that magically answer your question: "Yes indeed,

---

[10] I learned later that Tolkien hated literature written after 1500, so my paper was probably a bunch of drivel. However, I used enough authoritative sources to make a convincing argument to my professor, so I got the A.

third-year college student: here's how The Silmarillion borrowed from Milton's Paradise Lost!" Instead, you have to look for shorter subjects: you go into a critical edition of Paradise Lost and see if you can find individual words in that book that match words you're trying to write.

Before there was "Googling," there was indexing. That's a skill that still exists—especially in the textbook-writing world—but is often taken for granted by people otherwise. In essence, someone takes the time to read a text and identify specific topics within that text and where they're located so the reader might find them more quickly. What indexing is doing is identifying the most important words related to a topic you're studying. You find a lot of those words in the chapter names, headings, and subheadings of your basic classroom textbook. Indexes can provide you with a mental map to other fields of knowledge. If you use the right "magic words," you can cut down your search times considerably.

Keywords are all about concepts and context. Rather than look for specific terms, you're sometimes better off thinking descriptively. You're not going to find Lucifer or Satan in The Silmarillion any more than you'll find Melkor (a.k.a. Morgoth) in Paradise Lost. But you could find the concept of the "fallen angel" or its equivalent in the critical literature.

Today, if you do a Google search, you'll get 649,000 results for "fallen angel Silmarillion." In the paper-based world, there might have been that many sources, but you wouldn't find or want to use all of them; plus, you only had a week to research and write the paper. Therefore, you had to narrow down the search a bit by looking for other keywords: power, kingdom, hell, etc. As you dug through the critical texts, you sorted the wheat from the chaff and found which sources included more common elements than others. This connecting of keyword "dots" was essentially what indexes and card catalogs were doing.

Today, of course you can throw all those keywords into Google and find papers and entire discussions covering this very topic. It's almost like cheating.

Searches in the 21st Century

The indexing skill has value in the internet world as well. Let's say you want to find out what percentage of the federal budget is spent on NASA.

I've already provided you the keywords you need: percent federal budget NASA.

Or say you want to find a video with a particular quotation that you like. You can go to YouTube (a decent source for video clips, along with Vimeo.com and others) and do your search from there. You can input something like Kirk Star Trek no-win scenario and magically find the scene in Star Trek II: The Wrath of Khan where Admiral Kirk tells a lieutenant, "I don't believe in a no-win scenario."

But let's say you don't know what you're looking for. Again, it comes down to typing a set of the major nouns or concepts that, when combined, matches the gist of your query. A friend of mine is convinced that "everything is on the internet." He might be right. It might not make sense and you might not get the results you want, but the results you do obtain might help you clarify your query.

As you go forth, easily typing things on your computer, give silent thanks that you don't—unless you're in a college research methods class—have to create your own index or wander the stacks doing things "the hard way."

When Have You Researched "Enough?"

I'd love to tell you there's a hard-and-fast rule for knowing when you've gathered enough sources, but the honest answer is, even for an English major working among precision-minded aerospace engineers: it depends. However, the longer you  work in a job, the more familiar you become with "the literature" on your particular topic, and the faster you can locate the sources you need.

Generally, the shorter the document, the easier it is to lay your hands on the proper information or acquire it through a short interview with a SME. Longer documents, of course, require you to access a bit more information from multiple sources. The best advice I can give, having learned the hard way sometimes, is a mixed bag:

- Start with references directly related to your topic: meeting minutes, technical reports, or topical interviews.
- Depending on the scope of the work, you might need to provide some context for your document before you discuss your main point or topic. For instance, when I was writing papers about the Ares I-X flight test (2009), it was useful and necessary to discuss first the larger context of which Ares I-X was a part—the Constellation Program. I would then briefly discuss the Ares I crew launch vehicle, which the flight test was designed to help demonstrate. A technical paper might require a sentence or paragraph about the background material; a full report might include a full page or two.
- If you are dealing with a highly complex topic—say, nanotechnology or astrophysics—it is sometimes necessary to pull back the camera and go for a much wider view, talking about stars and galaxies or atoms first before talking about dark matter or molecular machinery.
- Much of your research will be driven by those three most important questions—audience, situation, and outcome—which you ask at the front end of the assignment: who is your audience, under what circumstances are they reading this information, and how do you want them to respond to it?
- When I was writing long academic papers for my undergrad and graduate degrees, I would get my hands on whatever seemed relevant and then stop when the sources were only tangentially touching on my topic or when they started referring back to articles I'd already collected. That worked pre- and post-internet, so it's still a valid strategy.
- Naturally, if you've got to get into the minutiae to write about some topics correctly or to clarify what a specific detail means, then go back and find the best source you can.

How to Write When Information Is Scarce

The methods for collecting information are straightforward and ideal when you have the resources and time available to learn what you need to learn. However, the real world being somewhat messier and less cooperative than the ideal, occasionally you will find situations where the textbook or standard operating procedure (SOP) way of doing things doesn't work.

This leaves you with that least-favorite problem: insufficient information.

The biggest problem with not having enough information is that it can make your writing feel vague, long on "vision," short on details. One reason you might find your content short on concrete details is that businesses and government agencies might have solid reasons for not sharing everything about their particular hardware. The reasons could include restrictions based on competitive, regulatory, national security, or proprietary concerns (a.k.a., giving away their "secret sauce").

Try, Try Again
If the reason you can't get the information is not one of the above, try again. Politely send another request to your SME(s) for the content. If they're on vacation, out sick, or otherwise unavailable, find out if someone else can answer your question. If the only possible person(s) who can fill in the blanks are unavailable, explain that to your manager or editor and ask them how they want you to proceed.

Is This Really Necessary?
One thing to consider before tracking someone down on their holiday to get a piece of information is whether you actually need that data in your document at all. Is the information critical to your content or just a nice-to-know fact?

Admit and Explain the Gaps
If I'm facing a gap, this would be my first-choice response. In the case of real-time journalism, I sometimes had to say, "This reporter contacted [Company X], but they had not responded by the time of publication," or something similar. Another thing I've had to do on tables of information is include a big "N/A" (for "not available"). Other blank-fillers I don't like but will accept include "Not publicly available," "Classified," or "Proprietary."

Don't Include or Explain the Information
I'm a pretty voracious data collector and will gladly fill in the blanks whenever I have facts to fit them. If the answer is "N/A," I've sometimes just deleted that row of the table rather than show a blank. In

this case, you just work with the data you have and say nothing about any gaps. With any luck, you can always go back and add it later.

Use What You Know

A while back, I was writing about a classified satellite and I was unable to find the spacecraft's mass (mass is the amount of material within a given object; weight is a measure of gravity's pull on the object). It simply wasn't publicly available. That doesn't mean the answer is "unknown." For example, while the spacecraft's mass was a blank, I did have information on the payload capabilities of the rocket it was launching on, so I could say it weighed "up to X pounds/kilograms."

Do Not Guess

Do not do this. An editor of mine and I strongly recommend against it. One might wing it when you're writing marketing copy if you have a general idea of how an organization talks about their product, but don't guess about facts because someone just a little (or a whole lot) more observant or knowledgeable will catch you on your error and call you on your BS, privately or—more likely—publicly. At that point, you have to make a correction and note the error publicly. That does not go over well.

As always, your content will come down to your audience, situation, and intended outcome. Does your audience need to know the information that only SME #1 knows? Can they achieve your intended outcome without that information? If so, go on without it.

If you have a report to publish inside an organization and you have the time to wait out the leave or vacation, there shouldn't be any call for incomplete answers. This is especially true of engineering organizations where data is often critical to the team's understanding of a product or situation. Something to consider if you find yourself facing a big blank spot in your content.

How Do You Organize Content?

If you're given a new topic to write about at length (one or more pages), but are uncertain how it should be organized, there are some practical ways to turn your complex subject matter into something useful for your audience.

You can start by asking your SMEs for clarity on what you've been asked to do. Assuming you've corralled your subject matter via audience, situation, and intended outcome, you also can narrow down the focus of what you need to write. For example, say you've been asked to write a paper about management approaches to address specific work situations. That doesn't mean you need to go back and read everything there is to know about management theory and practice.

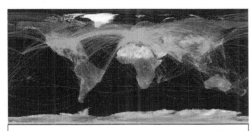

World Airline Route Map (source: Wikipedia)

You also need to orient yourself a bit after you've started your research. This means doing a little "mental mapping," organizing the content into manageable piles that make sense to you. You might find yourself connecting the new content to subjects you already do know. My parents worked at Eastern Airlines, so I always had a lot of route maps in the house. In my mind integrating content with what you already know is rather like adding a new city to the route system and then connecting it to several other cities already on the map.

Another approach to organizing material is "bucketing," a rather ugly neologism that means putting similar information into related mental buckets. After that, it's just a matter of arranging the buckets in such a way that the reader will understand what you mean.

Of course, once you've got your buckets, you might find that there is more than one way to arrange them, depending on the subject matter. These patterns become easier to identify as you encounter more and more new material. Here are some of the patterns I use when sorting new information:

- **Chronologically:** If your end user must act on your information in a specific time order, as in the case of making a recipe, performing a sequential task, or assembling a product, then it makes sense to put the information in that order. There might even be occasions where you have to write in reverse chronological order, as in the case of an incident report, where you start with a known problem and have to work backward to arrive at the original, root cause.

- **General to specific:** If your user must work with very complex, detailed, and difficult-to-understand information (say, redesigning a rocket engine), you might need to give your reader the "big picture" of how their work fits into the overall structure before delving into the specifics. This structure also works if you've got a very specific problem to address—say, a budget cut—and you want to provide the broader context for the decision before explaining why your specific item is being cut by X.

- **Specific to general:** This is how a criminal case or incident report is written up. You start by describing very specific actions or situations first, building backward to earlier causes, until you arrive at the overall "big picture," which is to answer why something happened.

- **Spatially:** When you're describing a piece of machinery or a site plan, you would want to describe the individual parts of the object or space in question. You might start in a general-to-specific mode first, explaining the overall plan or function, but then you need to describe how each part fits in or contributes to the whole. Or you might start front to back or top to bottom or, in the case of a house, starting from the front door and working your way through room by room.

- **Functionally:** This is similar to organizing information spatially, but applying the approach to a process with many moving parts moving concurrently, like a business. In this situation, you might end up using a "most to least important" order, where the different functions or departments are described hierarchically based on the politics of the organization.

- **Hybrid Topics:** You might encounter topics that are broad and complex enough to require more than one type of order to convey clearly. For instance, as in the business example, you might follow a product or service through its entire life cycle, starting with its initial design and working your way toward the customer purchase, or starting with surveying the customer and working your way back to the final product. Another example is a rocket flight. The papers I wrote for the Ares I-X flight test would often have to provide a general-to-specific picture first—what the Constellation Program was, why we were testing, and what the rocket would do to help the program—before providing a spatial description of the rocket, a description of the ground systems required to support it, and then the chronological sequence of the flight test itself.

In all of these cases, your goal should be to "tell a story" that makes sense to your readers or users. The good news is that your readers will generally have an idea in their heads of how your topic should work, so if you follow that expected narrative, they should be able to follow your logic and connect the same dots that you did in organizing the material.

A word of caution: it might be tempting to get so creative that you feel the urge to contradict expectations or provide a "surprise ending" for your readers. This is perilous for the nonfiction writer. Your users are reading your material to accomplish a specific task, correctly, in a particular manner or order; for the most part, they are not reading to be entertained. I add this caution only because I was so tempted once or twice early in my professional writing career, and I had to have operational reality explained to me. Consumers of technical communication do not want surprise endings, just the facts they need, in the order they need them, to do the job they set out to do. The more constructive thought you put into arranging the information on the front end, the less work your readers have to do on the receiving end. Trust me, they'll appreciate it.

Working with Equations...Egad, Math!

You might go through this whole information-gathering process, get your content organized properly, and pat yourself on the back for not asking stupid questions during meetings, but then somewhere in your collection of notes there might still be content that even I dread when working a tech job: equations.

Equations can be handled a few different ways. First, what sort of equation is it? Basic arithmetic (addition, subtraction, multiplication, division) you can and should be able to handle, at least. Algebra? Trigonometry? Calculus? Statistics? Some of those you might have encountered, some not. Whatever it is, relax. Equations rarely appear in technical documents without some context or explanation behind them. The most common way an equation appears in a document is to show what calculation process the SMEs used to develop or operate their product. At most, you might need to add a caption explaining the equation and the variables within it. If it's arithmetic, you can at least grab a calculator and check the math.

If the document uses or requires multiple sets of equations, you might need to sit down with the SME and ask what the equations are doing. You're really listening for key words that tie the equation back to the parts of the product or process you already understand. Most of the time, your SME will help you in these situations. You might take some ribbing for not speaking the language, but they did not hire you to do the math! They hired you to put the math in context so it makes sense in specific communications contexts. You can do this!

Part II: Processes

Chapter 4: Common Tech Writing Tasks

In this chapter you'll get a look at some of the more frequent (and easy) tasks assigned to technical communicators. And while your job title might say "documentation writer" or "proposal writer," there's probably a little caveat in your job description that reads, "Other duties as assigned."

Therefore, even if you weren't hired to write correspondence, news articles, meeting minutes, news articles, presentations, reports, meeting minutes, or web copy, these types of tasks could still cross your desk because, as they'll say, "You're the writer." I'll also touch on some skills it's good to have, such as managing shared online documents, version control, conference justifications, and travel reports.

What You Need to Know to Do Your Job: Tech Skills

Let's start with the basics. I have been swimming in the technocracy for a couple of decades now, and my experiences and technology requirements have varied a bit with each job. What follows is a general shopping list of software and hardware skills that technical communicators should have touched, worked with, or at least heard of to do their job. It'll probably be fun to go back and look at this list periodically for nostalgia's sake. (There are probably people reading this right now and thinking, "Fax machine? What's that?")

The lists below include my own experiences plus inputs from techieminded people I trust, including **Darlene Cavalier the Science Cheerleader, Anthony Duignan-Cabrera,** a new-media entrepreneur, and **John Ohab,** a social media guru (thank you!).

Software

- **Web Browsing:** Microsoft (MS) Internet Explorer (now Microsoft Edge), Safari, Google Chrome, Firefox, or some other web-surfing application.
- **Word Processing:** Microsoft Word. Oh, hush—you know you use it! Most offices can't live without it; and if they can, they've got some other word-processing software with an equally Byzantine list of functions that a technical writer usually knows inside and out.
- **Presentations:** Microsoft PowerPoint (PPT) is still the standard. I keep hearing from my presentation-wonk friends that

PPT "sucks," but Prezi or Apple's Keynote application have yet to replace it.

- **Spreadsheets:** Microsoft Excel or some other spreadsheet program. I understand there are a few good competitors out there, but I've moved from Disney to defense to NASA, and MS products still abound.
- **Email:** Gmail, Microsoft Outlook, or other email program. You have sent an email before, haven't you?
- **Desktop Publishing:** Adobe FrameMaker, InDesign, Acrobat, or some other page layout and graphic-design program.
- **Instant Messaging:** These include Facebook Messenger, Hip-Chat, and the text messaging application on your mobile phone.
- **Search Engine:** Yes, there is Google, but there are others still, such as Yahoo!, Bing, or the one I use—StartPage—because it supposedly protects the privacy of your searches.
- **Video Editing:** Apple's QuickTime or iMovie, Adobe Premiere Pro, Core VideoStudio Ultimate, or others.
- **Project Planning:** Microsoft Project or some other project-planning software.
- **Social Networking:** Facebook is still the leading social networking site, though it is also being closely followed by Instagram and other social networking sites (and apps).
- **Microblogging:** Twitter remains the 800-pound gorilla in this format, though they're getting less "micro" since they allowed up to 280 characters per tweet.
- **Really Simple Syndication (RSS)**
- **Online Document Management:** Google Drive, Dropbox, Box, or others.

Hardware

- Personal Computer (PC) or Mac computer with keyboard, mouse or track pad
- iPad or tablet PC of some sort
- Smart phone (iPhone, Android, Google Pixel, Samsung Galaxy)
- Webcam/GoPro
- Universal Serial Bus (USB)/flash drive
- Backup drive
- Fax (go ahead, future reader—laugh)

- Copier
- Scanner
- BlueTooth
- Digital Versatile Disc (DVD)/Blu-Ray player
- Videoconferencing software/hardware
- Digital Video Recorder (DVR)

Technical Concepts (phrases you should have heard of in the course of your work)

- Voice mail
- Telecommuting
- Virtual Private Network (VPN)
- Wi-Fi
- 3G/4G/5G
- Blog (web log)
- Computer programming languages such as HTML/XML/XHTML/Python/C/C# (bottom line being, you should have at least seen or touched some sort of computer code so when someone says "tag," you know what they mean)
- Cloud computing
- Voice to text
- Apps (usually associated with smart phones)
- Computer-generated imagery (CGI)
- Search Engine Optimization (SEO)
- Data visualization/mashups
- Intelligent personal assistants (Siri, Alexa, etc.)
- Geolocation
- Hashtags
- Semantic web (Web 3.0)
- Live streaming video/technology
- Blockchain
- Cryptocurrency
- Artificial Intelligence (AI)
- Robotics
- Dark web
- Memes
- Anything mobile
- Mobile, well, everything, is inevitable. So is programming for iOS and all Android platforms
- Also, digital tools that allow social sharing and e-commerce

The exciting, interesting, and scary aspect of all this is that the technological "necessities" for doing the job of technical communication keep advancing and improving. That puts the technical communicator on a dedicated course toward lifelong learning. And while I might be using some of the hot toys of my time, those toys (tools) will continue to evolve, which means you and I must be willing and able to adapt as well. It also means that the definition of "technical literacy" will continue to evolve. There is something vaguely unsettling, sad, and Borg-like about the fact that we must adapt to the machines instead of vice versa, but the good news is that some inventors, like the late Steve Jobs, are the same folks dedicated to making new technologies—if not "intuitive"—at least easy to use once a short demonstration or two is provided. I remain supremely impressed that I was able to use most basic iPhone functions without a manual.

As I pointed out in Part I, reading science fiction helps a new technical communicator—or anyone living in this age—because SF conditions the reader to accept that the future can and will be different. So perhaps the most important "tool" technical communicators can take with them is an open mind, one that is open to the probability that what you know today will be outdated tomorrow. And by all means, be ready to find new ways to communicate messages in a dynamic environment.

Online Document and Version Control
Related to understanding technology is coping with how it affects your content creation process in a team environment. Recently I've been using Google Drive a lot. Live, interactive online documents can create challenges for handling document version control. Don't believe me? Read on.

First, a Little Background
Having used Microsoft Word for 25 years, I confess to being a bit "old school" and "analog" in my approach to handling documents. Future generations will be more accustomed to documents that are electronic, "live," and continually changing. My mindset about content is based on print—books, reports, three-ring binders, and other content—which is expected to be finalized and "perfect" when it goes into production. Why? Because it's expensive to print multiple copies, especially if a product is going out to a large organization or the general

public. (Electronic documents, by contrast, are easily changed and relatively cheap.)

What this print-minded approach means from my point of view is that someone must be the owner of the "master" document, the official copy, the latest version, call it what you will. If you are that person, you are the "book boss." There is, as evidenced by the term "version control," a certain ownership or management view of documents. It means the document owner has the final say on how the "final" version will appear.

The analog approach to document control means one person has the "master" copy and everyone else receives a disposable copy. More to the point, with paper, eventually revisions come to a stop, and there will then be a final version, and that final version then goes to print, where it will remain in all its glory until the end of time…or at least until the next revision, which is often years away.

Even if you're handling Word documents and exchanging them via email, the "final" electronic document can go through several iterations before it finally goes to print, the archives, or wherever. Microsoft-based networks do not allow two individuals to "own" (work with) a document at the same time. If two people access a document from the same shared drive at the same time, one version often will get dumped when one user (the second person to access it) attempts to save their version under the same name. That, or the second person accessing the document will be blocked from using it until the other person exits. As of this writing (2020), MS Word still doesn't allow concurrent editing of a document. In this environment, as they say in the movie **Highlander**, "There can be only one" final document and one document owner.

Google Drive has its own word processing, spreadsheet, and presentation applications, which enable multiple users to access the same document simultaneously and edit in real time (they can then be exported as Microsoft Office files as needed). This was a major paradigm shift for many people, including me, who had a print-based vision of document control. Now, multiple people can make their changes in real time. Google Drive has democratized document "ownership," and the change process is still ongoing.

Pros and Cons

Hey, I was working on that! Some individuals like the ability to do concurrent editing. I'm still finding it to be a headache. As a document "owner," you still need to coordinate who is doing what, or you could find yourself facing situations where one person is doing a content review of a section and starting to make changes only to see that content deleted by someone else right before their eyes.

Fortunately, Google Drive does have little colored squares with initials in them at the upper-right of the screen showing who is accessing the document at the same time you are. Right next to the individual name icons is a little chat box you can click to communicate with others accessing the doc. That way, you can message them and say, "Hey, you just deleted section 3.3. I was working on that" and let the argument take off from there.

Who gets the last word? One concern I've had with documents handled in Google Drive applications is enforcing a "hands-off" policy when whoever owns the document says it's now official or "final." This is of particular importance when you're delivering something on a deadline, like a proposal. Ideally, everyone is in communication, so once the word has gone out, the document is exported to Office, Adobe, or a printer, and everyone keeps their keyboard and comments off the document after that. But what if someone wanted to make a change to the document of record after the fact? Fortunately, if this is a concern, the document owner can change everyone's access to read-only once it's been locked down.

You Can't Do That in Drive

As I mentioned earlier about version control hairballs, while Google Drive can accept uploads from and downloads to Microsoft Office, it doesn't have as many features or as much flexibility as the Office products. It's little things that most folks wouldn't notice, like formatting tools, layout, and tables or images. If you're just throwing a document together in a hurry, Drive applications are probably fine. However, if you want things like format to look or function a specific way, there's no substitute for the extensive set of tools Office has included over the years. It's an industry standard for a reason, and those of us who have grown up with the tool for 25+ years can become irritated when required to use another program that isn't as capable. If I want to do a really good cleanup of a document and format everything exactly the way I want it, I still need to export it to Word, make the necessary adjustments, and then re-upload it for the shared directory. Fortunately, the changes do upload when I make them. Maybe Google Drive's applications will catch up eventually, but for now, Word is still better at the little touches.

Version control. Here is where I go back to my book-boss mindset and grouse about the lack of authority in the democratized editing environment. Eventually, someone (usually a technical writer or editor) is going to have to go into the document last and put a final approval on it. This includes clearing out or addressing all the comments. What if the comments come from someone higher up the food chain and they haven't been resolved yet? Who has the authority to accept or decline a comment? The bureaucratic reality is that just because everyone can touch the document, that doesn't mean everyone should.

You can go back through the revision history and see who made what changes last, but that is a major headache. Sometimes it's best to establish writing and editing practices before the work begins so that everyone understands the rules of the road.

Final Thoughts

If you're in the target market for this book, you probably just read this section with a bit of eye rolling. Bear with me, because understanding generational approaches to technology is also an important insight into how office politics work. My Generation Xer method of editing (learned from Baby Boomers, who were also raised on print) is to have one person own the master copy and let everyone else mark up a copy and send it back to me for integration. The advantage of this approach is simply that it allows one document owner to keep an eye on the big picture: the overall content and flow, what's in, what's out, what's missing, and how things need to be said to ensure the document sounds like one person wrote it, not a dozen. If a single "book boss" cannot be designated because everyone wants to put in their two cents[11], there still needs to be a hands-off deadline, beyond which only

---

[11] Other words for this include "adding value" (the polite version) or "marking one's territory" (the less charitable version). I have a friend who purposely leaves small errors in the text so that a particular manager will jump to fix those errors rather than make their own suggestions and really screw up the style and flow.

one person is allowed to access, edit, format, apply a consistent style to, and finalize the document.

A dozen people can have a dozen good ideas, but it often requires the skill of one writer/editor to bring those ideas together in a single, coherent, consistent story the audience will want to read. If that means I end up using Microsoft Word to keep other people's paws off my work, that's what's going to happen.

Additional Thoughts on Version Control — Avoiding Hairballs

As you might have guessed, version control is one of the biggest headaches I face as a technical communicator. Oddly enough, the technologies that make document sharing so easy and storage space so plentiful also open up new and recurring nightmares for anyone working with those documents. An engineer I knew at NASA used to call paperwork problems "hairballs," akin to something cats cough up until they're gone. For me, version control is one big, nasty hairball.

The problem occurs when you have more than one draft of a document sent out via email distribution for edits, updates, or changes.[12] Sometimes you didn't create the extra draft(s), another person did. Which document then counts as the "master" or "live" copy?

It gets even more fun when you've got a document that runs a couple hundred pages and you've got a couple dozen people commenting on it. How do you move past this and make your life less painful? Below are some lessons I learned the hard way.

If possible, assign only one person to be the document owner. If you're lucky, you'll get to lay down the law and get yourself assigned to be the only person allowed to own, touch, or edit the official copy of the document. That way, anyone else handling a document can only make a copy and send the edits to you for incorporation. However, it's become less and less common in the era of Google Drive.

Use Track Changes. Microsoft Word has this lovely feature under the Review tab called Track Changes, which highlights any changes a previous user makes to a document. Track Changes is your friend,

---

[12] I freely admit that this is one of the downsides of using email vs. Google Docs or other shared drive/document system, but it eliminates a lot of the other headaches I already mentioned.

though in the spirit of full disclosure, I admit it can cause large documents to crash if there are too many changes being tracked. It is also good to accept changes on occasion to prevent a really big, important document from becoming prone to crashes.

If you are given a document to edit and don't turn on Track Changes, trusting an editor to magically see all of the changes you've made is a recipe for disaster. Still, if you're working with (or are) a contributor who has a mental block about Track Changes, you can always use the Merge or Combine Documents function, which will, as the name suggests, combine the contents of one document with another, with only the differences between the two showing up as tracked changes. It's ugly and can raise questions about which changes came from whom, but it can be done.

I get into discussions occasionally with people who inform me that Microsoft Word "sucks" and that there are better programs out there I should be using. On that matter, I will politely disagree. Plus, however much the anti-Microsoft crowd might prefer Mac's Pages app (which is still inferior for half a dozen reasons), Word is the most common shared document format out there, so you might as well live it, love it, learn it.

Include a date in the file name. You can ensure that people know which is the latest document simply by including the date of the version in the file name. If more than one person accessed the doc that day, you might have to add a time stamp (I use the 24-hour clock) as well.

Set rules for using file sharing services. As previously noted, online file sharing services such as DropBox, Google Drive, or ownCloud have made it possible for multiple people to access a shared document and edit simultaneously. People favoring this approach often do so because they prefer that only one file and one file name be used to prevent file sprawl. However, multiple users accessing the files make new versions more likely than ever. And these services are not foolproof (if you want to hear some colorful profanity, ask a NASA person sometime about finding a document in the agency-internal "Windchill" file application).

Here are my issues with these services as I've experienced them in the workplace:

Some services, such as Dropbox, allow multiple people to access the same document at the same time by downloading a copy instead of checking it out like a library book. Users can see what the "latest" version is by reading the update day or time in the system. However, problems crop up when more than one person uploads their edited version of the document at the same time. The first person to upload "wins," with the document of the second person going into limbo.

Another problem occurs if someone makes a bunch of changes and saves over the original master doc but those changes are rejected. However, it is entirely possible their changes caused other content or changes to be deleted or lost.

I realize that some of my reactions here are a factor of my age, my relationships with technology, or my attitude toward collaborative writing and editing. I use these file-sharing tools because they make some things more convenient. However, I'm still convinced that a document is likely to come out looking and reading better if you have only a single person doing the writing or editing.

Save your work! This issue comes up more often than it should, but it's still a reality. Say you've got multiple people working on a file that's too large to email (usually anything larger than 20 MB as of this writing) and you're at a remote location where a high-speed T1 line isn't available. In that case, you're left with the expedient of passing the file around on a USB drive or other external media. Here's what can happen if you're not paying attention:

- Person A makes changes to the document and saves it to the USB drive. The USB drive is then handed over to Person B.
- Person B downloads the document to his hard drive and makes changes. Before handing off the USB drive, however, Person B makes more changes and then saves them to his hard drive without changing the file on the USB.
- Person C now has the document. She might make changes to the USB version or not. Perhaps she saves the document to her hard drive, makes changes there, but neglects to update the USB drive.
- The USB drive is now handed back to Person A for final approval, only to find that some changes discussed by the group

are on the drive while some aren't. To try and resolve the changes, Person A, B, and C then discover that they all have slightly different versions on their computer, none of which match what was supposed to be on the USB drive.

In this case it's not just a matter of saving your work but saving it in all of the places where you need it to be. Saving a copy of a shared document on your hard drive is fine, but if it needs to be handed off, just make sure that you have saved the latest version in both locations.

Remember where you're working. Opening and editing a document from email also can be vexing if you neglect to take the file out of the temp files where computers save email attachments. As soon as you close the document, poof! It's gotten lost in the Temp File Forest of Fangorn. Good luck finding it again. In this case, it's important that you save email attachments to a known, recoverable place on your hard drive so you can find it afterward. Otherwise, you're most likely going to have to redo a few minutes' to a few hours' worth of work.

All this said, the keys to version control are attention to detail, memory, and consistent processes. Keeping track of all of these actions can help you avoid some seriously nasty document hairballs.

Some Basics about Business Correspondence

Now that you know what you're writing about, how to organize it, and where to save it, let's start with something simple, like correspondence. Organizations write formal letters or emails to make or respond to a request (or complaint); introduce a proposal; make a sales pitch; confirm a business arrangement; provide updates on the organization's status; request an extension on payments; and other activities that keep the business moving along smoothly. What follows are some guidelines for writing a letter on behalf of an organization or organizational executive.

As a starting point, hard-copy letters are treated differently from emails. They are more formal and often serve as an official document "for the record," with a specific responsible individual's name signed at the bottom. The basic business letter is usually no more than three to five paragraphs long and includes the following:

Date and Address

The date of an official correspondence is customary, as is the full spelling of the date, e.g., 29 May 2020 or May 29, 2020.

Usually there is at least one hard return between the date and the address. I was trained to add three hard returns (blank lines) between the date and address, but that assumes your letter is short enough to fit on a single page. If the letter is longer than usual, you can reduce the space after the date to one line to keep everything on a single piece of paper (8.5″x11″ or A4).

Next up is the addressee receiving the letter. This should include an abbreviated, proper form of address (Mr., Ms., General (Gen.), Colonel (Col.), or other. If you're writing business-to-business (B2B), or even as an individual to a business, it's usually a good practice to address your letter to a specific individual. Call the business, if necessary, to reach the correct person. I'm not fond of "To Whom It May Concern."[13]

Below the person's name, of course, should be the organization's name, then the address.

A fictitious example would be:

> Mr. Bart Leahy
> Heroic Tomfoolery, Inc.
> 123 Madeup Street
> Orlando, FL 32801
> USA

Salutation

This can vary. Some organizations include the warm-and-fuzzy "Dear Mr./Ms. X." You could also just use the individual's salutation— "Mr./Ms. X:" When in doubt it's hard to beat Emily Post for getting your etiquette correct, so refer to the "address" article mentioned in the footnote.

Opening Sentence(s)

This sentence should state the topic and purpose of the letter. If it's a friendly letter, as in a sales situation, you might make this a warm-

---

[13] See EmilyPost.com, "Official Forms of Address," http://emilypost.com/advice/official-forms-of-address/.

and-fuzzy greeting such as, "It was good to see you at the XYZ Conference [on X date]; I hope all is well with you." Another exception to the getting-down-to-business sentence first would be if you are responding to a particular piece of correspondence or on behalf of someone else, such as: "Thank you for contacting Darlene Cavalier. She has asked me to respond on her behalf."

Otherwise, your first sentence is doing a couple important things:

- Explaining the purpose of your letter.
- Setting the tone.

Your purpose will vary based on how you want your reader to respond:

- Learn – know the information
- Feel – respond emotionally
- Comply – follow directions
- Decide – take action
- Agree – advocate or accept the proposal

The variations are nearly endless, depending on your audience, specific business situation, and your intended outcome. The goal with American business writing, as with journalism, is to get the main point out in front of the reader as soon as possible. Other organizations and cultures might have differing approaches—including additional time spent on diplomatic greetings or inquiries into the reader's health or family—but if you're dealing with an American business or organization, the direct approach is generally acceptable and expected. "Time is money" being a very American view of things, the average business reader doesn't want to waste a lot of time digging through a lot of words to learn the writer's purpose. That said, we're not quite as far gone as the fictional Klingons in Star Trek, who skip all preliminaries and ask bluntly, "What do you want?"

Examples include:

- "This letter has been written in response to your letter dated May 23, requesting an extension for submitting your proposal. We regret to inform you that we are unable to grant an extension on this procurement."

- "Thank you for contacting Darlene Cavalier about Science Cheerleader. She asked me to respond on her behalf. We appreciate your enthusiasm for cheerleading and science, and we're happy to provide you with information about our organization."
- "This letter is to explain recent billing activity by XYZ Company and to reassure the Very Large Government Agency of America of the timeliness of our payments."

Body Paragraph(s)

Now that you've laid out your purpose, you can provide a more detailed explanation for the why, what, who, how, where, and when of the situation. Those may sound out of order (people are used to seeing who-what-where-when-why-how), but I believe the order I listed them makes sense. If you're sharing a decision of some sort, you want to start out with the "why," especially if it doesn't match up with what your correspondent requested. Or maybe it does and a why isn't necessary ("We'd be happy to refund your deposit—we're sorry to hear about X situation that kept you from buying X at this time and hope you consider doing business with us in the future."). If you are fulfilling a request, you might provide the individual with instructions for whom to address, how to do so, where to address their follow-up request, and by what date.

This could take anywhere from one to three paragraphs (longer, if your legal department gets hold of it). Again, try to keep business correspondence to a single page. If you're laying out a particular type of agreement or arrangement, you might be better off creating a different type of document, such as a work agreement, contract, or non-disclosure agreement.

Closing

Your closing should echo the tone set by your opening. This could include maintaining a positive, upbeat, we-look-forward-to-hearing-from-you tone to a conciliatory, we-hope-you-will-consider-doing-business-with-us-in-the-future attitude. Or you might be in the middle of a dispute and hope to end on an "up" note by saying that, "We (or I) hope we can resolve this situation to everyone's satisfaction soon." Your closing is, in effect, politely stating the direction you hope your correspondent will take upon reading the letter.

Signature Block

Your signature block should mirror the information you include in the address of the recipient. However, if you're printing on stationery that already includes your business's contact information, you can simply include your name and title.

Also, if you're writing your letter with print in mind, allow at least two (preferably three) hard returns below the closing sentence to provide you or the signer room to write their signature.

Identification Initials, Enclosures, Copies, and Postscripts

Often you can find other information on a formal letter beyond the signature block, such as whether the envelope includes an enclosure, a copy of a letter, or other materials.

Sometimes, businesses will include the initials of the individual signing the letter and the one preparing it, with the signer's initials in upper case and the preparer's initials in lower case. For example, a letter signed by Darlene Cavalier but originally prepared by Bart Leahy would appear as:

DC/bl

If you've enclosed another item with the letter—anything from a coupon to a contract to a full proposal—that should be noted.

If you are cc:-ing someone on the letter (short for "carbon copy," for those of us old enough to use such things), that would appear next, again with a blank line between the two. Sometimes letters are blind copies (bc:), meaning that a copy of the correspondence was sent to someone else within the organization but the addressee is not made aware of it and the bc: copy recipient's name is not included on the letterhead version, only in the file copy. A bc: copy will show this information and a "Copy" stamp in the signature block instead of an actual handwritten signature.

Postscripts are not common in most business correspondence (I see them a lot in sales pitches, though). They're included below the signature block, with one space between them. You might even throw in a post-postscript (P.P.S.), but this is not common and appears a bit unprofessional in my opinion. Simple enough?

Formal Letter vs. Email

If you or your organization prefers to correspond with someone via email instead of by paper or "snail mail," you probably don't need all of the components listed above. For example, the body of an email will not include the date at the top because that appears in the message information when it hits someone's inbox. An email might or might not contain the full street addresses of the recipient or the sender. Emails might not include cc:'s or bc:'s; they will not contain enclosures, but might include attachments. If you need to send something that would be better delivered as hard copy, a formal letter is preferred. The structure of an email, however, would remain the same.

How to Write a Complaint Letter

From 1996 to 2001, I answered guest letters for the Walt Disney World Guest Communications Department, what most people would call "Guest Letters." That was an interesting lesson in customer—sorry, guest—relations. I learned how people tried to get their way, using appeals to emotion, logic, or other methods. It was a first-class education in literary forms of argument.

As a result of this barrage of negativity (only about ten percent of the letters were from "happy" people), I learned how to write an effective complaint when my turn came to send one. Here are some recommended Dos and Don'ts if you plan to express your outrage through email or the U.S. Postal Service:

Don't

- WRITE IN ALL CAPS AND USE LOTS OF EXCLAMATION POINTS!!!!
- Use profanity, unless you're quoting an employee who used coarse language with you.
- Threaten legal action. This will take your complaint from the customer service department to the legal department, at which point you'd better be prepared to pony up for a lawyer because some corporate lawyers live for litigation.
- Go off topic. If your complaint is just one of many things going awry in your life, like your pet going missing or your car

being in the shop, those situations might be regrettable, but they are usually not relevant to the situation at hand.
- Make unsubstantiated allegations or otherwise lie about a business situation.
- Make personal threats of any kind. Those don't go to the legal department—they go to the police.
- Make unreasonable demands. Expecting a free vacation for you and your four-person family, including air fare, because your child got an owie from a sliver from a wooden beam is not realistic.
- Write letters for every little grievance. Complain about every transaction just to get "free stuff," and you'll get a reputation for being a difficult and, eventually, unwelcome customer.

Do

- Use spell checker.
- Include your return address, receipts, specific names, dates, and times regarding the situation in question, if possible.
- Stick to the facts—what went wrong, what the impact was, and what you expect for restitution.
- Suggest a reasonable service recovery or restitution, whether it be an apology or expenses incurred by an incident. Naturally if you experienced serious, grievous harm, an attorney might be more appropriate. We're talking here about minor service complaints.
- Write more than one draft, as you would with any document— we don't always provide our best, most cogent arguments while angry. The well-written complaint letter can elude even the best technical communicator if they're righteously angry.

How to Respond to a Complaint Letter

Now let's take the flip side of that situation and say you've been assigned to respond to a customer complaint. This might be a primary job responsibility, a secondary duty, or a one-off assignment. You might or might not get much guidance from your employer or leader about how to respond; sometimes you'll be asked to write the first draft and then someone else will review it. Some bosses just want to see something on paper to help them clarify what they want or don't want.

What follows are my insights on the business thinking behind answering complaints based on my past experience with Disney and other organizations. Before I write anything further, let me make this clear: The following content does not reflect the opinions or policies of the Walt Disney World Resort or any of my current or past employers. Any opinions are strictly my own.

Read the whole letter. This seems like a given. However, I've been caught off-guard by letters that start out badly but include some bright spot. Be certain to acknowledge that bright spot. Sometimes a customer or member of the general public has a long laundry list of points they want your organization to know about, but don't actually have a specific complaint that needs addressing—make sure you understand the whole story before shooting from the hip.

Thank them for writing. Courtesy first. You might not feel it, you might want to throw the letter into the rubbish bin. Just remember they can't see your face or hear your rage as they thoroughly insulted an organization you happen to like. Thank them for writing anyway.

Determine the writer's tone. Generally this is pretty easy to do, though as we've learned from the internet and social media, text is not always the most effective or efficient way to convey emotion. Nevertheless, you can look for some obvious words like "thrilled" or "enraged" to capture your correspondent's state of mind. This is also important for establishing the tone of your response. Happy people can get a happy letter. Serious people get a serious letter. Threatening people might get a serious letter or they might get referred to your Legal Department…or the authorities.

Determine the most important issue. This can be a challenge, especially in a letter or email that covers multiple concerns. However, the skill of being able to "read between the lines" is critical to responding to a customer concern. They might be irritated that their flight was late, for example, but what really set them off was the treatment they received from the desk agent handling their situation. How do you determine the most important issue? When in doubt, just look at what the customer spends the most words discussing. Sometimes they'll even tell you what their biggest concern is. Regardless of how many issues are in a letter, you need to identify the most important issue and make certain that your organization's response addresses that.

Evaluate requests for action or service recovery. Sometimes customers are writing just to make you aware of a negative situation. Sometimes they say they are simply making you aware but make a hint they won't be fully satisfied unless they are given something (often called "service recovery") to make them feel better. If you're in a product or service organization, they might want a refund or something free on their next transaction. If you're in a nonprofit organization, they might want you to change a particular policy position. Some people just want an apology. Then again, some people want to sue.

So how do you decide who gets what?

Service recovery has gotten complicated, especially with the advent of the internet, where people will share their "horror stories" online with anyone who will read them. And those "horrors" could include how a company responded to their complaint. On the flip side, if you end up being exceptionally generous with your service recovery, the recipient might share their joy online and suddenly you've got a hundred copycat complaints. This is why you often have to do research on a problem: were they actually there? Did they actually pay for the product/service? What was the input from the employee(s) involved? Do they have receipts? Audio? Video?

And what, exactly, do they want in response to their situation? Large organizations usually have preset responses, guidelines, and budgets for handling service issues and allow employees a certain amount of authority for providing service recovery before bumping the situation up the chain of command for approval (see below). A lot of this results from a constellation of proof on the customer's part, responsibility on the organization's part, and reasonableness of the stated request.

Then again, sometimes an apology is sufficient.

Determine if an issue needs to be escalated. If you've been asked to write a response to a complaint letter, that task might or might not be your regular line of work. The Walt Disney World Resort is large enough to require a whole staff of Guest Communications correspondents whose full-time role is answering letters, calls, and emails. Small or even medium-sized businesses might not get that many letters, so the person who's the best wordsmith in the office gets the job. If the issue is unusual enough, you might need some guidance from a leader on what should be said and how any response or service recovery needs to be handled.

If your regular job is responding to customer concerns, you already know the organization's service recovery guidelines. You might be empowered to provide that recovery without management approval, though you also might have an editor or a manager look over your work before you send the response. If you work at service-forward organizations such as Zappos or Ritz-Carlton, you might have broader discretionary authority than others. If, however, the customer is requesting or demanding something that it is not in your power to give, you might need to bump the request up the chain before getting a yes—especially if you think it's warranted.

The Goals of a Business Correspondent

Whether you call a department Guest Letters, Customer Service, or something else, the goal of the person providing the response is two-fold:

- Protect the interests of the organization.
- Keep the customers happy enough to keep patronizing the business.

It can be tricky to maintain a healthy balance between these two mandates. You want to serve the customer, whose dollars support the company. On the other hand, you need to be a responsible steward of the company's resources so that it's not defrauded. It is possible to err or become too zealous on one side of the equation or the other. "It's not my money" can be an invitation in your mind to give away whatever you want or make you paranoid about issuing any service recovery whatsoever. Sometimes, if you're in doubt, it's better to ask a peer or manager to get another perspective. At other times, you need to take a "hard line" on specific policies, whether you agree with them personally or not.

I'm Sorry vs. I Apologize

I go back and forth on word choices in apologies. In my mind, "sorry" is more sincere than "apologize," which is a colder, more formal word. One way or another, some folks want to hear "I'm sorry" or "I apologize" for whatever situation prompted the letter. However, depending on whom you ask, either word might get you into legal trouble because it might imply personal or corporate culpability. One nice word that avoids this issue entirely is regret, as in, "We regret that you had a disappointing experience with X." Not happy with that answer? Go search "I'm sorry vs. I apologize" on Google and prepare to spend a few hours sorting out the best way to say that you feel badly that something untoward happened to your customer without claiming responsibility.

How to Say No to a Request

There are any number of reasons why a customer's request might be refused. Their service recovery request might not match the circumstances—demanding a free vacation for four because someone stubbed their toe on a door jamb, for example. They might not have enough evidence of their problem—receipts, names, dates, the malfunctioning product, medical bills, or other specific evidence. Or they might be making a policy request that is unlikely to happen, like asking a defense company to stop making machinery that could be used for war. Or the correspondent might ask a nonprofit organization to include his or her favorite sub-cause in the organization's overall mission.

Regardless of the situation, eventually it comes down to giving someone the bad news. I'm not comfortable with that, but I've done it. The language can be relatively simple: "We understand that you would like us to provide you with X. However, your requested response to the situation you described does not fall within our service recovery guidelines." Or something like that. If the problem is one of insufficient evidence, you could throw in something like "Unfortunately, your letter did not include your original receipt. We would be willing to research your concern further if you will mail it to us." If the problem is one of policy, you might need to explain why the organization will not follow the correspondent's policy preference.

When a Response is Not Necessary

Sometimes no response is the best response. For instance, if a customer is outraged about life in general but doesn't have any comments about your organization, don't bother. Or maybe, again, they've sent some sort of rant about the state of the world and they want nothing to do with your organization. They haven't complained about your organization, they're not asking for anything, but they're just angry? Into the circular file it goes.

Closing Well

Again, try to match the tone of the correspondent or use words that put the correspondent in the mood you want them to have after they read your response. Happy people can get another thank you and a "hope you're our customer soon" sort of closing. Angry or disappointed people might require words to the effect of "We realize you have many choices when it comes to X, and we hope you will consider choosing us in the future."

The Reality of Business Correspondence

As I noted earlier, on the whole, happy people don't write letters. Treasure those compliments when you get them and make sure that if the customer recognizes or compliments specific people or departments, they and their leaders are informed about the happy customer.

If business correspondence is your full-time job, you will learn a lot about how people argue: which approaches they'll take to get what they want, what upsets them, and other important attitudes. You'll encounter a lot of bad language (vulgar, grammatically incorrect, or both). You'll see moments of joy and of high dudgeon. The bottom line is that, from a literary point of view, you are the "voice" of your organization. You have the opportunity to represent it well, to celebrate with your fans, and maybe turn around some of your detractors. It's an exercise in applied rhetoric, and it's a great education in writing clearly and well.

Writing to Elected Officials

Another form of correspondence businesses might use is a letter to an elected official. Why would you or they need to do this?

- **Appointment-making:** Your company CEO or Government Relations representative might want to make an appointment to meet your representative or senator. This is better done by phone, so focus on the items below.
- **Lobbying:** If you work for a government contractor ("Beltway Bandit" being the derogatory term, "Highway Helper" being the more polite version), it is entirely possible you might find an occasion to ask a representative or senator to fund a specific project or program. Specifically, your company might be lobbying for a "plus-up," which would be a budget increase to an existing program, or a set-aside, which would be new

money specifically set aside to pay for a product/service that your company produces.

- **Complaining:** Your representative or senator is voting or doing something that harms your company's interests. You want them to stop.
- **Thanking:** Your representative or senator has done something that helped your company's business. You want to express your appreciation.

You might not necessarily agree with your employer or your elected official, but you can still use a few specific skills and tactics to work through the process. To begin, if you've been asked to write a letter to someone in Congress (or Parliament, Duma, etc.), what tone do you use? How do you approach this work? My experience is with Americans and the American system of government and expectations. Your approach and tone could differ elsewhere. My apologies for my lack of knowledge overseas.

Keep Things Neat and Orderly

Realistically, a representative or senator will not be reading his or her own mail. That task will fall to his or her staff. Every staff member ("staffer") has a specific way of sorting the mail, with personal correspondence from the member's family or close associates likely coming first, followed by constituents, then junk mail. Constituent letters can move further up the list if they appear in a company-letterhead envelope; are addressed by a printer or neat handwriting; and do not include unnecessary commentary on the exterior ("Angry constituent letter enclosed" is probably a bad thing to write). And while an email might seem the more immediate way to contact someone in Washington, a plain old paper letter on company letterhead makes more of an impression than an email. Think of how much junk email your spam filter weeds out. Now multiply that by a few hundred thousand, and you might have some idea of the volume Congress receives on a regular basis.

Start with Respect

This seems like a no-brainer, but even if your employer is unhappy with the way an elected official is behaving or voting, it would serve you well to write in a direct, respectful manner. Don't include insults, innuendos, or echoing of allegations heard at the water cooler, in the media, or on the internet even if found to be true. Irritating someone—particularly someone in power—is a poor way to get them to read your letter. By respect, I don't mean being obsequious, begging, or fawning. I do mean using proper titles, avoiding familiarity or insult, and assuming that said elected official has an informed, educated vocabulary. You might not agree with that assumption or believe it; regardless, assume so in your writing anyway.

Get to the Point

Congressional staffers are busy people. They are not going to have the time or patience to read a ten-page polemic on all the perceived errors your elected official has made. Focus on one topic, and mention that topic in your opening sentence. As with any constructive feedback—if that's what you're providing—it's good to follow the situation-impact-outcome format. That is, you state the problem, explain its impact to your company, and explain what you would prefer your elected official do to rectify the situation. This approach works for lobbying or complaint situations. For additional insight into formatting a formal letter, refer back to the section on writing complaint letters.

Concentrate on Topics That Interest Your Reader

Members of the U.S. Congress, whether they be in the House of Representatives or the Senate, have very specific interests in their jobs. Most importantly, they are interested in issues that directly affect their constituents (district or state), including jobs or public safety matters, which could, in turn, affect their ability to get re-elected. Also, do a little research: most members of Congress belong to one or more committees or subcommittees related to specific aspects of public policy. If your representative/senator is on the Armed Services, Foreign Relations, or other national security-related committee or subcommittee, they are more likely to pay attention to issues or arguments related to that particular topic.

Be Realistic about Your Expectations

Understand the Constitutional or jurisdictional limitations of your representative or senator. There might not be much a member of Congress can do about a Supreme Court ruling or about a law passed by your state or local government. However, they do have some influence over which types of laws or budgets are passed in their area of action, especially if they are on the committee that handles your issue.

That said, throwing in a comment like "I pay your salary" won't sway an elected official much better than it would with a police officer who pulls you over for speeding. Another thing to consider is that your letter is unlikely to change your elected official's point of view, especially if you are opposing an issue that is a core belief for them. However, your letter can at least make your displeasure known.

Avoid Some Basic Errors

As I've noted in previous sections, there are some obvious things you should not do in any business letter: don't be rude, don't use profanity, don't write in ALL CAPS, etc. But seriously, I can't stress this enough: don't make threats. A threat made toward a business will attract the attention of the police. A threat to a congressperson or senator will yield a visit from the FBI, Department of Homeland Security, or Secret Service. Seriously, don't even hint at it.

Follow Up

It can take a while for mail to get to a congressional office, sometimes over a week, even when sending from an address within the 48 contiguous states, because congressional mail is scanned for bombs, anthrax, and other threatening items (see previous section). Also, even if your company's letter is read right away, it can take a week or two for a staffer to write back to you. Writing as a private citizen and under a corporate signature, I've usually received responses within three to four weeks. If it has been three weeks since you mailed said letter, it might not hurt to call the member's office to verify they've received it. And, again, if you want a more immediate response or conversation, you might want to call the member's office and arrange an appointment. That's a whole other set of protocol, so I recommend reading The Citizen's Guide to Lobbying Congress.[14]

Closing Thoughts

It is a fact of life in the United States that the federal government is involved in more and more aspects of our daily lives, personal and professional. Appealing to the government to redress grievances is included as a fundamental right in the First Amendment, so businesses have this opportunity just as do individuals. The trick, as always, is to

---

[14] By Donald E. deKieffer. Chicago Review Press, 2007.

frame your argument in such a way that you are more likely get the result you want.

Journalism — News Framing and Acquiring

In 2016, I picked up a side job reporting for SpaceflightInsider.com, a news site specializing in all things space: NASA, Department of Defense, commercial space, what have you. While I was not educated formally as a journalist, I acquired enough knowledge and experience to be hired. The primary challenges of the trade, I've observed, are tactical (acquiring the information) and strategic (framing the news). In journalism, tactics often precede the strategy, as the details of a story will affect how you tell it.

Tactics for Getting the News

Watching missions "live." Space activities happen in a lot of different places, from Cape Canaveral in Florida to the halls of Congress, the Jet Propulsion Laboratory in California, the outer solar system, or even stars millions of light-years away. It's not like Spaceflight Insider had a huge travel budget; nor was I able to put on a spacesuit, hop in a spacecraft, and fly out there to interview someone (if only!). Instead, a lot of my reporting was handled by researching and observing channels available on the internet.

For example, I covered launches that flew out of Tanegashima, Japan, Vandenberg Air Force Base in California, and of course from Cape Canaveral Air Force Station, which is 65 miles away from home. I didn't actually drive or fly out to each of these launches on every occasion. Instead, I did my preliminary research about the mission and its payload on the internet and then, when launch day came, I watched the proceedings live online, another service Spaceflight Insider provides. Mind you, I could have gone to most of the launches in Florida, but occasionally I've had other commitments. My attendance is not always necessary.

Person-on-the-street "interviewing." One thing that most space reports require is a quotation from one or more mission participants. Some of these comments can be extracted from existing media releases. Depending on my angle or connection to the story, I could also email people I knew in the industry and ask them to provide me their perspective without having to stick a microphone or recorder under their face.

Capturing imagery. Thanks to something called an essential tremor, I am not the world's steadiest photographer. I could capture decent images with my iPhone, but it was often easier, again, to acquire public-domain images from the internet and attribute them appropriately. Jason Rhian, the founder of Spaceflight Insider, also had a team of outstanding photographers who could get into places I couldn't and who took gorgeous, high-quality pictures on site.

Bringing things to life—from a distance. While I can do background and primary research online, would I have preferred to see these events and speak with participants live? Certainly. However, like I said, my employer didn't have an unlimited travel budget, and the internet made accurate long-distance reporting feasible. Whether I'm writing on site or from half a continent (or solar system) away, it is still quite possible to bring a story to life without being there. That's where the magic of writing comes in, and that's why I took the job. The creative—not the making-up-fake-news variety—part of covering space comes from writing vividly about the events as they transpire. Does the writing access the reader's senses? Emotions? Imaginations? Great: you're doing your job.

Framing the News

Some stories tell themselves, especially technical or scientific "firsts." Other topics require a little more work. Writing about an event is much easier than just a topic or, say, a report. Still, there are times when even a news item doesn't exactly jump with excitement. So how do you make a news story or other article interesting when the topic doesn't seem that exciting?

Sometimes you've got a one-sentence news item: So-and-So died, Company X bought Company Y, or New Product Z will be released tomorrow. Assuming you're not writing for Twitter and your publication expects more than 140 characters but less than 250–500 words, how do you fill in that blank space? This can be particularly challenging if, at first glance, the main point of the story can be or is summarized in the article's title or first line (as journalism teaches). What you need to do is dig a little deeper.

Obituary. The bulk of a news article after the opening sentence is used to provide details and context for the story. In the first instance—the death of Famous So-and-So—one needs to explain why this individual's passing  warrants your reader's attention beyond a standard blurb in the obituary section. What was the decedent's connection to the reader's community or interests? Were the circumstances of their death mysterious, expected, or unexpected? Is there a "human interest" angle, such as the individual's charity work or sterling reputation? How were those demonstrated? Or was the deceased a figure of controversy? What was his or her impact or most notable contribution while alive? And so forth.

Business notice. This could be a simple business story, from one company buying another to a single company opening a new location or line of business. Where does the "angle" come in? Why should someone care beyond the headline or opening sentence or paragraph? Again, you're looking to meet the reader's interests. Is the business new to the reader's community? Will the business activity result in more jobs for the area? Fewer jobs? Was there some controversy about one company or another? You can capture a hint of some of this in your headline, but again the content beneath your opening line is going to be where you provide the rest of the story.

New product announcement. The day after a new product/service announcement is easy because you can talk about what the new item is, what its features are, and how it differs from what the company has done before or what's on the market now. But what about the day before an announcement? How do you cough up 200–300 words on something you know nothing about? Again, your best bet is providing context for the announcement. What has the company been known for doing up to now? Has this announcement been highly anticipated? Have there been any hints or (reliable) leaks about what the product might be? If the company has made product announcements before, what has been the reception and ultimate product outcome?

Other thoughts. Is there any controversy or question surrounding an event? You could look at this as "digging up dirt," or you could look at it as "getting the whole story." Either way, there must be some reason your readers should be interested in why X is happening—also called a "hook." Your job is to find that hook.

Any story you write can be expanded by adding quotations from the people involved, relevant statistics, or informed explanations about what comes next. The goal, of course, is not to make stuff up—find the content you need to fill in the blanks. The creative part also comes from deciding which blanks would be most interesting to your readers to fill.

White Papers

White papers are a regular output in the technical world—especially in the aerospace, defense, or other tech industries.

What Is It?

A white paper is a short document, usually two to ten pages, that proposes a solution to a particular problem—technical, political, social, or other—using an organization's existing capabilities. Essentially, it's a marketing document.

Why Write One?

Sometimes a U.S. Government agency puts out Requests for Information (RFIs) seeking inputs on a particular technical problem they are facing. Sometimes your organization has identified a problem that they feel needs to be addressed and for which their particular widget or expertise is the solution. In the case of a solution to a technical issue, a company will share just enough proprietary information to provide the general outline of their solution (unless they classify it or add a bunch of proprietary notices to it). The idea with a white paper is usually to attract attention: "Hey, we've got this great idea, contact us directly for more!" And the "more" would be, for example, a full-blown proposal for money or a formal request for paid work.

What's the Format?

Below is one format for white papers I used at NASA, along with the content and length guidance. Some of the language is mine, some of it was forwarded to me.

ABC Widget for Solving Problem X

Executive Summary

This is an overall summary of your white paper (three to four paragraphs, no more than one page). Ideally, this should be written last to make certain that you've covered all of the main points of your proposal[15]: the problem being solved, summary of the technical approach, benefits of your approach, and a bottom-line cost and schedule. Your paper title should be short, descriptive, and easily understood by a non-technical audience.

Introduction

This should be a short paragraph or two (two to four sentences each) describing the problem you are attempting to solve.

Background

This section should describe why the problem you are solving is important and to whom—i.e., who needs this solution, what benefit(s) they will derive from it, what approaches have been used to date, and why a new approach is needed (three to five paragraphs).

Methodology

Here is where you describe your approach to solving the problem at hand (five to seven pages). This should include the physical, technological, or operational principles involved in your solution, what the individual components will do, and what the anticipated results or outputs would be. In addition to a description of your approach, this section should note where your solution results in innovations or improvements in one or more of the following areas:

- Technology
- Management
- Integration
- Cost

---

[15] There are other schools of thought. Some writing gurus suggest you write the summary first so you have a clear idea of the "big picture."

- Schedule

If you are using this white paper as the basis for a proposal, this is a good place to do a "sanity check" on your content to make certain you are answering the questions a solicitation or RFI is asking.

Other items you might wish to cover are:

- **Description of the team:** These are your personnel and key partners—who you are, what sorts of similar problems you've solved previously, and why you are ideally situated to solve this particular problem.
- **Description of facilities:** Labs, special test equipment (STE), or other facilities your team has access to that will allow you to execute your solution.
- **Description of costs and schedule:** What your solution will cost to implement, what that money buys, and how long it will take to execute.

Conclusion

The conclusion should summarize the key advantages and the benefits of your approach (three to five sentences).

Presentations

Psychology Today notes that public speaking is something that many people fear worse than death. Determining why people feel that way might be an interesting academic exercise, but for now I'm going to make a couple of assumptions about you, my readers:

- If you're a technical communicator, you will have to give a presentation at some point.
- If you know enough to write about something, you can talk about it.

If you're someone who fears speaking worse than death, hopefully the advice below, coming as it does from a fellow professional, introvert, and recovering giver of bad speeches, will help you deliver presentations more easily without undue pain or suffering.

Preparation

Congratulations! You've just been asked to give a presentation about "X" for your boss and half a dozen of her peers. Aside from finding out who the audience is, you'll also want to know the situation (need for or context of the presentation), how you need the audience to react, and how much time you've been given to talk. You know: audience, situation, and outcome.

Mind the time. The amount of time you've been given to talk is important because that gives you an idea of how much content you need to prepare. If it's a one-minute status update, you might be able to do that from your chair without even standing up or needing a Power-Point slide. A five-minute presentation means you might or might not need any visual aids—ask if you need them. At the 15-minute mark, you'll need considerably more time to prepare because you'll have more content. In most cases, I'd say Content is King, but when you're giving a live presentation it's best to let time be your guide. The more time you have, the more detail you can and should provide.

Outlining. There are some folks who absolutely hate "outlining." This is one of those times you might want to accept the inevitable and do it anyway. You might have the whole thing structured in your head, but it helps to put it on a screen or on paper. Also, there is the chance that your supervisor will want to see what you plan to cover before you get too involved.

While you're working on that outline, my military friends and family have reminded me more than once to do the following:

- Tell 'em what you're gonna tell 'em.
- Tell 'em.
- Tell 'em what ya told 'em.

This isn't very different from the five-paragraph essay we learn starting in middle school: introduction, three main topics (more on that in a moment), summary. Exit.

Why only three main topics? Okay, sometimes you can't always do it that way. An all-day meeting might cover five or more big topics. However, your audience won't remember much more than three, so when possible try to narrow the topics or main points down to those three.

How do you structure those main topics? As a starting point, consider reviewing the section on "How Do You Organize Content?" (Chapter 3). In a business setting, your topic is usually self-organizing. If you're discussing a timeline, you talk about things in chronological order. If you've got a new organization or "org" chart to discuss, you work from the top down or bottom up, as you see fit. If you're discussing a new rocket, you might start with the engines and work your way up to the payload. Again, your topic will have its own logic, and if you're familiar with it already, you'll know how to organize the content.

Stay relevant. You might really like your topic, and you might be passionate enough to be tempted to share everything that you know. Don't. Thinking about your audience, you want to make sure that you share facts that matter to them and fit within the context of the meeting.

This is where context or situation matters as much as your time constraint. Are you making a presentation for informational purposes (a new policy or regulation that affects the work), entertainment purposes (informing everyone about the company picnic), or decisional purposes (management needs to decide whether to keep funding your project)?

If you're there to entertain, keep your tone light.

If you're sharing information on a new process or regulation, depending on what it is, keep the content and tone factual and professional. For example, never joke about Human Resources regulations: those folks have little to no sense of humor whatsoever because failure to comply can cause the organization to be hauled into court and cost them (or you) serious money.

If you're there to persuade, your demeanor and content should be professional, upbeat, and on point. Your audience needs to hear why your proposal is a good thing, why not approving it would be a bad thing, and what's in it for them if they approve it.

Rehearse, rehearse, rehearse. This requirement will vary from person to person and speech to speech. You can probably give people a one-minute update on your work status without notecards or staying up all night practicing in front of the mirror. For five-minute talks,

I've been known to scribble my outline in my journal to get my thoughts ordered before the meeting, and then get up and wing it after that. Of course I also had some time at Disney and other organizations that provided good training for speaking in front of audiences.

I'm not saying you can go to a meeting with absolutely no idea of what you're going to say. That would be unprofessional and more than a little awkward to have a blank look on your face when you're called upon to speak. Plus, if you're fumbling around, you're wasting other people's time, especially the boss's, and that is a Bad Thing. At the very least, if you're in a meeting where there's a possibility you might be asked to speak, the people in the room will want to know about something you're working on. You should know the status of your own work and be able explain how it's going. Disney taught me that "I don't know" is almost never a good response. "I don't know, but I can find out" is better.

So, semper paratus: always be ready.

Finish on a high note. Your get-off-the-stage line should direct your audience's attitude or attention in the direction you want them to go. If you're there to entertain, end on a high note or have them looking forward to what comes next. If you're there to inform, ask if everyone understood or has questions. If you're there to persuade, ask for the sale or say something like you're looking forward to receiving your audience's approval.

Relax. I had a friend in grad school who would get hives or hyperventilate at the thought of talking in front of the group. Stage fright is no fun, that's the truth. I had it when I was younger until I tried several tricks that kept my mind focused on the task at hand. Maybe one of these will work for you.

Remember that in this situation you are the expert. Your audience is looking to you because they don't know what you know—if anyone should lack confidence, it's them—you're the one with something to share.

Assume you're among friends. Okay, depending on the situation or your relationships with your coworkers or fellow students, this might not be the case. However, if the situation is more or less friendly and you're on good relations with the people you work with, then you're just sharing information with friends, not facing the Inquisition.

Pretend the audience is not there. This is easier on a stage with bright lights and a darkened auditorium.

Breathe.

Open with humor, but only if appropriate.

Practice making a mistake. Yes, I'm serious. Why do this? A lot of people fear public speaking, and if they see you make a mistake and humorously recovering from it, you will come across as more sympathetic and relatable. It loosens you up and makes you (and your audience) more tolerant if anything else goes awry.

Prepare your slides. I try to keep my PowerPoint presentations to one slide per minute. There's nothing particularly sacred or special about that number. If you talk faster, and the content warrants it, go faster. If you're showing a lot of images or graphics, you can usually have more slides because your audience isn't reading them, they're paying attention to you and what you're saying.

Speaking of reading: NASA's internal presentations are often notorious for being text-heavy because presenters try to get everything about a topic onto one slide. The idea being that the whole story would be in the PPT if someone missed the presentation and wanted to print it. Again, unless you're at NASA and your manager tells you to do this, don't. Put at least some of your content into the Notes section of the application or make your own handwritten notes. If you put all the things you mean to say on the screen, people will read the screen and not listen to you. Therefore, if you've got a lot of information, provide the main points on the screen and provide the details in your color commentary, i.e., the stuff that is not on the screen. Or, if you have a chart, table, or illustration, the explanation of the chart should go into your notes, which you share aloud. If they wanted or needed to read a paper, you'd be giving them the document and not giving a talk, right? If you've been asked to speak rather than just forward a document, it's generally because the content will be explained or received better with some sort of immediate human presence in the room. Often this is because people will have questions about the content, which cannot be answered in a memo or other document. (Not sure if a meeting presentation is the best way to share information? See the section in Chapter 6 on "Intra-Office Communications.")

Prepare for questions. Again, you're there to deliver information in person, so the expectation is that you will respond to questions and allow time for your answers. That's when it's helpful to know your stuff. If you're reporting about your work that week, you can usually answer a question with a minimum of preparation. If your questioner has something more detailed in mind, you might need to follow up with them "offline," meaning after the meeting.

If you're presenting a topic that requires a decision, however, you might need to have answers prepared for really tough questions. The more contentious the issue, the more likely you are to be asked questions that make you uncomfortable. Audience members could be questioning your assumptions, your data, your conclusions, or even your motivations. The trick, as always, is not to look like you're taking it personally, even if it is personal and you do feel that way. Count to ten in your mind…and know your stuff. If you can anticipate questions or objections and have answers to counter them, you've got it nailed. The questioner might not like your answer, but that's not entirely your problem. And you can smile as you dismount.

Minor hint from a high school theater jock: Don't eat chocolate, milk, peanut butter, or dairy products right before you're scheduled to go on. Just trust me on this.

Again…relax. No one, to my knowledge, ever died from giving an office presentation. There might be times when you wish that were the case, but stressing or obsessing over the experience won't do you any good. Watch or read something funny before you go on. Visualize yourself giving a flawless performance and winning the argument. Whatever it takes to get your head in the right place to speak in front of a group of your fellow humans. I'm not a speech coach, I'm an English major, but I've had enough experience giving presentations to know that I usually recover just fine from them once they're done.

Reports

In 2017 I received a reader letter from a student who had questions about the types of reports I've written for NASA. Below are some of my answers.

What Types of Reports or Manuals (If Any) Did You Have to Prepare While Working as a Tech Writer for NASA?

When I worked at Marshall Space Flight Center (MSFC), 2006–2012, I wrote a variety of conference papers, which were essentially status reports on the status of the Ares Launch Vehicles and later the Space Launch System (SLS). These reports covered different aspects of the vehicles, from specific elements such as first stage, upper stage, or boosters to the overall program or the test flight program. On occasion, I also contributed to or edited internal planning documents such as the Certification of Flight Readiness (COFR) or Systems Engineering Management Plan (SEMP). On rarer occasions, I wrote internal documents in response to Congressional or White House (Office of Science & Technology Policy/OSTP) inquiries about the progress of the program.

As a freelance writer (2014–present), I've written, contributed to, or edited internal planning documents for future exploration programs, such as the agency's Mars exploration plans. Another project I worked on was a summary of technology development roadmaps, which are essentially NASA's best attempt to describe what future technologies are needed in space exploration and how long it might take to develop them. Other work has related to education and outreach, such as informing internal or external customers at another NASA center of what sort of progress or contribution their group has made.

Who Were Your Target Audiences?

These vary by product. Conference papers are usually for other engineers in the aerospace field (American Institute for Aeronautics and Astronautics (AIAA), Joint Navy-NASA-Air Force (JANNAF), International Astronautical Federation, among others). Internal planning documents are meant for higher-up managers, who want to know how a program plans to manage its business and operations, such as systems engineering or approving a flight test. Intra-government reports would go to staff members of the legislative or executive branches wanting to understand how NASA was justifying a program decision or expenditure. Outreach products can go to internal audiences, such as other NASA centers unaware of what X center is doing or to external audiences, such as industry or academic institutions interested in partnering with the center or looking to use a particular technology.

Are There Any Legal or Ethical Issues You Need to Be Aware of When Writing?

Most technical papers dealing with rocket propulsion and guidance are subject to the International Traffic in Arms Regulations (ITAR), which are designed to prevent hostile nations from getting hold of information they could use to make weapons and attack us. Those papers go through a review by an export control officer to ensure that they aren't revealing too much of NASA's "secret sauce." Those restrictions are loosened somewhat for papers delivered to conferences that require security clearances, like the JANNAF meeting. Congressional or presidential inquiries can be treated as "controlled unclassified information" (CUI). This happens if the questions relate to policy matters like, "Should we cancel funding for X Program?" Sometimes I couldn't share those responses with my employer because of the CUI rating, even when the content could affect job security—mine or hers.

In other situations, if I had to write an internal technical report and my employer was competing for a contract to build a piece of technology mentioned in the report, I'd have to "firewall" myself by avoiding communications with the manufacturing side of my employer about the report.

Even outreach products can be scrubbed for legal or other sensitivities. For example, a NASA center might be negotiating with a company to use their technology or for the company to use a particular piece of NASA tech but hasn't concluded those negotiations yet, so any reference to that company might get scrubbed from a report.

These are just some of the variations.

Even in non-space settings, internal and external reports will often have a similar structure:

- Executive summary
- Introduction and purpose of the report
- Results
- Conclusions or recommendations
- Appendices and related data

Reports of any kind can be subject to content restrictions beyond national security. For example, the owners of the report might be more concerned about disclosing proprietary information, such as pricing methods, future plans, or advantageous business practices. In all cases, report writers will rely greatly on their audience, context (situation), and intended outcome to drive their content and tone.

Meeting Minutes

Whether you're supporting a large engineering organization or a member of a nonprofit group, if you're a technical writer, the odds are better than even that you will be asked to record the minutes at a meeting, especially if there is not a designated executive assistant or other clerical employee dedicated to the task. I've encountered technical writers who take great offense to such requests and, in fact, refuse to do meeting minutes because they see the work as demeaning, "beneath their station," or other such responses.

"That's Beneath Me!"

I politely disagree, for a few reasons:

- I don't like to say no to a work request because it makes me appear difficult or unresponsive.
- If I'm in a meeting, it's likely that I will be taking notes anyway, so it's not like I'm going out of my way.
- If the meeting is for a group or department I normally would not work with, it's an opportunity to:
  o Learn more about what they're doing.
  o Make myself known to that group and, potentially, expand my network or scope of work.
- All work has its value. And while, yes, it might seem like asking the tech writer to write meeting minutes is akin to sending a Ferrari to make a two-block drive to the grocery store, it's still an opportunity to excel and prove your worth.
- On several occasions, my willingness to take meeting minutes led to additional tasks later because:
  o I had shown my willingness and diligence in helping on the previous occasion.
  o I was now familiar with the subject matter and so required less ramp-up time.

So, really: think twice before making the prideful choice. If you're the company CEO, you might have a point if someone asked you to take the minutes. Otherwise, you're there to help, so help.

How to Take Minutes

If you took notes during high school or university lectures, you know how to take meeting minutes. Unless you know shorthand, are a professional stenographer, or are a rapid typist (I think I manage 70–100 words per minute, which is about average if you've taken a keyboarding class), it is likely that you'll be summarizing what people are saying rather than recording what they say word for word.

If I am new to the group or organization and have been brought in at the last minute, I am usually given a little more leeway in interrupting, asking questions, or asking for people to repeat something they said. Also, if the group wants you to write down something word for word, then they need to give you the time to write things out verbatim and even read the content aloud back to the group so that you can confirm you got everything correct.

Another key point when taking notes is to be objective and avoid commentary unless asked for it. Most of the time, you are there to record what happened, not share your feelings about what is being said or who is saying it. You need to remember that your notes and comments will be read by people outside your organization, so clarity, accuracy, and diplomacy are usually your best tools when sharing minutes.

Related to commentary is analysis: explaining what things might mean beyond what was specifically stated in the meeting. You might have knowledge of the subject matter in question, you might not. If you feel something said in the meeting requires explanation, you can add your explanation to your minutes. However, if you are new to the group, it is likely that your minutes will need to be reviewed by someone else before they are sent out to the team. This should not be seen as an automatic judgment on you or your abilities. The reviewer might simply need to verify that what you wrote is accurate.

Lastly, if the meeting you're attending is sensitive, confidential, or otherwise restricted, you should verify that you are authorized to be in the room (do you have the appropriate security clearance, for example?). Follow the wishes of the meeting's presiding authority and only share the information you learn with the people designated to see it. You might be asked about the content, but depending on the level of sensitivity, you might not even be allowed to describe the subject matter—to do so could put you at risk of disciplinary action, termination, or legal prosecution!

In the end, being asked to take meeting minutes should not be seen as an insult, but rather as an opportunity to learn more and to show your value to your customer(s).

Web Content

As a writer, I maintain a professional site and a personal page. I'll freely admit that Heroic Technical Writing gets at least 20 times the audience that BartLeahy.com receives. The primary reason for that discrepancy is content focus.

What's It All About?

I've written personal blogs under various guises for years now, and their readership has always been minimal, mostly because a lot of people don't know me, nor do they necessarily care about my opinions regarding books, movies, politics, relationships, or the events of the day. However, the success of Heroic Technical Writing owes a lot to some sage advice I got from Hugh Stanley, who runs MyKick-Start.com, a business information site based out of Huntsville, Alabama. His advice amounted to, "You need to write a blog about something you know really well."

Mind you, my personal blog is about something, but that something comprises my opinions about whatever interests me at a given moment. The best way to acquire an attentive and loyal blog audience is to write consistently and with high quality or insight about one particular topic of interest to others. If you're interested enough to write well about one thing consistently, you will attract an audience also interested in that subject.

What HeroicTechWriting.com—the blog and the book—is about is providing practical advice on the professional, business, and personal aspects of technical communication. Is there a demand for such advice? According to my internal stats, there's at least 20 times more demand for my thoughts on tech writing than on any other topic, so there you have it.

Who Is Your Audience?

Having content is important, but so is having an audience in mind. My primary audiences are in-school or fresh-out-of-college students pursuing careers in technical communication. My secondary audience comprises other technical writing pros who might benefit from my experiences.

What Do You Want Your Audience to DO?

Heroic Technical Writing is written as a public service for my audience and a writing outlet for me. It did not start out that way. Originally it was going to be a marketing site to bring in customers to my freelancing practice. The primary purpose of a business site is to attract customers. The blog was simply a way to share my knowledge of the technical writing business. My customers eventually appeared through network contacts and word of mouth, but the blog remained.

What do I want my audience to do with the unsolicited advice I dispense?

The goal, of course, was that they would find it useful enough to act upon. Sometimes it's enough to know my audience is reading and avoiding problems I learned the hard way. Now, of course, the blog has a secondary purpose in addition to dispensing advice: selling this book. (You did buy it, right? Or at least get it from a library?)

However, regardless of your particular content, any website you create should have a specific aim:

- If your goal is selling stuff, you should include prominent links and shopping pages that make it easy for them to purchase your products or services.
- If your goal is advocacy, you should include position papers and opportunities for people to understand your cause and "get involved."
- If your goal is sharing your creative output—news releases, fiction, music, paintings, handicrafts—around the internet, you should include hashtags, sharing buttons, or other links that allow your readers to distribute your content far and wide

(and maybe donate so you're not always giving your work away for free).

- If your goal is to facilitate discussions about specific topics, you should provide robust forums or chat services that allow interested audiences to communicate with each other.

Your audience, writing context (situation), and intended outcomes should be factored into your website so your content allows your audience to do what you want to them do with the content you provide.

Editing

Technical writers are not just creating content. Sometimes we spend a lot of our time editing other people's work. When I'm given existing technical material to edit, I have some basic items that I look for to make the content more engaging, robust, and easy to read. These are the types of edits I do when I'm asked to "Make this sound like English" and am given carte blanche to change things my way.

Content

- **Make sure your content is on point:** This means the content should relate to the primary topic at hand as well as your audience's expectations.
- **Ensure that the main point is up-front:** Scientists and engineers often assume the purpose or benefit of their particular project is so obvious it does not need to be stated up-front in plain language. I disagree. I go into a document thinking like a non-techie manager or a bureaucrat, which is close to my actual role. I need and expect the "so what?" text to be up-front. The "so what" should read something like, "We are building X Widget to make Y process better, cheaper, faster and achieve end result Z."
- **Ensure that the content is complete and makes sense:** Sometimes you might encounter a document where explanations are left out; background material that would be better up-front is buried later; or the order of operations seems contradictory or confusing. If that's the case, call them on it and attempt to clarify: "Did you mean to say…X?"

Mechanics and Copyediting

A content edit is about making certain that the content is correct, makes sense, and fits together. This differs from copyediting, where you're just looking at the mechanics of the document: grammar, spelling, punctuation, and formatting. I have yet to restrain myself from doing copyediting while doing a content edit, and generally, if I'm given free rein to fix the document, I'll be expected to do it anyway. The challenge with doing too much copyediting during a content review is that you might end up wasting time fixing minor nits on a sentence or paragraph that is going to be deleted anyway.

Sometimes you need to educate your customers on the difference between content and copy editing and determine which one they want. You might, for example, suggest a content edit first to ensure that the document has all the information it should in the proper order before you go in and do copyediting on the next draft. This is not to say you shouldn't copyedit, but be judicious about it if the content is due to go back to the SME for review.

- **Enforce active voice where feasible:** Some organizations are stylistically allergic to using any sort of individual or even corporate voice. "The magnet was moved" is more common than "The team moved the magnet," and it makes for dull reading. Passive voice adds unnecessary words and dilutes the message. If your organization is similarly averse to having actual people in their prose, see if there are ways to make the widget active: "The Space Launch System allows larger payloads to be launched into space and ensures increased science capabilities beyond Earth orbit."
- **Keep subjects and their actions close:** For some reason, technical folk find it tempting to add a lot of explanatory text between the subject of a sentence and the action the subject is performing. Here's a made-up example:

The five-segment reusable solid rocket booster (RSRB), using polybutadiene acrylonitrile (PBAN) propellant aboard and providing immediate, increased thrust during liftoff, burns for a little over two minutes before being jettisoned.

The subject in this case is the RSRB. And while there are a couple of gerunds in there (using and providing), the actual verb the RSRB performs is burns. There are 14 words separating the actor from its action. Again, the impact is diluted. There are a couple of ways you can fix this, including breaking up the sentence into a couple of sentences or moving the words around so the action is closer to its subject:

The five-segment reusable solid rocket booster (RSRB) burns its polybutadiene acrylonitrile (PBAN) propellant for a little over two minutes, providing immediate, increased thrust during liftoff before being jettisoned.

There are doubtless many other ways you can tweak this sentence to make it shorter. The point is: to make the action more immediate, you need to move the actor and his or her action closer together: The...RSRB burns.

- **Maintain parallel structure:** This could happen in a couple of different ways. For instance, you might need to make certain that the first word in each item of a bulleted list is a verb. Another thing you might need to do is ensure items of equal importance have equal length as well as a similar structure. For example, if you're describing a series of objects, you would describe them in a similar order, say, by physical description, then by function, size, capability, and safety features. Sometimes adding subheadings can keep this order consistent and ensure that each attribute is covered.
- **Unify writing styles:** It's not uncommon for multiple people to write a document and for word choices, tenses, and even tone of "voice" to change dramatically as the content shifts from author to author. The trick, as always, is to make certain the entire document reads as if one person wrote it. The simplest way to ensure a consistent style is just to read the entire document and ensure that it reads in a consistent style that you can live with (even if it is not necessarily your style).

Other items can and do come up when you're editing, such as ensuring that acronyms are spelled out the first time they're used, but these are the sort of things I've conditioned myself to spot and fix given the opportunity to do full-scale technical editing.

How Do You Justify Attending a Work Conference?

This might seem like a radical topic change after all the discussion about writing, editing, and document version control. However, when I worked for the government contractor industrial complex, I spent a surprising amount of time writing up justifications for individuals (not just myself) seeking approval to attend business conferences. It becomes part of the job, usually listed under "other duties as assigned."

Why is this so difficult? I'm not certain, but perhaps the tips below will help you when you're writing your own (or your boss's) legitimate justification to attend an event that just happens to be in Orlando, Las Vegas, Vail, Edinburgh, et cetera.

As with travel reports, employers want to know they're getting their money's worth and not paying for air, hotel, and M&IE (miscellaneous and incidental expenses) just so you can ski the slopes in Vail, Colorado, or water ski in Maui, Hawaii. You might do some of that in your free time, but ideally, you're there to work. Here's what you need to focus on while discussing the work portion of your business travel before the event.

Education

Most conferences provide sessions that are directly related to new techniques or information for people in your particular field. Be sure to list the specifics of the classes you plan to attend, their topics, and how attending them can benefit you and your organization by applying said content. If you have a current project requiring a particular skill you need, so much the better! Be sure to cite the project and skill needed in your justification.

Updates on the Industry

One of the functions business development folks fulfill at industry conferences is collecting business intelligence: what are your customers doing? What are your competitors doing? What are your partners doing? How can any or all of that activity be used to your organization's advantage? Sometimes organizations use conferences as opportunities to make a big announcement, such as landing a new contract or unveiling a new product or service. All of this activity affects your organization's competitive position, directly or indirectly, so it's important to be mindful not just of what your group is doing, but what everyone else is doing as well.

Networking and Sales

As you'll come to realize later in this book, I'm a big fan of networking. Conferences are an excellent opportunity to build your face-to-face network, which includes contacts and peers within your industry, faces that you can connect to names, and people you can call if you have a question later about Topic X.

Part of learning what the neighbors are doing can include a certain amount of business development:

- Identifying new potential customers or business opportunities.
- Learning about new needs from current customers.
- Expanding your organization's existing work or lines of business.
- Identifying new potential partners.
- Making actual sales.
- Signing business or partnering agreements.

All of these activities are possible but not necessary components of your participation in a conference; however, the more of them you can do while participating in one will build your case for attending. Your trip report is where you discuss what you actually did compared to what you stated you would do during the justification process, which I'll discuss next.

As for the skiing, water-skiing, and other activities you might happen to do while on business travel, don't get too carried away and, if you're very wise, don't share too much of it on social media.

How and Why to Write a Trip/Travel Report

If you're self-employed, you are unlikely to write a trip report. However, if you're working for someone else and they send you somewhere on business travel, you might find yourself completing such a report. The basic point of a trip report is to summarize what work-related activities you did with your time so that your employer can verify they got some value from sending you on that trip.

The Basics

If you are sent on business travel, the obvious purpose at your destination is to advance the goals of your organization. Often, a company will have a standardized form for you to complete upon returning from your trip. It will include specific data, such as where you went, how long, how many people you talked to, and what was discussed.

If you're on a marketing trip—say, by staffing the company's booth at a convention—the narrative part of your report will include a summary of what types of contacts you made, what you talked about, what sort of "intel" (intelligence) you gathered from or about your customers, and what potential value that information could bring to the company. If you made an actual sale, even better! That should be mentioned first.

Side note. If it seems odd that a technical writer would be sent to staff a convention booth, I should explain that I did this for both the Department of Defense and NASA. In the DoD world, such travel was one of my "other duties as assigned" tasks in the business development (a.k.a., BD or marketing) department. At NASA, I was part of Education and Outreach, which again meant going to events and talking with the public about NASA programs. So if you're nervous about talking to people and you're applying for a BD job, you might want to ask if convention booth staffing is part of the job duties. The answer is likely "yes."

Other business travel can be proposal-related. In that case, your report will most likely state whether or not the proposal was submitted on time, what and who worked well, who or what did not, and maybe suggestions for the future.

You also could be sent out to help write documentation or some other communication product. Again, your report should summarize the level of success you and your coworkers achieved.

Closing Thoughts and a Reality Check

If you're working for the corporate headquarters (a.k.a. "the mother ship") and you're visiting a branch office, you might find yourself receiving some negative attitudes or complaints from the field office. Given that everyone sent on travel might have to write a travel report, you could also be treated as a "spy" and conversations could cease when you enter the room.

None of this is particularly nice or rational, but it is reality. The best things you can do while on travel are simply:

- Do your job well.

- Be polite with the people you encounter.
- Don't be defensive about, nor try to encourage gripes about HQ or your department. If people in the branch office have feedback about you in particular, by all means listen with the intention of improving yourself. Otherwise, just nod and pass the information along.

And while it's not stated directly, you are allowed to have fun in your off time on these trips…just not too much fun.

Chapter 5: Complex Tech Writing Tasks

This chapter covers some of the larger, more complex projects tech writers see: the ones usually listed as the primary duties or reasons to be hired. These include technical documentation, proposals, strategic communication, and instructional design. Proposals are an exceptionally complex endeavor, requiring a mix of technical and marketing writing as well as understanding the government proposal-writing ecosystem. Things become more challenging from here.

Documentation

There are several types of documentation, the most common being requirements, technical, and end-user documentation.

Requirements

This is the type of documentation developed when a team is determining whom a product will serve, what it will do for them, and how. It will include:

- A list of the users, how they would interact with the product, and for what purpose (also called use cases).
- A definition of the overall system architecture and development methods.
- A description of how the development team will do its work (who will be in charge, what will be developed first, what might be added as additional features if there is time or money available).
- A schedule showing how long the development process will take.
- A concept of operations (CONOPS) for using the product.
- A list of development participants, roles, and responsibilities.
- (Eventually) A detailed description of the types of data to be acquired and how it will be used or evaluated.

The audiences for design documents of this sort are often technology managers, who want to ensure that a development team knows what it's doing, their resources are being used wisely, and the work is proceeding according to plan.

Many types of engineering—such as my favorite, launch vehicle propulsion—use requirements documents to make the design process more systematic and ensure that everything has been accounted for before people start coding software or "bending metal."

Technical Documentation

This is the serious, in-the-weeds content that communicates, engineer-to-engineer, or engineer-to-manufacturer, about how things should be designed or built. Unlike requirements definitions, which can be done without a lot of formal training in an engineering discipline, technical documentation usually requires hands-on experience with the tools, hardware, software, processes, and terminology needed to do the job. I had to turn down a job in software documentation because it would've taken much too long for me to get up to speed.

These are the types of jobs that often go to "engineers who can write"; don't laugh, English majors, they exist. For example, if you see a technical documentation job that includes in its experience requirements an engineering degree or time spent in the military, they are looking for someone who can write engineering content by engineers for engineers or by technicians for technicians. This is not my thing, needless to say, but if you're an engineer or technician transitioning into technical writing, it might be for you.

End-User Documentation

This is the type of documentation most people are familiar with. It's the book or online help module people refer to when someone tells you to RTFM ("Read the Frickin' Manual!"). It's a step-by-step process document that walks a user through how to operate or employ a piece of software or an engineering product like a toaster or even a launch vehicle. User documentation often employs a dual-form organization, meaning it's broken out by activity, but is chronological when describing individual functions. It includes possible cautions and warnings, which appear before a step is taken so the user is aware of a problem prior to taking any action. It establishes technical nomenclature and provides a glossary of those ever-present acronyms. It also ties the product's operational functions to work functions or outcomes.

To write user documentation, you have to become familiar with the user's actual work processes:

- What their primary tasks or outputs are.
- How they normally encounter the product.

93

- How they will receive their instructions. (Are they at their desk? On a factory floor? In a machine shop? Will the instructions be in print? On a computer? At a kiosk? On a mobile app?)
- How often they are likely to use it.
- How problematic or dangerous errors are if they occur and how they can be addressed.
- How they handle exceptions or unusual situations.
- What personal safety equipment (if any) they wear while handling the product.

User documentation is the supreme example of "translating Engineerish into English" and is often the most challenging and people-intensive technical writing you might do. The complexity exists because you must be able to absorb what the engineers are doing; advocate for the user if the product is creating problems, confusion, or dangers; exercise diplomacy when challenges arise between the developers and the end users; write user test cases that make sense for the users' work environment; operate as a guinea pig (test subject) for the user test cases; and keep the documentation updated as product or version upgrades arise.

Selling Your Program More Effectively

Proposals, white papers, and other persuasive documents are a decent way to earn money. Technology programs often need a technical communicator's help to bring in money or to make sure the funding doesn't go away (as in the case of government-to-government documents). What follows are some suggestions for improving the strength of your case.

It's Not All about the Tech

You'll catch me saying this more than once, but it bears repeating: you cannot talk only about your technology and what it does and hope to win your case.

Yes, if you read a request for proposal (RFP) or questionnaire from a government agency, they might ask for something direct like "Describe your program and its outcomes to date."

Simple, right? Not entirely. This is where you need to do some history writing and yes, I will dare to say it, marketing.

For instance, you might be tempted to dive right in and talk about your product's features, as in this fictitious example:

> The Gargantua XL 01 SuperProgram processes data at 500 mega-burps per second in a Linux/UNIX environment and can calculate orbital parameters within .4449321q43 arc-seconds per minute.

And yes, to an engineer who uses your program that might make all the sense in the world. However, this approach makes one critical and quite probably fatal mistake: it assumes that another engineer is reading it.

Depending on the size (dollar amount) of the program in question, you might have a much more diverse reading audience. They will most likely have a technical background of some sort, but they might not be specifically versed in your tech.

Ideally, rather than starting with what the technology can do, you want to talk about what problem your particular technology will solve. That's not to say you won't have the opportunity to brag about your 500 megaburps; you will, but not right away. What you want to tell your reader is that the Gargantua XL 01 SuperProgram allows rockets or spacecraft to get to their target or destination with a precision ten times greater than anything currently flying, or that your widget will reduce the likelihood of an error from one in ten thousand computations to one in a million.

Or instead of a computer program, you might have a rocket to sell. What makes your vehicle better than any other rocket out there? Who benefits? How much money is saved? How much more capability does it provide? What types of missions does it support better than any other competitor? Is your technology faster, better, cheaper, or more efficient than others? In which ways?

If the format of your proposal or white paper allows you the freedom to provide background, I'd explain things in the following order:

- What is the problem being solved?
- What has been done before?
- How is your particular gadget/vehicle/process different?
- How is your particular gadget/vehicle/process better?
- What are the benefits or outcomes for users working with your gadget?

Keeping It Simple

Let's say you're writing a fact sheet to lobby Congress. As I noted earlier, staffers on Capitol Hill tend to be young (mid-twenties); they might or might not be familiar with the history of your organization, cause, or equipment; and they are notoriously overworked, often covering multiple issues for their particular member of Congress. This is not meant to bash congressional staffers, it's just a reality you have to face. Given those realities and the likely constraints on their time and attention, you need to keep your language clear, simple, and relatively free from jargon.

How does this affect your writing? First of all, you will need to reduce the amount of technobabble. Speak in more generic, non-engineering terms about the technology and its benefits, which might mean using "computer chip" instead of "integrated circuit" or "rocket" instead of "launch vehicle." I can imagine someone saying, "You're dumbing it down!" or "You're making it less precise." Okay, fair enough. If there's a reason you need to specify "integrated circuit" rather than "computer chip," explain that terminology briefly and move on.

Remember that the goal is to reach your audience and win them over. If they spend five minutes puzzling over what you mean, you've lost them. Most staffers are college educated, so you don't have to be condescending, but you should be clear. For instance, you probably don't need to provide the dictionary definition of what an algorithm is (if that's what you're supporting), but you should take a sentence to explain what your algorithm does in its designated environment.

Graphics are good. If you have the time and a good graphic designer available, you should include relevant graphics that depict or amplify the story you want to tell. For example, include a high-quality, computer-aided design (CAD) drawing of your hardware if that's what you're selling; use bar charts to compare your performance with others, line charts to show trends for why your tech is necessary, or area charts to show how much smaller your program's operational footprint is compared to others'.

Discuss People

This can mean several things:

Show off the team. If you're writing to the government and you want to show who the players are on your particular project, you should name them and their locations—this is important for members of Congress, especially, who will want to know which districts or constituencies benefit from funding a particular program. If one or more of your team members are leaders or "celebrities" in their field, you should note that as well.

Show off the beneficiaries. Your widget/process undoubtedly benefits someone, or you wouldn't have built it. You should mention targeted beneficiaries first—the people who will most benefit from your work—and then move on to secondary beneficiaries. Lastly, you can talk about future beneficiaries or customers. This is especially important in Small Business Innovation Research (SBIR) or Small Business Technology Transfer (STTR) proposals, which include a section that specifically asks how you will commercialize your product or service beyond the designated government customer(s).

Ideally, the benefit of your product should be specific, measurable, achievable, relevant, and timely (SMART). If you tell your reviewers that "everybody on Earth will benefit" from using your product, you'd better make a convincing case. (Hint: it's usually better to do some realistic research on your intended target market and work the numbers from there.) And, again, pointing out the geographical locations of known or anticipated customers and beneficiaries can help a member of Congress (or their staff) better justify supporting the program.

Underpromising vs. Overpromising

The technological wizardry available today gives me hope for a better future. However, the risk exists for inventors to overpromise on the eventual outcomes of their inventions. This usually happens when engineers get ambitious about anticipating their secondary effects.

Hypothetical: Company X's new widget reduces the cost of launching a rocket from ABC Space Center. The ambitious engineering marketer then goes on to presume lower launch costs from ABC Space Center will resort in more launches, thereby improving the local economy in the municipalities closest to the center. While possible, that might be taking things a bit too far...and in any case, local business development would be an extra, potential benefit, not a guaranteed, primary goal. Another type of overpromising might be one that promises zero defects or 100 percent availability or some other impossibly optimistic outcome.

On the other hand, a technical team can get so focused on the specific application for their particular widget that they miss out on identifying how the widget could, with a little tweaking, work in another market or technology area. As Gene Kranz says in the movie Apollo 13, "I don't care what something was designed to do, I want to know what it can do!" This type of creative thinking is especially important when discussing potential commercialization opportunities.

Ghosting the Competition

Many times your program will be competing against one or many others. If you know who your competitors are, you should do some research on them. That way, you know the advantages and disadvantages of your product/service compared to theirs. Usually you don't cite the competition by name, just identify why your approach is better than Approach X. This practice is called ghosting. Then you need to provide reasonable rebuttals to their advantages and show how your product/service has the key advantage(s). If there are criteria where you know your product or service has an advantage (even if it's not a requirement of the RFP), mention those as well as key differentiators of your product or service.

Closing Thoughts

Again, it's a common mistake in the engineering and tech communities to cite capabilities and features and then assume the technology will speak for itself. You can't just talk about what your widget will do, you have to explain why it's better, faster, or cheaper than any other competing product and why that should matter to the customer. Providing those answers can make a difference when there are dollars and jobs on the line.

The Tech is Great, but What's It Good For?

The Great Courses website includes a class on "Becoming a Great Essayist," which I bought to help improve my skill set. One of the more important things the professor shared was the need for the essayist to make his or her observations on the world relevant to the reader. Otherwise, the writing is just a self-indulgent exercise for the writer.

The Questions One Doesn't Ask

This problem often comes up in technology-focused companies and organizations. Not to pick on my friends at NASA too much, but unaskable questions can be a frequent problem among aerospace engineers (the folks we frequently misname "rocket scientists").

If you talked to the various Ares Launch Vehicles managers—boosters, engines, core stage, etc.—each of them would proudly share the performance characteristics of their particular part of the rocket, how it functioned, and how it did things better for the overall system. So far, so good. But eventually I'd move up through the system and get to the point where I'd ask, "What is the program good for?" and the conversation would uncomfortably stop. Apparently, one did not ask that sort of question. It was obvious, wasn't it?

I recall having the "What's it good for?" conversation with an engineer who was one of the experts on Big, Beautiful Rockets, and after some embarrassed squirming, he finally came out with, "Because the rocket will help get us closer to the stars." He then added, "But you can't say that in what you're writing." Which was true, because sending people to the stars was and is not NASA policy. That was why he worked on rockets, though, and it helped me narrow down the questions I needed to ask.

To his credit, my customer heard me out and tasked me to do some research and writing on why going to the Moon, Mars, or other destination was a good idea and, more to the point, a good use of taxpayer dollars. That sort of content eventually made it into some outreach pieces, so my poking did some good, even if the program was eventually canceled.

Are You Admiring the Widget or Planning to Sell It?

To keep SMEs and other customers on target, it's helpful to ask variations of these questions:

- Who is our audience?
- What do they care about?
- How does Cool Widget X advance or improve what our audience cares about?

You're concerned with the "So what?" of a piece of writing, whether you're writing a blog, a bit of marketing copy, or a letter to an elected official. The other variation of this is asking about the WIIFM ("What's In It For Me?") for the audience.

The risk for any organization is that they become so enamored with the features of their particular widget, software, or idea that the benefits get lost in the noise. Or the benefits are taken as self-evident. Or worse, the features are seen as benefits without any further explanation necessary. This is why branding and strategic communication matter. While the bulk of an organization might be focused on the doing—the what and how—there must always be at least one or two individuals who keep their eye on the ball regarding who the customer is and why they should care about what the organization is doing.

The features of a given technology are obvious. The benefits are not necessarily obvious for the end user, the general public, or bill-paying customer; and those audiences do not always overlap. I recall asking a scientist a feature-and-benefit question about a telescope I was helping him write a proposal for. He restated a couple of different ways that it would be capable of visibility over a specific spectral range. Not being an astrophysicist, the benefit was lost on me. I asked, "Is that good? What will it enable the telescope to do?" That last question probably saved me because he said, "It helps us see more of the universe." Aha! I could work with that.

Helping Techies Articulate Product Benefits

The bottom line with this sort of work is that engineers are often tech- and task-focused (that's why they are in those careers, after all). They know what they need to accomplish and how to go about it. It sometimes takes open-ended questions to get responses from them to help them sell a product. These include:

- Who do you define as the end users or customers? Are there multiple types of customers?
- What are the customer's priorities?
- What are the customer's key measures of performance?
- How is this product better than what's been done before (based on the aforementioned performance measures)?
- What tasks/outcomes will the new tech/widget/product allow your customers to do that they have not been able to do previously?

Don't be surprised if you get some push-back on these types of questions. Engineers often look down on marketing (the practice or the people) as "fluffy," unconnected to reality, or worse, unethical. They also don't like to overpromise on performance. Check out Dilbert if you ever need examples of these attitudes. You can win over those reluctant audiences by not overpromising, merely sticking to the technology as they're designing it. The goal is to sell the product, which keeps everyone doing their job. At the very least, your feature-and-benefit discussion should help answer that ever-important question: "Why should your audience care?"

Marketing Materials/Flyers

Most of my marketing materials have been for highly technical customers, such as NASA or DoD contractors. As a result, the writing isn't always "sexy" or exciting for the average reader. However, regardless of your product, you need to be able to do a few things very quickly:

- Explain what your product/service is and what it does.
- Explain the benefits of your product/service.

The Products

In fact, you might end up starting with the chief benefit of your item and a picture of it, then let the details fall out from there.

Marketing materials are usually brief:

- Business cards
- Postcards
- Double-sided one-sheets
- Tri-fold, one-sheet brochures
- Two-page foldouts

Other marketing materials might appear in a folder or packet that contains one or more of the above. But what do you put into one of those materials? As with many products described in this book, your content will vary by your audience, situation, and intended outcome.

Audience

Your audience members will vary greatly, especially if you work for a large, publicly owned corporation or a government agency. You will often need to communicate the value of your products or services to elected officials, legislative aides, other industry or government agency representatives, and members of the voting (or share-buying) public. Regardless, your marketing messages will be based on your industry and the way your organization prefers to position itself.[16] Again, your audience is going to want to know why they should trust your product/service or do business with your organization. What you're doing is determining what is most important to your audience, and how your product/service meets those needs.

Situation

How will your audience encounter your marketing material? On the floor of a trade show? Through an internet banner ad? In the field? In an elevator? At a rocket launch? Any or all of those circumstances will determine the size, shape, appearance, and emphasis of your marketing (or education and outreach) materials. A full-scale booth might incorporate demonstration videos of your product, full- or subscale models of the product, one-page flyers, business cards, and other portable giveaways. Technical customers with more time to read might receive a folder full of detailed spec sheets and other materials. Members of the general public attending a large convention or trade show might receive a business card and a quick "elevator pitch." Your readers' situation or context will determine the form of your marketing products.

Outcome

Another determining factor in your marketing materials will be your audience's relationship to your organization and how you want them to respond to your materials. As I noted earlier, your audience might do one of the following:

- Learn – know the information.
- Feel – respond emotionally.
- Comply – follow directions (unlikely in a marketing situation, but still possible if you're working for a government agency).
- Decide – take action.

---

[16] For an excellent reference on company positioning, I highly recommend How the World Sees You: Discover Your Highest Value through the Science of Fascination and Fascinate, Revised and Updated: How to Make Your Brand Impossible to Resist by Sally Hogshead.

- Agree – advocate for or buy the proposal or product.

To have your audience (reader) take action, you will need to provide them with information that will help them take the action you seek. If you want them to buy, you'd include a price. If you want them to visit your website, you'd include the URL. If you want them to advocate on behalf of your cause, you might provide a congressional phone number for a motivated individual to call.

The point of all this being: marketing materials need to accomplish your intent using a minimum of text and—most likely—a maximum of evocative imagery. The goal, more often than not, is to make a sale or intrigue someone enough to ask more about whatever it is your organization is selling. Are you ready?

Creative Briefs

A creative brief is a product that marketing agencies often develop to clarify how a company, project, product, or service is to be marketed to its intended audience(s). The point is to ensure creative people such as artists, graphic designers, copywriters, and other individuals all have the same understanding of how they should communicate about the project or product in question. Usually the brief is developed with a specific advertising or marketing campaign in mind. Some of the basic items or questions[17] to be included in a creative brief could include:

- Client name
- Project synopsis
- Prepared by (who developed the brief)
- Creative brief outline
- Background/overview
- Campaign objective
- Target audience
- Product/project key messages
- Most important thing to say about the product/project
- How it should be said
- Supporting rationales and emotional "reasons to believe and buy"

---

[17] This list was compiled from creative briefs I've worked on with my mentor D2 and Cynthia Dailey at ScribbleSpace. The content is used with permission.

- Additional resources needed to assist creative development
- Partnerships, Alliances, Sponsors
- Creative Assets (logos, color schemes, fonts, etc.)
- Schedule

These questions might sound straightforward, but many creative briefs go through multiple cycles before the brief originator(s) and the customer(s) are satisfied with the final result. Once the answers are agreed upon by all concerned, the creative team can begin on the actual campaign designed to sell the product.

Strategic Communication

"Strategic" communication is content written about an organization or program that is designed to build support among the organization's stakeholders and encourages them to support the goals of said organization. "Stakeholders" are people with a direct financial, technical, or policy interest in an organization or program's success. To engage in strategic communication, then, is to share information about a program, project, or organization in a way that matters to the stakeholders and enables them to better understand and support the work the program is doing.

This is different from "pure" technical writing because the precise concern of the audience (or the writer) is not with executing the technical content of the activity. Instead, the concern of the strategic communicator is to advance the business and public support interests of the program itself.

So what do you need to know to be a "strategic communicator" instead of, say, a documentation writer? Within NASA, the difference was in the user and audience of the information. In both cases (strategic communication and documentation), the goal is to communicate specific, useful information of a scientific or technical nature in such a way that the audience can act upon it in the way the writer intends. However, rather than focusing on the technical activities you are focusing more on the "why" or the benefits of the technology that enable stakeholders to advance their own goals. Another term for this, which you might hear in the political world occasionally, is "messaging," where you try to get out the "messages" that you want others to think about when they hear about a project or organization.

Does this sound like blah-blah-blah or business doublespeak? I apologize. It's a little philosophical, and I've more or less taken it for granted.

Let's say the program manager is going out to talk to a group of companies that would like to join the work she or he is trying to do. They are going to want to know things such as:

- What are the business opportunities they might explore in the program?
- What are the deadlines for submitting proposals to do new work?
- What sort of progress is the program making?
- How many workers might your organization need for future work?

These are the sorts of statistics (technical information) your audience wants. Yes, the technical aspects of the project are important to provide context (where are you going, how, and why?), but your emphasis as a strategic communicator is to provide information the audience can use to plan for the future, lobby their congressperson, encourage their employees, or propose future business.

"Strategic" communication, then, is about sharing technical information (a message) that helps your organization's supporters justify supporting the work you are doing. It requires a slightly different mindset from documentation writing because while documentation exists to ensure that users of a technology or process use it correctly and safely, strategic communicators are providing information so stakeholders can accurately and honestly support your cause.

Think of it as the sort of messaging corporations like to do when there isn't a crisis happening: "This is how we'd like you to think of us."

Admittedly, this is a little more "fluffy" than traditional technical writing, and I confess that I prefer it in many ways to documentation. It is more philosophical, for one thing. It requires a different type of creativity because it is dealing with different types of actions: social and political rather than technical. With documentation, you want to make sure each audience member understands and uses your information in precisely the same way so the technology works correctly. With strategic communication, you are aiming for your audience to take some action on your behalf. You are not always certain what that action will be, but in the end, you want your audience to advance your cause, whatever it is.

If you are looking for a writing job in a technical field, but are more interested in winning hearts and minds, strategic communication might be for you.

Instructional Design Materials

My primary line of work for the last few years has been in the instructional design field. What, exactly, is instructional design? InstructionalDesign.org says:

> [Instructional design is the] process by which instruction is improved through the analysis of learning needs and systematic development of learning experiences. Instructional designers often use technology and multimedia as tools to enhance instruction.

In practical terms, that means I'm helping deliver classroom materials, such as facilitator (trainer) scripts, PowerPoint presentations, workbooks, activity materials, and handouts. My first experience with this work was at Disney University, where I was teamed with instructional designers to develop management training classes.

The instructional designer works through a systematic process, sometimes called ADDIE (Analysis, Design, Development, Implementation, and Evaluation). You start by analyzing what the skill gap is; what the target audience needs to learn to address that gap; who the target audience should be; and how they might apply the skills or knowledge they need. Once all that gets worked out, the process moves toward creating an outline for how the training experience will flow, in what order, and with what emphases. When the outline is approved, the course material is developed in detail. Depending on the extent of the material, that development could involve any of the products I listed above. At the tail end of the development process, the training experience is launched with its intended audience, and is evaluated for effectiveness and future improvements.

Instructional design is a great way to make a living. If you're an introvert like me, but you're interested in teaching others what you know, this is a nice compromise because you get to write the script for someone else who talks in front of a class. I've been fortunate to work with some highly skilled instructional designers, and I've written classes on anything from launching fireworks to taking reservations to reading financial statements. I learn as I go, so it's a humbling process. If you're interested in pursuing ISD (Instructional Systems Design), here are the bits of wisdom I've learned so far:

- Consistency is key, especially across the training script, PowerPoint, workbook, and other materials. Visual consistency is often achieved with the help of a graphic designer, who develops the look/feel of the class across products. Content consistency is up to you: making sure content flows in the same order, asks the same questions, and provides the same answers all in the same language.
- Your writing "tone" should fit your audience, situation, and intended outcome. This is something you develop in connection with the customer. It could range anywhere from serious to hilarious, but regardless it will reflect the customer's organization and the content.
- Your content will determine the flow and organization of your training. Does your audience need to just "learn it" so they can pass an exam or follow some new policies? Do they need to "apply it?" Is the content intellectual, skill-based, personal, or physical (kinesthetic)?
- Straight lecture for four to eight hours can put people to sleep. Adult learners, who have a wide range of experiences, will engage with content differently from school-age students. I noticed this about myself when I attended graduate school eight years after I finished my B.A. Like many adult learners in a professional environment, rather than just absorb the material and memorize it, I was interested in understanding how it applied to my daily work, so I asked a lot more questions. It's important to allow time for participants to discuss and apply the material as they go.
- Speaking of straight lecture, my ISD mentor Dede (D2) is fond of keeping new lecture sections down to no more than 18 minutes—essentially the length of a TED talk—before you pause to discuss and learn.
- Don't be afraid to use analogies, especially if your material is utterly new to the participants.

- Listen to your trainers if you get a chance to interact with them, or better yet, sit in on a class or two. They can tell you (or you can see for yourself) what's "not working," either for them or the class.

Responding to Government Proposals

Improving Your Proposal Writing

Proposal writing is a common, often-lucrative method for a technical writer to earn a living. It can be a high-stress, tight-deadline environment, where the pressure is on to win. The writers, SMEs, graphic artists, and managers contributing to the effort are all aiming to win the contract…as are similar teams at their competitors. Customers get my best effort in the form of proper formatting and on-point prose, but I still have no idea what goes through the minds of Source Selection Boards or other reviewing authorities to guarantee the proposal will win. As a result, I do not and cannot guarantee my proposals will win. What I can offer are tips to help your proposal rise above the usual engineering textbook.

Don't be boring. What's boring in the proposal world?

- Providing bland descriptions of your technology or approach: we will do X, we will do Y, we will do Z.
- Reciting statistics—say, about your Mean Time Between Failures performance or how many widgets your ABC Machine can crank out in an hour—without explaining why those performance numbers are a benefit to the customer.
- Parroting the solicitation language back at the evaluators without adding anything that explains how your proposed product or service addresses that language.
- Reciting your company's or technology's history of doing whatever it is that needs doing.
- Using a lot of passive voice.

I can hear some of you saying, "But, but, BUT! That's what they asked for!" Yes, yes. And a lot of engineering proposals require the reader to be immersed in the latest software, propulsion, nanotechnology, or robotics wizardry. Technobabble is unavoidable. All reasonable points. Some of your readers might even enjoy reading dry engineering descriptions. That is no excuse for boring other readers.

State your advantages. Now I'm imagining my engineering readers thinking, "Oh, great, here comes the marketing guy trying to add razzle-dazzle and BS to a sound technical proposal!" Not at all. Luckily for my engineering colleagues, I don't know enough about their hardware to overpromise or make up capabilities. I take the proposed engineering work for what it is. I merely suggest that engineering writing can be made interesting without being misleading or confusing.

So how would I improve things? Let's start with that first bullet: providing bland descriptions of your technology or approach. Trust me, I'm a fan of clear and direct language: no fuss, tell me what you're going to do. However…before you explain how you're going to build your widget or set up your team, it would help to start the proposal and each technical section with an overview paragraph or sentence explaining what you will do, the context of your approach, and why your customer should want to use it. For instance, engineering proposal writers might assume the reader knows as much as they do about the hardware so they don't need to explain everything. I beg to differ.

For a hypothetical example, let's say you have a software development approach that enables software to be developed at an error rate of one per million lines of code, which might be ten times better than the industry average. You might know that, but do your readers? They might, but even if they do, that advantage is worth restating. Or you might have a technology that improves the ability of a telescope to see eight times farther than any instrument built to date. However, if you only describe the technology and its capabilities but stop short of explaining that difference, advantage, or outcome, you miss the opportunity to highlight why your proposal stands out. If you leave it to the reader to understand the implications, they might not know, causing you to miss out on a great opportunity to sell your product or service.

Show how you're answering the mail. Yes, it's good to show your reviewers that you read the solicitation by parroting some of their requirement language back to them, and it's often helpful to sprinkle in some of those keywords to show you're giving the customer what they want. However, it's more important that your proposal "answer the mail" by showing how your solution matches the intent of those magic words and your customer's priorities. Some of that is reflected in the RFP evaluation criteria. If your customer's primary emphasis is cost, you want to highlight all the places where your approach saves money up-front or in the long run. If your customer's primary interest is in your past performance, you shouldn't only recite a list of everyone you've worked for before, but your results...hopefully all good ones. If your customer is looking for the latest gee-whiz high technology, you want to be able to show the newness of your approach or research.

Communicate clearly and directly. Passive-voice writing makes me crazy. It's the difference between "The magnet will be moved" and "The engineer moves the magnet." Another headache for the proposal readers (who are reading other proposals than yours) is confusing them such that they cannot tell what the subject is or what action it's performing. Example (fictitious):

> The mission of the new Constitution class vehicle, with its need to advance rapidly across multiple star systems over the course of days, can be advanced by employing the Consolidated Machinery Warp Drive.

There are all sorts of things wrong in that sentence—on purpose—so you can see how they can be improved. First of all, what's the subject here? The mission of the starship or the starship itself? What's being advanced? One clue is that prepositional phrase: "of the starship." So really, "the mission...can be advanced." You could fix this by saying:

> The new Constitution class vehicle's mission, with its need to move rapidly across multiple star systems over the course of days, can be advanced by employing the Consolidated Machinery Warp Drive.

Okay, that's a slight improvement, but let's dig a little deeper. There are still way too many words clogging up the space between the subject and the verb. I added an extra bit of ugliness here by making the verb passive: "can be advanced" vs. "advances."

> The new Constitution class vehicle's mission, with its need to move rapidly across multiple star systems over the course of days, advances by employing the Consolidated Machinery Warp Drive.

Better? Maybe. But do we really want the mission to be the subject of this sentence? If you're writing on behalf of the company making the warp engines, you really want the actor here to be the warp drive. So let's do some more serious rearranging and add some more verbs to make it clear what's being done to what:

> The Consolidated Machinery Warp Drive advances the mission of the new Constitution class vehicle by accelerating the ship rapidly across multiple star systems over the course of days.

Now we've got a much more active sentence, with the Consolidated Machinery Warp Drive—the product you want to sell—being the first thing discussed and the subject of the sentence. And look! The verb is the next word. And two words later? There's the thing being acted upon: the mission. This is what English professors call classic SVO (Subject-Verb-Object) construction, and it's one of the easiest sentence structures to read. In this case, we have SVO (the warp drive advances the mission) followed by some explanatory text afterward, which might or might not be needed. The most important things I did with this editing exercise were:

- Clarified what is done and who or what is doing it, identifying the actor of the sentence.
- Moved the verb closer to the actor.
- Moved the object of the verb closer to the action so it is clear what the subject is acting upon.

Explain how **it is done.** If you're an engineer and all this seems like too much thinking, just concentrate on who is doing what to whom (SVO) and leave the wordsmithing to your friendly neighborhood tech writer/editor. The important things here are to make your writing clear, active, and understandable.

Do some additional reading. For more insight into how to improve your writing, the best editing textbook I've ever read and used is Style: Lessons in Clarity and Grace by Joseph M. Williams. It's the inspiration for the wordsmithing exercise I described above and is well worth the time and money by providing additional ways to improve your prose.

Government Contract Types
Beyond getting the words right, it helps to understand the business and contractual environment within which your proposal operates. The U.S. Government issues different contract vehicles for different types of efforts. These contracting methods are set up to make it easier

for the contractors to bid (and bill) and to make it as cost-effective as possible for the government to pay without busting the budget. I won't cover every single variation of the contract beast, but I'll share enough to give you the big picture.

Cost-Plus

Many large, difficult development projects (especially at NASA) have been set up as "cost-plus" contracts. A cost-plus contract means the contractor will be paid for its incurred costs (labor, materials, travel, and other direct costs (ODCs)). They'll also—depending on specific performance expectations—receive an extra fee, which is an award for completing the work to or above the government's expectations. You'll see these contracts called Cost Plus Fixed Fee (CPFF), Cost Plus Award Fee (CPAF), or Cost Plus Incentive Fee (CPIF), the latter two of which are awarded if the contractor does the work better, faster, or cheaper than originally expected.

Cost-plus contracting gets a lot grief in the aerospace world because it can allow or even encourage costs to balloon rapidly over time. However, if the contractor is being asked to build something that's never been built before, it can make more sense. The incentive or fixed fees could be withheld if the contractor doesn't do the job with the speed, quality, or promptness the customer expected.

Firm Fixed Price

Firm Fixed Price (FFP) contracts mean the contractor is expected to work for a predetermined amount, out of which they are expected to recoup their material, labor, and other costs as well as profit. FFPs are good for contracts where the product or service being delivered is a known quantity.

Time & Materials

Time and Materials (T&M) contracts are good for activities such as refurbishments or painting, where the full amount or duration of the work is not yet known. Because of the unknowns involved, reporting requirements and government oversight of billable hours and materials can be more stringent than usual.

Indefinite Delivery/Indefinite Quantity

The Indefinite Delivery/Indefinite Quantity (ID/IQ) contracts are often service-related contracts for activities such as engineering or communications, where the customer has existing but unpredictable needs (downtimes, surge). Work under ID/IQs is often issued under a series of task or delivery orders, where the contractor receives a minimum payment if the customer does not use their services, and a contract ceiling above which the contractor cannot bill. If the contractor hits their billing ceiling, the government customer might raise that ceiling or extend the contract if further services are needed. I've also seen fixed-price contracts with ID/IQ task orders, where the government will not raise the funding ceiling. In those situations, the onus falls on the contractor to "work smart" and estimate their costs well while still offering a bid that will beat the competition.

You can find more details at WinGovernmentContracts.com, among other places.

Why should a technical writer know this information? If you're writing proposals for a government contractor, you need to understand what type of contract your organization is bidding on and what language you should include to ensure that the government feels its needs are being met. Contract knowledge is especially important in situations where the scope of work is unknown but potentially expensive. If the most important evaluation criterion of a solicitation is the cost, you need to be able to emphasize how your company can minimize cost in a dynamic or uncertain environment.

Deciphering Government Solicitations

One of the first (and sometimes biggest) headaches a proposal writer can face even before sitting down to write is figuring out the format of the proposal. This might sound trivial, but the government—and contracting businesses—bounce noncompliant proposals all the time because they weren't written in the proper format. Proposal preparation and writing, then, is an advanced version of that lesson you learned in kindergarten: follow the directions.

While the specific tips here are geared toward government solicitations, the general principles can apply to the nonprofit and commercial sectors as well.

Reading the Directions

Depending on the length of a solicitation and the depth of your involvement in preparing the proposal, you might be able to read the entire set of proposal instructions in a couple of minutes or it might take you all day if you're looking at an RFP that runs several hundred pages long.

Multi-page government solicitations often have standard instruction sections, labeled alphabetically A through M. The letters have little to do with the section name, that's just the format that's been used—at least since World War Two, but knowing how government works, they've probably had something similar since the American Revolution. In any case, when the A–M categories are used, they mean the same thing agency to agency because the government likes consistency…and really, so do contractors. If each agency used a different order and format for each individual RFP, it would take even longer for government to get things done than it already does. And anyway, why reinvent the wheel each time?

So with that format in mind, let's take a look at some of the sections that affect the proposal writer most directly and most often.

Section C — Statement of Work. This is the work your organization is expected to do. Your proposal responses will need to address the contents of section C in the order and format used in Section L. Much of this content will be handled under your Technical Approach section, if applicable.

Section L — Proposal Preparation. Section L provides the format for the proposal. It will include things like what font and margins to use (the U.S. Government likes 1 inch margins and 12-point Times New Roman as its primary body text font), proposal section names, section contents, header and footer requirements, Export Control notice language, and page length requirements. This is the section I usually look at first because I like to get the format together to sort out my thoughts. Based on section L, I will create a proposal "shell" that the content creators can then use as a starting point for their work. Sometimes I'll include the content instructions underneath the section headings to help prompt the content writers as well.

Section M — Evaluation Criteria. In this section, the government agency will tell you how it intends to "grade your paper," i.e., tell the bidders what its most important criteria are when judging the quality of their proposals. The most common figures of merit are technical approach, management approach, past performance, and cost. However, agencies also might evaluate proposals on things like small business participation, uniqueness of the technical solution, partnerships with other agencies, safety, workforce qualifications, and proposed schedule. Cost is almost always a factor, but you'd be surprised how often it is not the most important factor.

Section M is important because it affects the depth of your content and the amount of marketing language you use in your proposal. The government agency will sometimes help you out in Section L by specifying a higher page count for those areas where it wants more detail. Again, it boils down to following directions.

And all this is not to say you should not read the rest of the solicitation. You should at least become familiar with the other sections of the proposal, as they might affect, in some small way, your delivery of the final product.

What to Do When the Solicitation Makes No D@mn Sense

On occasion I will admit to being stymied in my efforts to "translate" government proposal instructions into an organized proposal. Sometimes it is obvious multiple people wrote the instructions and they did not consult each other prior to getting the RFP out the door, thereby making conflicting or confusing requests. I've been in situations where each person in the proposal "war room" had multiple college degrees and none of us could figure out what the government meant in the RFP. Sometimes, to quote Star Trek, "There's no correct resolution, it's a test of character."

That said, if you are still in the question-and-answer period prior to proposal delivery, you can email the contracting officer and ask for clarification, keeping in mind that any questions and answers will be readable by all of your competitors as well. (Related topic: if the solicitation is asking for content that affects the technical aspects of your response, you might need to be careful about how you word your question to the contracting officer—otherwise you might inadvertently reveal to your competitors some of your company's technical approach or your "secret sauce.")

If you are past the Q&A period, you're going to have to take your best shot, focusing primarily on what the government wants done. In that case, Section C might overrule Section L to have the proposal order make sense, or vice versa.

Again, most of proposal writing amounts to following the directions. Even if you're proposing an actual space vehicle, the fundamentals of proposal writing are not rocket science. The government wants a product or service; they want your company's best solution and offer; and they want it in a prescribed order and format. Nail all of those, and you're halfway there.

Getting to the Heart of the Matter in a Technical Proposal

How do you choose what's the most important information to share in a proposal? How do you know which facts are most important to your audience? Which arguments will persuade your audience to choose your proposal over another? Sometimes a lot of your thinking can be guided simply by reading the non-technical words you do understand, parsing those words, and asking the right questions.

Say you've got a bunch of technobabble in front of you…

> Energy from the power cell is controlled by all three modules and routed by shielded conduits to a prefire chamber, a 1.5 cm diameter sphere of LiCu 521 reinforced with gulium arkenide. Here the energy is held temporarily by a collapsible charge barrier before passing to the actual LiCu 521 emitter for discharge out of the phaser, creating a pulse.

If most of that was gibberish, one magic word might jump out at some of you: phaser. This is, of course, an excerpt from the Star Trek: The Next Generation Technical Manual. The point is not to pick on my friends Rick Sternbach and Mike Okuda, who wrote a book to help authors writing Star Trek stories or scripts understand how the fictional starship Enterprise works (in theory). In the case of this paragraph, the text is explaining how the hand weapons work.

For an intellectual exercise, let's say you worked for a company that manufactured phasers and needed to include this information in a proposal to win the contract to make them. We can take this paragraph one section at a time. Again, the point here is not to help you write proposals for Starfleet (though that sounds like an awesome job in my world), but to walk through the thinking process of translating Engineerish into Marketing English.

> Energy from the power cell is controlled by all three modules

Energy from the power cell is controlled by all three modules, you say? How might that be an advantage? That might be a sign of redundancy, which translates into safety or reliability.

and routed by shielded conduits

Shielded conduits? Aha, extra safety. Or durability. This is important, especially for a combat weapon, yes?

to a prefire chamber, a 1.5 cm diameter sphere of LiCu 521 reinforced with gulium arkenide.

There are a few directions you might go here:

- The prefire chamber is 1.5-centimeter sphere. This is a pretty small area. That might convey light weight, increasing the utility and handling of the weapon.
- The sphere is made of LiCu (lithium-copper) 521. Is that a useful alloy? Durable? Easy to manufacture? Resistant to high temperatures? What makes it special?
- Gulium arkenide—what the heck is that? Another futuristic alloy made in the 24th century, no doubt. It is a reinforcing alloy—presumably strong, but what else? Lightweight? What other properties of this 1.5-centimeter sphere are worth highlighting and marketing?

Let's move on to the next sentence…

Here the energy is held temporarily by a collapsible charge barrier before passing to the actual LiCu 521 emitter for discharge out of the phaser, creating a pulse.

This is obviously a process statement, describing how the power cell of the phaser works—the battery, if you will. You've got a collapsible charge barrier—what does that do? It's a barrier, so presumably it holds the energy in place until it's ready to be used. Why not say that for the non-engineers on the proposal review board?

And note that you're using a LiCu 521 emitter, which is the same material being used for the power cell. How might that be an advantage? Since your company is already working with the alloy on one part of the phaser, they presumably have the expertise to make the other, and they also can buy and shape the alloy in bulk, which would be cheaper than one-off buys.

In the end, you need not be an engineer to write for engineers. You do need to identify the key properties (features) of the technology or service you are trying to sell and be able to translate those features into benefits that will match your customer's needs. If you can't deduce the advantages of your company's technology, ask. Engineering is a human task performed to achieve human aims. Your subject matter experts should be able to explain to you how their hardware or software works and why their work is better than others. Then it's up to you to make the words fit together well.

Marketing Language in Proposal Writing

Proposals are marketing documents. This should be something everyone knows, but you'd be surprised how often that knowledge doesn't result in effective proposal writing. Below are some thoughts on how to ensure your proposal readers are getting the most "bang for the buck."

Showcasing Your Market Advantages

Most RFPs from the federal government require the following sections in their responses:

- Technical Approach
- Management Approach
- Past Performance
- Cost

In each of these sections, you have the opportunity not only to explain what your widget or process is, but to jazz up the language by including details or support statements that show why your organization is the perfect entity to solve a particular problem.

Technical Approach

The technical approach section is where you describe your solution to the RFP's problem. Whether Agency XYZ needs a part, product, system, or service, the customer is expecting the best outcome they can get for the best price. Marketing language here would focus on why your solution is best for the customer. The key is to argue from your strength(s):

- If your product is a proven, known commodity, you emphasize its reliability, industry acceptance, or availability.

- If your product is less expensive to make or operate, you emphasize cost.
- If your product is more efficient than others, you emphasize the ability to produce multiple activities quickly, operate easily, or reduce consumption of resources (e.g., money, part count, time, energy).
- If your product's greatest value is its advanced technology, you want to emphasize the improvements its new approach could make (faster, better, cheaper—pick two). However, this approach also might need to include some sort of hedge to calm fears about using an unproven product. If your product or approach is new, you can mitigate that risk by pointing the customer to your superior performance or staff in the Past Performance or Management sections.
- If your product and all of its competitors are nearly equal in technology, quality, or capability, you need to emphasize some other aspect of your organization to help you stand out, such as the quality or experience of your people, your level of service, your past history with the customer, or price. (Note that I put price last. If "lowest bidder" is the primary consideration, by all means, go there; however, as I noted previously, Section M of a typical federal RFP will tell you what the most important factors are in an award decision. If technology is the customer's #1 priority, you want to talk about why your technology is superior. If price is the customer's #1 priority, you will probably need to provide more detail in your cost proposal to show that you have accounted for everything and that your lowest bid is, in fact, realistic.)

Some managers will employ ghosting in their proposal language. As I stated earlier, this is where, if you know your competitor(s) and how they approach things, you make slight digs against their approach by explaining how your approach is superior to process X (without naming your competitor directly, of course). Just be certain your approach is superior. I'm not a huge fan of this tactic, but then I don't like negative advertisements in elections and people who use them still get elected, so if you think it's necessary and appropriate, ghost away.

Management Approach

This is where you talk about the people who will ultimately do the work and how they will be organized. You might be required to provide a paragraph-long bio or full resumes of your best and brightest team members. In either case, you shouldn't just copy and paste from an existing resume or bio and consider your work done. Your team members' background information should be customized to emphasize the types of relevant experience they have for completing the task you're proposing.

I've observed over the years that a company's management approach has become increasingly important. This is especially true with agencies issuing more firm-fixed price (FFP) or performance-based contracts. In both cases, the government doesn't always know what product/service it wants, only what outcome they want and how much they're willing to spend. In that case, a company's management approach becomes paramount: the customer will want to know who is doing the work, how they will be organized, and what processes or procedures are in place to ensure the work is delivered as promised.

Because programs and companies can vary greatly in size and scope, I won't attempt to name all of the different types of management or team structures here or suggest which type will work for which situation. However, as with your technical section, the important marketing-language rule here is to focus on your strengths:

Experienced staff. This is an advantage when the customer is interested in reliability and in-depth knowledge of their operation. It's not always an advantage when the customer is looking for new thinking.

Relationship with the customer. This is an advantage if you are familiar with how an organization runs and are on good terms with them. It's not an advantage if your relationship has been contentious or if you have had performance problems recently.

Educational background. Having a lot of team members fresh-out of college is an advantage in scientific or high-tech proposals where new thinking is expected; also, many scientific projects require Ph.D.-level educations to handle the work. It is not necessarily an advantage if the customer is more interested in hands-on field experience.

Team structure. Is your team "lean and mean" to ensure low cost and quick communications or is it "deep," with enough varied SMEs to call upon in case you need "bench strength" for specialized problems or surge situations? Again, the low-cost alternative doesn't always win, especially on high-cost, high-risk programs.

Supplier or subcontractor base. This one can get overlooked, but if you're a prime contractor and depend on a lot of subcontractors, the quality of those team members matters. Also, if your team consists of multiple categories of small businesses (8(a), Minority Owned, Woman Owned, and Alaska Native, to name a few), the customer can ensure that you and they get credit for subcontracting work to those types of companies.

Past Performance

This is simply your track record to prove you've done a specific type of work before or have done work of similar difficulty or scope successfully. The marketing angle here is pretty straightforward, as you want to point out the similarities between your past work and the proposed work as well as how well you've performed on those projects. You have done well, haven't you? Okay, maybe one of those projects wasn't your company's best experience. If you have enough other jobs, you don't necessarily have to include that customer and can use another. If you don't have any alternatives, what are you doing to fix the situation? As in most situations, don't lie about your past. Don't claim to do things you haven't done, and don't try to make a connection between past work and the proposed work if it doesn't relate.

All that said, again: play to your strengths. In situations where the government is asking for something risky and high-tech, they will rely as much on your past performance as technical approach because past performance can be verified.

Cost. If you met your cost estimate or came in low, that's a good thing.

Schedule. If you consistently met your proposed schedule or delivered early, those are good things.

Quality. If your delivered product service required very few "do-overs" due to workmanship or service issues, by all means, note that.

Do you know how you stand with your customer(s)? Do your front-line and project management teams have ongoing, positive relationships with them? Are you delivering the product or service they expect? Do you send your customers satisfaction surveys quarterly or annually to get some hard numbers? If the answer to all of the above is "no," depending on your past performance can be risky because you don't know what your customers will say, and the awarding agency will follow up with your references to determine if what you said matches the customer's reality.

Cost

I've worked for companies where the technical writer never touches the cost section (or volume), either to restrict the sharing of the company's costing data or there was no need because the section consisted entirely of spreadsheets, which are the finance manager's responsibility. If you are called upon to write or edit the cost section, the language will usually include justifications for the costs your company submits or explanations for why your cost structure is better than the competition's. Since the cost section is usually prepared by and for finance people, your goal in this section is to make your company's costs appear as clear and reasonable as possible. If something doesn't sound right in the explanations, ask.

Concluding Thoughts on Proposal Marketing

The "marketing" aspect of proposal writing comprises the messages or themes you include throughout your proposal document. Therefore, as with any marketing product, you want your messaging to be consistent. This can be challenging if you have multiple people writing the proposal, in which case it's good to have a kickoff meeting to discuss your themes and messages before everyone starts writing. For example, if the people writing the management section are convinced that the strength of your proposal is the quality of your machining, your customer will be confused if that machining isn't mentioned in the technical section. Your strengths also should be highlighted in your Executive Summary so the customer knows what to expect when they delve into the details. You don't just want to explain what you do; you want to show why you do it better than anyone else!

Tips for Effective SBIR Proposal Writing

Many of my customers are small aerospace firms that pursue opportunities for Small Business Innovation Research (SBIR, pronounced by spelling out the initialism). SBIRs are competitive programs wherein the U.S. Government provides seed money to help a small business develop a new technology in a specific area to help them bring it from a lower-level technology readiness level (TRL) to a higher one and, eventually, to the commercial market. Assuming it works, the government gets the benefit of the technology in question. The following advice is for engineers as well as tech writers responding to SBIR opportunities, so feel free to pass this along to your engineering friends.

Program Overview

Most SBIR RFPs have two or three phases. In Phase I, the company is typically doing research, as the concept they're developing is so new there's not even a way to turn it into a concrete product (hardware or software) yet. All you're doing in Phase I is establishing the technical merit, feasibility, and commercial merit of your proposed idea with the specific government agency issuing the SBIR as the customer. The proposed work—usually a technical study—takes six months to complete and the award is less than or equal to $150,000.

In most of the Phase II proposals I've seen, the company is describing a demonstration model of some sort, which they will build over the period of performance. The work lasts up to two years and could be awarded as much as $2 million.

In rarer cases, an SBIR will go into a Phase III effort, where the small business translates their government-focused widget into a commercial product. The issuing agency does not actually fund Phase III, though some agencies may help a small business commercialize their product through other funding—sometimes through another agency in need of the technology.

STTRs

There is another type of proposal in this field called the STTR (Small Business Technology Transfer Research). These are awarded to companies that team up with a non-profit research institution, such as a laboratory or an academic institution. The primary rule is that the small business prime contractor must perform at least 40 percent of the work while the research institution must perform at least 30 percent of the work. The goal in STTR opportunities is to facilitate quicker transfers of pure research activities into real-world products. Most of the work I've done has been in the SBIR realm, where a single company is doing the work, so that's where I will focus.

SBIR Proposals

The government's SBIR site provides its own insights into how to write effective proposals for this program, and I encourage you to read it.[18] What follows are my thoughts when turning out these documents.

Have a product or idea in work or in mind before the RFP comes out. The SBIR opportunities typically come out once a year—for example, NASA's SBIR window of opportunity is open from November to January, with contracts awarded in April. This gives you a predictable time of year to start gathering ideas. Ideally, your team has been coming up with ideas and doing some of the pre-writing for how their idea(s) will work before it's proposal-writing season. It's not that they need to have all of the writing done before the proposal comes out, but it makes life easier for everyone if you're not making up everything on the fly. Of course that happens, too, as more people besides the original inventor get involved. Still, it's good to have a brainstorming session with the team before the RFP hits the streets.

Have a definite product outcome in mind. Phase I usually doesn't involve creating a product, but simply developing a study that will lead to a concrete product to be demonstrated in Phase II. These proposals fund specific, applied research on a designated product, not basic research where you're not certain of the outcome.

Know your industry. Part of your proposal will include some sort of "literature review" where you describe what work has been done on your topic previously. Once you know what's been done, you can be clear about what hasn't been tried before and what you can add that's new.

Advance the state of the art. As I noted up-front, the "I" in SBIR is for Innovation. That means you should be advancing the state of the art in your particular field and doing something new that results in a

---

[18] See https://www.sbir.gov/sbirsearch/detail/358863, "Proposal Preparation Instructions and Requirements."

substantive, even dramatic, performance improvement. By contrast, you would not do an SBIR proposal for something common like actual nuts and bolts unless your approach was unlike anything seen in the industry before. You're working more on the middle range of the TRL scale, ideally TRL 3 or 4 so that by Phase II you're able to demonstrate some sort of working model or "breadboard" prototype of your product. The NASA Institute for Advanced Concepts (NIAC) organization is geared for ideas still in the theoretical stage, like "warp drive" or equivalent ideas.

Solve a problem with specific customers in mind. You want to have a specific customer in mind when you're coming up with your bright idea. Multiple agencies put out SBIR solicitations; and within NASA and the Department of Defense there can be specific groups within those agencies seeking proposals for particular technology areas. Obviously, then, you need to start with that specific government customer. From there, you need to think about the following:

- Who else within that particular department or agency could benefit from your widget?
- What other government agencies would benefit from your widget?
- How could your widget be used in a commercial environment, and who would most likely use or benefit from it?

Demonstrate that your organization can do the work. It's one thing to have a bright idea, it's another to have the skill set(s) needed to do the job. You need to identify what types of tasks must be done to achieve your goal and then demonstrate that you or other people in your organization have those skills. If not, you might need to do a little subcontracting, either from academic institutions or another small business. Usually, you can't call up your local Big Aerospace company. That would sort of defeat the purpose of the money being given to small businesses, right?

Have a realistic plan. In addition to having the right skill sets to do the work, the work itself should be well thought out. You must identify your project's outcomes, how long the work will take, who will be needed to do the work, and how much the work will cost. In short, you have to show the government what they'll be getting for their money. NASA, DoD, and other agencies don't just give out money to small businesses to keep people employed: they want their problem solved, and they want to know that at the end of your contract, they will receive something that shows if their problem is solvable.

SBIRs are very competitive, so it's best not to count on them as a primary source of income for your company. These are meant to fund your in-house, creative research ideas, not keep the lights on. With all that in mind—good luck and go do great things!

Doing Effective Business Development Research in Sam.gov

 One task proposal writers in the government contracting sector do between bids is search for new business development opportunities. One of the key tools in this search is Sam.gov (formerly FBO, short for Federal Business Opportunities). This website helps companies search for proposed or current solicitations from government agencies seeking specific products or services. The Sam search engine is robust, enabling users to search opportunities based on multiple factors, which is important because the U.S. Federal Government is a huge organization with multiple agencies and sub-agencies, each with its own special business needs.

Parameters for a basic search include:

- Posted date, which includes a drop-down menu that allows you to search items posted anywhere from the last couple of days to the last year.
- Set-aside code to search for opportunities set aside for small businesses, woman-owned businesses, historically black colleges and universities (HBCUs), and other special categories.
- Place of performance, including specific states or U.S. territories.
- Type, which allows you to search for current solicitations, pre-solicitation notices, or even past awards of opportunities so you can see who won a specific contract.
- Keyword/Solicitation # is a text window that allows you to search for specific solicitation numbers if you happen to know them or to search for specific topics.
- Agency, which allows you to search agencies (e.g., Department of Defense, NASA) or sub-organizations within those

agencies (e.g., Defense Logistics Agency, Marshall Space Flight Center).

Advanced searches allow you to get really specific with your opportunity search, as they add the following:

- Multiple states (as opposed to the single-state searches in the basic search window).
- ZIP code.
- Set-aside codes (again, you can check more than one as opposed to only one on the basic search screen).
- Opportunity/procurement type (again, you can check more than one box).
- NAICS code – tasks designated for businesses with specific North American Industry Classification System codes.
- Specific product/service codes, e.g., weapons, hand tools, furniture.
- Justification & Approval (J&A) Authority is an interesting one. FBO does not just post opportunities for work but also announces awards of contracts or notices for when the government feels a specific contract must be awarded to a single or large company rather than a small business without a competitive bidding process. Such a condition is usually called a JOFOC (Justification for Other than Full and Open Competition, pronounced JOE-fock). This is a situation where the government believes only one specific company or type of company can do the work. To issue a JOFOC or single-source award, the awarding agency has to comply with specific parts of the Federal Acquisition Regulations ("the FAR") and state its case for why it is awarding a contract in a particular way. As a search parameter, you can check boxes that show contracts awarded based on specific need: only one responsible source, unusual or compelling national interest, or international agreement.
- Posted date range.
- Response date.
- Last modified.
- Contract award date.

127

You can see, then, that Sam is a useful tool for doing opportunity and historical research. How detailed you want to get in your search depends a great deal on your business's particular needs. With keyword searches, the tricky thing is to use the right terminology—do you call things what the customer is likely to call them or what industry calls them? And even when you narrow down your search parameters, you can still find yourself facing a couple dozen pages of different, potentially related opportunities. Because the uses of Sam are so varied, I offer the following general tips for those of you asked to "go look for business."

- Again, use keywords as the government uses them. As a backup, use industry terms.
- Focus on actual solicitations rather than pre-solicitation notices because pre-solicitation notices, while they provide useful information on agency intentions, usually don't have money behind them yet.
- That said, there are times when it's useful to go through Requests for Information (RFIs) or "Sources Sought" notices. These are notices of interest by a government agency: they know they need a particular product or service, but they don't know how much it might cost or how complicated it might be to build the product. It's sort of like doing the government's homework for them. Responding to an RFI is a way to show off your company's skills and get its name "on the list" should an actual contract solicitation be released.
- If you're doing an active search for opportunities that you can write a proposal response to now, I wouldn't go back much farther than 90 days. The reason being, if it's an active solicitation, proposals rarely have due dates more than 90 days out.
- Keep in mind your proposal team's bandwidth: how long is the proposal document expected to be? What is the due date? How many people do you have on vacation at the moment? Can you get a good proposal together in the time allowed?
- Are you already doing the sort of work sought by the solicitation? That will determine how easy it is to show your relevant past performance or value proposition to the customer.
- Does the opportunity represent work your company has wanted to get into but hasn't yet? If so, you'll need to

show how your business's experience is still relevant and could add value. You also might need to find an organization (as a prime or subcontractor) to be your partner on the proposal—and that takes time to set up as well.

- Be on the lookout for signs that a solicitation might have been written with one particular contractor in mind. Officially, the government is supposed to have full and open competition; in reality, the companies closest to a particular agency are most familiar with that agency or command's needs and so are usually the best able to meet the need. Examples of solicitations that seem "custom-made" for one particular company include a lot of very specific business requirements; a large proposal page count with a very short deadline; or specific clearance or business location requirements for the personnel that usually only an existing on-site contractor can fulfill. It's not that you can't or shouldn't compete in those circumstances, but it's best to be aware of the uphill battle you might face and the challenges you'll have to overcome to prove your company can offer a product or service clearly superior to the on-site contractor. And who knows? That solicitation just might have been written for you!

Government contracting is its own special flavor of business, and it can take a while to learn how it works. However, once you learn the ins and outs of how the game is played, your business development process can become easier and more effective.

Part III: People and Politics

Chapter 6: Working With People

What You Should Know as a Technical Communicator: Soft Skills

The biggest challenge with any job will be the people.

This is not to say everyone is evil or that you'll spend most of your time fighting politics. However, your verbal and non-verbal soft skills can help you navigate challenging work situations, from sales calls to working with new customers, networking at business functions; interacting with managers and subject matter experts; giving and receiving writing feedback; and handling work situations with difficult people.

Meetings

I'm not a fan of meetings, to put it mildly, but they're a fact of life. Meetings occur for a multitude of reasons. At Disney, they had project team meetings, departmental meetings, and occasionally division or even company-wide all-hands meetings. In a

NASA context, you might have meetings with your senior customer (say, the director of a department), your customer's manager, and then your actual customer to find out what's going on at various levels of the organization. If you're a contractor, this could happen, plus you'll have to attend meetings at the various levels of the company you work for. Generally, meetings occur for one of several reasons: (1) learn the status of what everyone is doing, (2) share technical information that's valuable to a given project or activity (NASA calls these Technical Interchange Meetings, or TIMs), or (3) make a decision when there is a question about how to proceed.

So how do you approach a meeting?

Don't talk unnecessarily. I've got to confess, this took me a while because as I moved from my twenties to my thirties, I started attending more meetings and also shifted to becoming more of an introvert. As a result, I started enjoying meetings less. I also started using my reasoning. For instance, I realized that if I stopped asking questions that someone else had already asked or answered, or if I wasn't talking just to hear myself talk, the meeting wouldn't last as long. It's your call: if you like being in a room with fluorescent lighting and a bunch of people all talking about their activities, Godspeed, keep talking. However, if you're an introvert who wants to get back to writing ASAP, the less you talk, the better.

Identify which questions you can ask later. There are times when you have a burning question, but it might be better to shut your mouth and listen before asking. For instance, if you want to know the meaning of an acronym people are using, the meaning might come to you just through experience. Or you might learn more by listening to the context of the conversation. Or, if it's not a major detail but something you might want to know for future reference, you can ask a coworker after the meeting. The guiding principle here is: If you can look it up somewhere, you don't need to ask about it in a meeting. This lesson is in direct contradiction of the next one, which is...

Do speak when necessary. This is a tougher call, especially for an introvert like me, but there will be times when I need to know something. It usually happens when someone is saying something that affects my pay, my job security, or my future work. Whatever button it is that sets you off, eventually there will come that moment when nobody in the room is willing to ask a question everyone wants to know the answer to, and you have to decide whether you will raise your hand or stay ignorant like everyone else. A former coworker of mine groaned whenever I raised my hand because he knew I was about to ask a direct or uncomfortable question. For example, one of my favorites is, "Is this [process/paperwork/meeting/social gathering] really necessary?" You never know: the answer might be no, which would save you some aggravation, wouldn't it?

Another thing I'm willing to do is ask a question that might make me look stupid. That's hard for some people. No one wants to look stupid. However, if you've got a question about something that can only be answered in the context of that meeting ("What does that mean?" "Does this mean our benefits will be cut?" "Did our schedule just get extended or cut?"), ask it. Yes, it might take extra time. Yes, it might sound like an obvious or for-dummies question, but odds are if you're asking the question, you're not the only one wanting to know. Generally, the best time to ask a question like this is if the topic is about to change and the answer hasn't become obvious through the ensuing conversation.

Managing Conflict

Perhaps someone is slow to provide you the information you need to finish a project. Perhaps someone is pushing you to deliver something that isn't ready yet. Perhaps someone is being unnecessarily rude or curt with you when you have done nothing consciously to earn their disrespect.

Well, the workplace isn't junior high or high school (I can't vouch for everyone's experience on this point). However, punching someone or pulling their hair out are usually bad responses because any or all of them are likely to earn you a suspension from work, termination, or a lawsuit rather than detention. The business world requires people to talk out their differences of opinion.

How do you approach your difficult person? One of the few things I remember from my conflict management class at Disney is that you should—politely, respectfully—describe the behavior that concerns you without accusing or being snippy, explain its effect on you, request a specific, different behavior in the future, and then await the other person's response. Seriously, I don't have anything better than that, but it can't hurt to try. If you're worried about how your comments will be perceived, bring in someone with authority above the two of you and use the above method. Otherwise, you might end up letting things fester or having a toxic feud that makes the workplace uncomfortable for everyone. Your call.

Working with Individuals

A lot of the time your content will come from SMEs, who might not have a lot of time to talk, don't like talking about their work, or think their explanations are so brilliant they don't require repetition or further explanation. It will be up to you to be true to your product and to get the answers you need. That will mean asking (politely—I'm a big fan of politeness) someone with a Ph.D. or a "Vice President" in their title to slow down and clarify something you don't understand. That is where your diplomacy skills must come in, and you must be willing to echo them a bit and say, "I'm sorry, but I don't understand what you just said. Did you mean…?" Then explain what you thought you heard from the SME or the big boss in your own words until you arrive at a common understanding.

Working with Groups

Proposals are a typical example of when you will have to work in a group. Sometimes you're theoretically locked into a "war room" until a high-pressure proposal is completed by the deadline. You'll have multiple people talking in your ear or looking over your shoulder as you try to type what they're saying. In such situations, you must maintain your cool and (again, politely) push back when people are making unreasonable demands on you. What's unreasonable? Unreasonable demands would be things like asking you to type two things at once; answering last-minute requests to stay at the office overnight when you've already said you have an appointment or other commitment after work; someone changing content that is flat-out incorrect; or someone changing the scope of a project without warning.

The Unexpected

Your coworkers will surprise you. Someone might pull you aside and tell you about some personal problem they're having. Your boss might pull you aside and ask you if you're okay when you think you've been acting normally. You might have to tell someone you can't hire them or their invoice is out of order. You might have to apologize for some comment an executive in your organization made on TV or in a meeting that offended a customer. In my personal case, I found that my time in the retail and hospitality industries gave me a solid foundation in customer relations.

However, what if you haven't had experience working with thousands of guests in one of the world's most high-demand tourist locations? The short version of the Disney philosophy comes from that magic word, "guest." When you're working with a client, customer, vendor, or other business acquaintance, you need to think of them as someone you would have as a guest in your own home: you act hospitably to the most reasonable extent you can. When they become unreasonable (rude, insulting, profane, violent), you have more freedom to be firm in kind, but even in the rude, insulting, and profane stages, you can still focus on maintaining your politeness. Your goal is to maintain a relationship, not intimidate someone to win an argument.

As much as I hoped my career would consist of me sitting at a desk, writing content, that was wishful thinking. The content comes from people, and the end users are people, so you can't avoid "soft skills" in your quest to develop good technical communication products. The challenge isn't always "overcoming" your people challenges but working around or with them. You can't avoid people by becoming a technical writer. Learning how to work with them is an absolutely necessary "survival skill."

Elevator Pitches

The first part of dealing with new people on the job or potential customers or employers is simply introducing yourself. As part of that introduction, the most important thing you can do as a business practice is to develop an "elevator pitch." The idea being that you make a good impression while introducing yourself to a stranger in the time it takes to ride between floors in an elevator.

An elevator pitch is usually a single, memorable sentence or two that helps explain who you are, what you do, what sort of problems you solve, how you add value for your customers or a combination of those. The elevator pitch is the central message of your overall marketing approach. It should be included in any of your bios, and marketing materials, regardless of the amount of time you have to introduce yourself or include extra details.

For example:

> "Hi, I'm Bart Leahy. I'm a freelance technical writer. I translate Engineerish into English. I help technical organizations that don't need a writer full-time develop proposals, technical documents, or other content. Could you use someone like that on your team?"

Simple, right? Obviously your pitch will not be mine, but it should be brief, pithy, and easy to say, understand, and remember. Note that it includes a request for the individual's business. That's an action step that puts the ball in their court.

You should think through your elevator pitch because it should simultaneously encompass who you are and what you do as well as who you want your customers to be and what type of work you want to do. My work is obviously focused on "translating" between engineers and non-engineering customers. Your elevator pitch will reflect your abilities, interests, and target market.

Don't forget to practice saying it aloud, wordsmithing until it comes out clearly and comfortably, and in a tone that is comfortable for you and easy on the ears of the listener.

Cold Calls/Sales Calls

My father was a sales representative for the original Eastern Airlines (EAL). As one of EAL's Florida experts, he spent a lot of time doing sales calls, which amounted to visiting hotels and attractions around the Sunshine State, making sure they had all the system timetables they needed, and in general reminding them that Eastern was around and looking to do business with them.

What Does a Sales Call Look Like?

Dad was trying to sell seats on airplanes. I'm trying to sell technical writing services. Regardless, the process of sales calls doesn't change too much, despite the differences between industries and products.

You might or might not enjoy "cold call" sales, where you try to make sales with individuals you've never spoken to before,[19] but they are often necessary. When things get quiet for a freelancer, you need to reach out to new potential customers or check in with your existing customers to see if you can dig around for more work in your preferred or chosen market. It's a delicate balance sometimes. You want paying work, but you don't want to look desperate or pushy. The goals of a sales call are simple:

- Make a connection with your customer.
- Maintain your connection with the customer.
- Look for opportunities for future sales.

Make a Connection with Your Customer

Cold calling can be done in other ways besides dropping by an office out of the blue. There are conferences and trade shows, for example, where people are expecting to talk to individuals looking to do business. Regardless of where a "first contact" takes place, that contact should include making a good impression; dressing and speaking professionally; being prepared with business cards or brochures; and having a quick, to-the-point "elevator pitch" that explains who you are,

---

[19] As opposed to a "warm" call, where you've already established some sort of relationship with the potential customer in question.

what sort of problems you solve, and how you can help. Some folks bring along stand-out promotional items.

However you get the prospect's attention, even if you make a positive impression in your initial conversation, that doesn't mean you'll get work right away. You might get a referral to the person who makes the decisions. Or, in the case of a small business, you might be talking to the decision maker and they don't have any work for you now, but you have gotten your foot in the door. Cold calling requires persistence.

Maintain Your Connection with the Customer

Maintaining the relationship requires a combination of "small talk" (the nemesis of many introverts) and serious talk. The small talk means simple things: learning and remembering your point of contact's name, where they're from, their interests, and any personal details you can remember as conversation starters on future visits (favorite sports teams, hobbies, free-time activities). And yes, it doesn't hurt if you just try to make friends with your customers. Friendships and closer connections make it easier and more fun to work with customers in the long run.

There are multiple software programs out there that you can use to track your sales contacts. You can use Microsoft Excel, if you're lazy or cheap. Or, if you've got a reasonably good memory, you can just remember who is who and what their lives and needs are.

Look for Opportunities for Future Sales

People in the sales profession will always emphasize the need to "ask for the sale." That means you need to ask a concrete, yes-or-no question like, "Can you commit to X activity?" or "When can I expect to hear from you about writing for X project?"

If you're like me, you might not always be comfortable asking for money. But you've got to eat, too. And there are psychological tricks you can play on yourself to work around this. The most important thing for me to do is to ask for the work. This shows you're more concerned about helping the customer. The money will come after that.

Another thing you can do when looking for work is avoid making your customer feel uncomfortable telling you they don't have any work for you. Rather than force your customer into an uncomfortable

137

corner by asking, "Have you got any work for me?" you could ask instead: "Do you know anyone in need of a writer at the moment?" This opens a couple of opportunities for your customer:

- They are free to refer you to another department within their organization or even at another company.
- If they don't know anyone needing technical writing assistance, they can save face by saying, "No, but I'll keep my ears open" or "No, but I'll be happy to recommend you if someone needs help."

Ensuring the Next Sale

The trick, of course, is developing your reputation with the customer to the level where they will be willing and eager to recommend you to another organization. That requires you to do two things:

- Do good enough work that a customer can recommend you professionally.
- Develop a good enough personal relationship with the customer that they will recommend you personally.

The second item might seem minor, but it's not. Humans are emotional creatures. It's easier and more believable for a customer to recommend your services if they appreciate the quality of your work and they like working with you. I wish it were a simple matter of pure merit, but it's not.

So as you're working through the mysteries of translating Engineerish or Sciencese and getting your style and grammar right, remember you also have to pay attention to the sales aspect of your life as a writer.

Working with New Clients/Customers

Let's say you've done your cold calling, you've worked the rooms and events, and you've finally landed a potential customer who's interested in hiring you. Let's assume they call you using the business card you gave them. What next?

The early part of the discussion usually involves the customer introducing him or herself and a brief background about how they got around to contacting you. The talk also can include an explanation of their business, what they do, who their customer is, and so forth. This part of the talk can last anywhere from a couple minutes to a full hour.

Eventually you get to the Big Questions, the ones that relate to actual, paying work. For me, work encompasses some basic characteristics, which I've managed to consolidate into a nice, alliterative set of four Ps that form part of the organization of this book:

1. Product
2. Process
3. People
4. Politics

Note that I've numbered these criteria. That's on purpose because you should probably cover them in order.

1. The **product** actually covers two areas: the types of products, services, or content you have to write about and the actual deliverables you're producing, such as proposals, white papers, or marketing flyers. If you've never worked with the company or industry before, you'll need to get background on those (you can do some of that in your free time, some they might pay you for). You'll also learn through this early part of the discussion whether the customer's needs are a good fit for your skill set or not: the content, the products, or the deadlines. This would be worth knowing before you dig into some of the detailed logistical questions.

2. **Processes** include determining how you will be writing—remotely or on-site; interviews or editing of SME-written content; deadlines, number of review cycles, folders, naming conventions, email addresses—as well as how business will be conducted: how often should you invoice, do they require a non-disclosure agreement (NDA), what rate are they willing to pay, when is your Red Team (or other) review, when is your deadline?

3. **People** are pretty straightforward: you want to know whom you'll be working with, who your SMEs are, who will be responsible for what, who has final approval of the content, or whom to contact if there's a problem. If you've never worked with the customer, you might want to take a few minutes to gauge their attitudes toward the work you're doing, toward your role, or toward life in general. Yes, if you're an introvert that can mean a little bit of "small talk," but it's all purpose-

driven because you want to know how you'll be interacting with this customer in the future.

4. **Politics** is a slight variant on people, but this is where you have to start poking at potential challenges: if there is a disagreement on content, for example, who is the "tie breaker?" Is there a historical challenge with the customer your client is writing a proposal to? Is there serious, well-known competition that needs to be challenged or "ghosted?"[20]

Cover these items, and you'll have a pretty solid idea of what you'll be facing. If you hear the answers you want to the questions you ask, you can then ask the next-most important question: "When do we start?"

How to Make Small Talk in Business Networking Situations

Introverts—of which I am one most of the time—usually dread small talk.[21] In general, "small talk" is simply idle chatter designed to interact superficially without asking deep, controversial, or personal questions about the other person.

Large social gatherings, such as business networking events (or office parties where you don't know a lot of people) are often where small talk is not only appropriate but sometimes necessary. If you're an extrovert, you probably enjoy most social gatherings and this section will be bewildering to you.

What DO People Talk About, Anyway?

I actually asked this question on Facebook once because, honestly, I don't always know what "normal (non-workaholic, non-space) people" talk about. Small talk in the U.S. means discussing innocuous things like sports, television programs, or the weather before you jump right into wowing them with your latest, genius sale-making idea. I'm a science fiction, history, and philosophy book fan. Not all of those are mainstream interests. I follow some sports and am quite

---

[20] This type of "ghosting" is different from disappearing from a party. This is where (as discussed in Chapter 5), if you know your competitor(s) and how they do things, you make slight digs against their approach by explaining how your approach is superior to process X (without naming your competitor, of course). Just be certain that your approach is superior.

[21] This is not because we hate people, we just prefer to interact with them in smaller quantities.

conversant on matters related to Star Trek or Star Wars. Does that mean I follow the culture that carefully? No.

A cousin of mine suggested that if I wanted to engage in small talk, I stick to discussing other people's health, their families, or, yes, the weather...again, innocuous stuff.

Still, you could flip that small talk on its ear a bit to be a bit more memorable in future discussions. For example, by observing that everyone talks about the weather, but nobody ever does anything about it. I did get a strange look from someone who complained about the rain and I responded, "I'm sorry, our weather satellite is broken."

Of course you might not care or remember what people at an event actually talked about. Little hint: if you're in a roomful of strangers, you don't always need to talk: just nod occasionally and ask appropriate follow-up questions: "What did that mean to you?" "How did you feel about that?" People like talking about themselves, so asking open-ended questions about others doesn't require talking nearly as much as when you try to make up witty or memorable things to say about yourself.

Another thing to do is to casually walk around with food or beverage in hand and listen to what other people are discussing to see if there's a conversation you might consider joining. Your level of energy will go up if you feel you hear a topic you enjoy or have a question to ask or something interesting to contribute...just make sure you're invited to join the conversation first. Usually a nod or question asked in your direction is sufficient.

I've said this before, but small talk usually means avoiding larger discussions such as politics, sex, or religion. You might get more animated or interesting discussions talking about hot-button topics like those, but this can be a social risk, depending on the crowd and the occasion. Do you want to start an argument at someone's wedding or the company picnic? I don't, but that's me.

How to Prep for Small Talk

One thing that can help the socially uncomfortable is to go in with a plan...or with a set of topics you can talk about that meet the usual sports, TV, or weather-level of chitchat. I am much better at "business networking" activities than purely social events because at a business event because I'm on a mission and free to talk about my work, which is a lot of what interests or animates me. Purely social occasions mean I have to talk about myself and my life when I'm not at work, and that's not terribly interesting to a lot of people or nobody's darned business much of the time.

There are a few ways you can go in "armed for battle."

- Read up on what's going on in the world of sports (who's winning, who's losing), maybe specialize in the activities of one particular team or sports figure.
- Find out what's popular on TV and get at least a general idea of what's happening on the show and who the main characters are. Again, you might not care about most of what's on TV, but you can fake it until you make it.
- Go see a movie you like and watch the trailers, so you can be familiar with what other shows are out there.
- You might have a hobby (mine is reading, and more recently, community theater) about which you're passionately interested. Talk about that instead.

You can also show up prepped with open-ended questions so that you get other people to talk more than you. Open-ended questions mean something that requires more than a yes-or-no answer. These might include:

- How do you occupy your time?
- What's your favorite team? How are they doing?
- What are you watching on TV? And here's a more interesting question for introverts to ask: what is it about the show that interests you?
- Set a goal for meeting or speaking with a minimum or maximum number of people.
- Come in with an interesting, short, funny story about something that happened to you—again avoiding stories related to sex, religion, or politics. Just share something brief and amusing to set other people at ease. Odds are, you're not the only uncomfortable person in the room.
- If you're attending a business-related function, have business cards handy. Talking business can put you in a work frame of

mind, which can be very different from a simply social mindset. I learned the hard way that this is a little awkward at purely social occasions.

Calling It a Night

There are things you can do to avoid making social gatherings endless hours of agony. You can set yourself a time limit for your attendance. My social energy threshold is usually expended in about two hours, after which I need to retire. This is not a bad amount of time, as it usually gives you an opportunity to interact with many people, it doesn't look like you just came for the food, and it has a cutoff time.

If you're going with someone else—a friend, preferably—it's good to set that expectation up-front. When it's time to go, you can depart quietly or let the host(ess) know you had a great time and it's just time to go.

Bottom line: social functions are often unavoidable, as is the idle chit-chat that comes with them. Also, attempts to avoid them can cause you other problems, so it's best to put in the effort so you're not always the wallflower by the punch bowl. You might not learn to like it, but you can learn to at least get better at it.

Intra-Office Communications

Communicating in work situations is a bit different from social occasions because at work you very much have an aim in mind. The question is, how do you communicate? There are times when it's better to walk down the hall and have a conversation rather than lean too heavily on technology. As a former NASA customer of mine once said, "Emailing isn't communicating." Still, it's a question worth asking: when can something be handled by a simple email or a phone call, and when do you need to have a multi-party teleconference or face-to-face meeting?

To make this simpler, I've put this into table form. If you can answer yes to most or all of the questions in section I, you're probably safe with an email, text message, or a phone call. If you can say yes to most or all of the questions in section II, an in-person visit is worth considering. If you can say yes to most of the questions in section III, a formal, face-to-face meeting or video teleconference might be most appropriate.

Group	Question	Text	Email	Phone Call	Cubicle/Office Visit	Teleconference	Face-to-Face Meeting/Video Teleconference
I	Is it a quick question?	X	X	X			
	Is it a question of fact?	X	X	X			
	Is it NOT an emergency?	X	X	X			
	Are you just sending a document?		X				
	Can the subject be handled by only two people?	X	X	X	X		
	Is there little to no controversy attached to the subject?	X	X	X	X		
II	Will the subject require less than an hour to discuss?			X	X		
	Can the subject be handled by 2 people?			X	X		
	Is it something you'd rather not discuss in the cubicle farm?			X	Office		
	Is it something you'd rather not commit to email?			X	X		
	Does the subject have personal/emotional weight attached to it?			X	X		
	Do you need an answer soon/immediately?	X		X	X		
III	Is it something that needs to be addressed by four or more people?				X	X	X
	Will the subject require an hour or more to discuss?					X	X
	Does the subject have organizational controversy or legal implications attached to it?						X
	Do decisions/votes need to be documented formally?						Face-to-Face Meeting (Site Visit)
	Is it something that's easier to convey in person, either because the other person needs to see something or because it's more easily conveyed visually?					X	VTC
	Is the individual (or individuals) required for a decision not immediately available in person?						X
	Are travel funds tight?					X	VTC

These are my personal guidelines, I hasten to add, though they're based on my observations of corporate behavior in a variety of environments (Disney, DoD, NASA, Nissan). Situations can change and sometimes a memo will cover it. But most communications professionals will tell you face-to-face communications are better than electronic, and voice is preferable to text.

Human beings are very dependent upon facial expressions, body language, gestures, tone of voice, and other nonverbal clues to determine how well our messages are being received. Essentially, the more emotional, financial, or legal weight to a topic, the more you're going to want human beings facing each other in the same room to read all of the verbal and nonverbal components possible. Just as you wouldn't propose to your significant other via text message, so also you probably wouldn't resign from your job that way, either. Okay, some people do, but that's not the most effective way to handle things. If communications were easy, a lot of writers would be out of a job.

Being a Team Player: How Do You Define It?

I am probably the wrong person to be writing this. As a corporate employee I was not always seen as a team player as defined by my managers. That can be a problem, especially at review time, because their definition is what matters, not necessarily yours.

My Definition of "Team Player"

I was (and remain) focused on my work when I'm in the workplace. In my 20-something or 30-something mind, that meant doing my job well, helping my coworkers when asked, and generally being a productive citizen. However, sometimes this was insufficient.

My Managers' Definition of "Team Player"

If I didn't like the job I had—which happened a few times before I got full-time writing work—I was sometimes less than diligent. I'd arrive and depart exactly on time. Or I'd find whatever assignments would require messenger duties to keep out of sight of management for the maximum amount of time. In short, I did the bare minimum. To managers, that was not being a "team player."

I can't say I was easier for managers to deal with once I did like my job. Then, all I wanted to do was the job: writing. I was diligent, thoughtful, thorough, and enjoyed my work. However, problems arose when managers wanted me to appear at meetings, mandatory random training, or office social gatherings (birthdays, engagement celebrations, or other events). At that point I'd start pushing back because I had a deadline or, in my biased opinion, something more important to do.

I learned that lesson the hard way: Managers don't like to hear no.

Once in the meetings, I could be difficult, too. In one office I got so notorious with my questions that on one occasion "the Bart hand" went up and the manager just saw me, shook her head, and said, "Yes, Bart. This is necessary."

Lessons Learned
I settled down eventually. I learned if I wanted to reduce the amount of friction I experienced with my managers, it was better if I just did what they asked me to do rather than ask "Why?" all the time. Call it a little bit of playing the game.

Another thing that helped was talking with my peers and managers about how management defined being a team player. That's usually the best route as you're starting a job or even while you're interviewing. Even if you think you've got your priorities straight, your managers might have other ideas. And like it or not, if you're in a corporate environment, they're the ones who have the authority to decide what your priorities are—and whether you're doing them satisfactorily or not.

When Working with SMEs Goes Badly
In 2013 I gave a talk about subject matter expert (SME) "horror stories" from the tech writing trenches. If you've done the job for any amount of time, you no doubt have your own. These are mine. The point is not to justify bad behavior—mine or theirs—but to share some lessons learned to prevent you from handling similar situations badly.

Example #1: Battle of the Egos
When I worked in the Disney IT department, I needed a programmer to give me some information for a software development document. I

kept asking, "Hey, Mike! Where's the info I need?" After a sufficient number of inquiries of this nature, Mike got irritated with me and snapped, "Why are you pushing so hard on this? No one's going to read what you write, anyway." To which I replied, equally impolitely, "Why are you working so hard on that code? No one's ever going to use it."

Okay, that wasn't my most diplomatic moment, but after our tempers cooled, he did give me the information.

Example #2: The Genius

A few years ago, I was assigned to help write an internal proposal within NASA. The SME was a bit put out that he was sent a writer at all. "Look, I've got a Ph.D. in X, and I've taken a seven-day course in proposal writing. I know everything there is to know about this business." I bit my tongue on that occasion, but I found it amusing when a proposal reviewer complained about the language in a section of the proposal the SME had written and wouldn't let me touch. "This is dry and a bit condescending. Did your technical writer read this?" For what it's worth, I did edit that section later and the proposal did win.

Regardless of the horror stories, the bottom-line lesson here is that this conflict and the one before it arose out of a lack of mutual respect. It's important to respect the value your SME brings to the table, but it also helps if that respect goes both ways. Sometimes that takes a while.

How Should We Work with SMEs?

Americans tend to be very informal, and it's tempting for us to just walk into someone's office or accost them in the hallway and ask them something. However, if you work in large, formal, bureaucratic organizations, it is good to remember a little etiquette and protocol. Protocol means you follow the official chain of command to communicate with Subject Matter Expert X, via formal email invitation or via appointment made through their assistant. Etiquette means you approach such matters politely.

In practical terms, this means you should set a formal meeting with an agenda (topic, context, and questions stated up-front) so the SME knows the reason for the discussion. You need to show up for the meeting on time. You need to stick to your agenda and end on time.

Their time is as valuable as yours—probably more, depending on what they make per hour.

This protocol-based approach will not guarantee that the SME won't let his or her conversation wander, share too many details you don't need, or let the meeting run long on their own ("Back when we were working on the space shuttle…"). The side stories are often a bonus in your work because they can be fascinating, but you might need to interrupt (politely, of course) and say, "You know what? This is an interesting story, and I'd like to hear the whole thing once we're done. But right now, I really need to know more about X."

At the conclusion of the interview, ask the SME to review the content (proposal, press release, white paper, or other document) that you wrote based on your discussion. This is a good time to set some expectations regarding the easiest way to give and receive feedback: phone call? Track Changes in an emailed Word document? Drop off a hard copy at the SME's office? It's also good to state when you will need the SME's inputs. And, as always, thank them for their time.

Technology now offers us many different ways to **communicate** with each other, some with differing levels of engagement and effectiveness. Some people prefer Post-It Notes. Some like text messaging, which to me is the worst method for getting things done, but it suffices when you're in a hurry. Email is a little better because people are more likely to type better and more formally in front of a grownup-size keyboard than typing quickly on those little-kid keys on their smart phone. The next-best method of communicating is that old standby, speaking on the telephone: you know, what we used to use our phones for before we started playing Angry Birds or Candy Crush with them. The most effective method for human beings is still speaking in person, face to face. Usually. There are some people who don't like a lot of people around and are more comfortable conversing by email. Look at this as an opportunity to apply the Golden Rule to communications: communicate with your SME as they would prefer to communicate. You should be a little more accommodating toward their style of doing things since they're helping you.

What Questions Should We Ask?
Before we start asking a SME questions out of the blue, it's worth considering when we shouldn't bother them. A manager at Disney got

frustrated with my constant inquiries and asked me, "Bart, did you try looking it up first?!" Having learned that lesson the hard way, my sanity check now is to ask myself, "Is this a question of fact? Can I Google this or look it up in an internal document somewhere?" If the answer to both of these questions is yes, I won't bother the SME.

You should also do your homework to some extent: learn the nomenclature, the flow of technology in your area of work, and the everpresent (at least in the space business) list of acronyms. The effort is worth it because learning the basics of the SME's language helps you in several ways:

- It prevents you from asking stupid questions ("What's an engine?").
- It helps you to understand the answers the SME is giving you.
- It allows you to get past all the little or simple questions, and get to the more important and interesting questions the SME can answer best.
- The SME is more likely to take you seriously because you've taken the time to learn his or her business and to get things right.

So what are those more interesting questions?

- The how or why behind particular technical decisions.
- Localized knowledge; for example, how do they do or think about things at Marshall Space Flight Center differently from how they do them at Kennedy Space Center?
- Networking or referrals to other sources: "Hey, Phil! Who worked on the aerospike engine for the X-33?"
- Sanity checks or clarifications of content you've written based on their work or interview.

Concluding Thoughts

I love my job. Technical writing is a constant opportunity to learn things you never knew from some very interesting people who are a lot smarter than you on particular subjects. They aren't always as nice as they could be—though most of them are happy to share their knowledge with you—but if you can stay humble enough to admit you don't know everything, working with SMEs is pretty easy. They add value by providing depth and context to what you write. You add value by translating what they share into the clearest, most effective prose you can so their work can go forward. And if you can get past some occasional conflicts of personality, technical writing really is the most interesting job in the world.

In 2013, my employer's primary method of communicating was to call me up or drag me into a room with a white board and do a brain dump (lecture) for an hour. I then went back to my desk, translated what I'd heard, and emailed the document to him for a sanity check. It was a good system for him, and he appreciated my ability to translate Engineerish into English. That manager also didn't like me to use any more than five major points in any deliverable. In that spirit, allow me to close this section with the following five reminders for dealing with SMEs:

- Give and expect respect.
- Establish and follow protocol and etiquette.
- Communicate with SMEs as they would like to communicate.
- Do your homework first so you can ask better questions and don't waste the SME's time.
- Listen to the SMEs and write clearly and correctly with the best words possible so that you're both adding your best value.

The Good Parts about Working with Subject Matter Experts
A respondent to an online survey I posted on Heroic Tech Writing said that "Interactive skills and depth of listening even appear unpleasant." Wow. I guess he had a point: I've often shared my "horror stories" when dealing with SMEs without sharing the good side. My intention is (usually) to show how technical writers can make our lives more difficult by testing the patience of an eminent, busy SME by not being prepared before we ask them questions. However, let's talk about some of the bright sides of dealing with the "experts." It's not all bad, really!

As a technical writer, it's been my good fortune to interview or write and edit for some very bright people in the science, space, and technology industries. These individuals include (among others) David Anderson, Darlene Cavalier, Barbara Cohen, Steve Cook, Mary Lynne Dittmar, Dan Dumbacher, Jeff Foust, Jeff Greason, Jason Hundley, Mike Griffin, Loretta Hidalgo-Whitesides, John Horack,

Les Johnson, Ray Kurzweil, Bruce Mackenzie, Todd May, Tim Pickens, Carolyn Porco, Sian Proctor, Phil Sumrall, Paul Spudis, George Whitesides, and Robert Zubrin.

The point is not to name drop, but to give you some insight into why I've enjoyed my chosen career. It's one thing to read what these people say in the news, it's another to talk with them directly, pick their brains, and get wisdom from people who are actually advancing the state of the art in their particular field. They're doing exciting things and working on difficult problems that interest me and make my content exciting to write.

I would also say that given the prominent positions these people have achieved, they have learned the importance of making their difficult subject matter accessible to members of the public. They can speak by analogy or clarify complex subjects in ways that don't require equations. They help me learn.

On other occasions, these individuals have shared their visions of what the future of their business might be like: what we might do, where we might go, and what those discoveries might mean for humanity. The ideas in their minds have the virtue of expanding my own horizons. Those kinds of discussions are exhilarating for a space geek like me. It's an opportunity to hear what the future might be like and what sorts of wonders we might find there.

This is not to say it's always easy to work around serious subject matter experts. Often due to my English-focused education, I have to ask them to repeat some things or ask them to "bring it down a level" until what they're saying makes sense to me. That's my problem, not theirs. But again, it's a privilege to obtain information from SMEs, and I make my best effort to ask pertinent questions that get the most information possible from them without wasting their time.

If you're sincerely interested in your content, talking to the people on the leading edge of that content can be rewarding and fascinating. And, as an extra bonus, those discussions make your writing that much better because it is informed by people who are the experts in what they do.

Giving and Receiving Feedback on Your Writing

This is a sensitive subject for many writers, me included, because our words are what we get paid for, what we take pride in, and why we do what we do for a living. How dare someone change them or correct them? I don't know about the rest of you, but I for one know that I need editors, badly. Writing is not easy for many people, which is why I have a job in the first place. But for those of us who find writing enjoyable, the editing process can be a sensitive proposition.

I did not appreciate the value of a good editor until I got paid to write for a living. That was in 1996, when I started answering guest letters for the Walt Disney World Resort. I had a lot of bad academic habits from writing papers for English literature professors: verbosity, convoluted sentences, "scholarly" language, and other university-based literary sins.

In a professional setting, when I'm getting paid or on a deadline, I now generally let editors do their thing. I am not as gracious when my reviewer makes the content worse. This happened to me a few years ago when an engineer took a serious hatchet to my work because it was not written as an engineer would write it. Everywhere an active verb was used, he switched it to passive. If my sentences had been short, he made them longer. If I used a colloquialism or more generic, less Engineerish term for a piece of the rocket, he reinserted the technical name of the widget. It was like hearing fingernails squeak across the blackboard. I was not amused.

If this had been a technical paper, for a technical audience, I probably would have pushed back only a little then let it go. However, in this situation, the engineer was making my job more difficult because I was writing a document meant for the general public: a non-NASA audience unfamiliar with the intricacies of aerospace propulsion engineering. I finally found a solution: I just accepted all his changes and started over again with my translation efforts, informing my final customer of what I'd done.

The biggest challenge I faced with that particular reviewer was that he felt my writing wasn't "correct" because it wasn't written the way an engineer would write it. Perhaps he did not understand that this was my point, my strength, and my actual reason for being there. If engineers could write in a way easily understood by the public, NASA wouldn't have hired me in the first place. I felt as if he was questioning the rightness of my work, and considered snarling something like, "When I have the impertinence to question your engineering, you can edit my writing style." As I recall, I was a little more restrained than that, but I did explain that he'd made my job a bit more difficult that day and left it at that.

Still, that experience taught me something about setting expectations up-front with my editor. If I don't lay out any requirements up-front, a good editor is likely to dive in and tear apart the document at every level.

Giving feedback was another matter. Training a coworker proved an excellent way to help me lose my bad habits. I started out doing some rather rude things, such as going after a coworker's style. That was unnecessary. If the meaning of the content is being conveyed and the grammar is being used correctly, I had to learn to leave it alone. If the word choices someone makes are not mine, so be it. It also goes without saying that rude or snarky comments are unnecessary unless you have that kind of relationship with your customer.

As a professional writer, there are situations where I will ask my reviewer to look at spelling and punctuation only. Sometimes I need a content or comprehensive review. Regardless of the level of edit I request, I need to thank my reviewer for their time and effort. Most of the time any corrections they make will have improved my work. I need to accept any changes in the spirit of self-improvement. It sounds great on paper, and most times I can even think that way without grumbling. It is harder to respond that way when writing fiction or poetry, when I'm trying to conjure up my personal view of the universe. But that's another story.

Do You Need a Diplomacy Filter?
Sometime in my twenties, I started realizing that people could get hurt or offended by my choice of words in a business document. I wasn't insulting people (deliberately) or using vulgar language. I was, however, a tad blunt and not always aware of some of the sensitivities people can have toward how I phrased things. From that point on, if I found myself in a situation where I thought I might get into trouble, I made certain to have my writing reviewed by my "diplomacy filter." Do you have one?

What kinds of documents would benefit from a diplomacy filter?

- Anything being sent or posted for a mixed audience. This "mixing" could include multiple genders, nationalities, ethnicities, social statuses, languages, educational levels, sexual preferences, or political leanings. If you're sharing information or a specific viewpoint, do so without going out of your way to offend or condescend to any group, deliberately or inadvertently (unless that's your style…in which case, good luck with that).

- Related to the above, any document that addresses an issue of employment, ethics, pay, benefits, employee conduct, customer relations, proprietary information, or corporate viability…in short, anything important or politically sensitive.

- Anything related to corporate culture. This, again, goes to political sensitivities and how people conduct themselves and how company management perceives itself.

- Any document related to disciplinary matters. These will usually be handled by a member of management, human resources, or even the legal department, depending on the size of the organization or the nature of the offense.

- Refusal of a deal or financial transaction, service recovery request, favor, or any other situation where you have to tell the individual receiving the document "No."

- Product safety issues. The goal here isn't to sugar-coat a situation, but also not to assign blame, especially if all the facts are not in yet. If all the facts are in, it's best to be clear and emotion-free as much as possible so that you're laying out the problem, consequences, and response, fix, or work-around, if known. Again, legal might get involved here.

You want a diplomacy filter when your words could produce negative reactions based on the audience, situation, and potential outcome if you use the wrong words. In short, that could be darn near everything. However, some situations are more fraught with social pitfalls than others; hence the list above.

Stay diplomatic, everyone! There are worse things you could do.

Is Coworking for You?

As an introvert, I've learned to love working from home. I get to set my own hours, play my own music (or not), arrange my environment as I would prefer it, and don't get interrupted by a lot of talking when I'm in the middle of a hot deadline or train of thought.

That said, technical writing is one of the "knowledge economy" careers that works well in a coworking space. In case you haven't heard of coworking before, it's working in a shared office space with individuals who have their own business or work for multiple companies but otherwise would work from home. Why would you want to join and pay to belong to such a community?

It's a Quieter Alternative to Starbucks, BUT...

I've made the rounds at Starbucks, Panera, the local library...whoever has free Wi-Fi or breakfast, sometimes just to get out of the house. However, while Starbucks has Wi-Fi and allegedly good coffee[22], it's often noisy and not necessarily wired for someone trying to write or edit content. (However, while I find them too noisy, my editor reminded me that some people are just fine with working there). Coworking sites are often converted industrial or office properties that have been made over into comfortable shared work spaces. They're made for work.

On the other hand, coworking sites differ from rented formal office space, such as you might find at places like Regus, because they coworking sites tend to feature open floor plans and an atmosphere that is built with more socializing, networking, or collaborating in mind.

Office-Based Networking

Why on Earth would an introvert want to work among all those people? Aren't we happy to finally have the luxury of working from home?

Two words: business contacts. Depending on the types of customers you support, you might meet potential clients or people who know potential clients.

---

[22] Unlike many writers, I don't drink coffee, so I'll have to take others' word for it.

And there's this: not every work-from-home business is run by an introvert.

So really what you have in a coworking facility is the "social" aspect of an office without everyone reporting to the same boss(es). You're free—or even encouraged!—to talk with others to find out what they're doing and see if they might have an opportunity for you to help.

Downsides

I've only really been to a couple of coworking facilities, though I've done research and other writing for a local startup coworking place (ScribbleSpace) in Orange County, Florida, so I have a general idea of the different types of environments you can find. Some coworking places can be louder than others, some will support a different "culture" because of the nature of the people working there or how the place was organized.

One coworking place I visited was rather messy—chairs and tables all over the place, random paint splashes on the wall—and noisy, with loud music playing that did not appeal to me.

Another issue—for me, anyway—is the "cruise director" mentality, where coworking managers feel they have to create activities or events to keep the members engaged. Those types of events can be off-putting at times, just as they are in a regular nine-to-five office, and you can be made to feel "guilted" into attending. I had enough of that in corporate America, thank you. But hey, if you miss that aspect of working in an office, there's probably a location that can do that for you. And because you don't work for a coworking space but at one, you're not obligated to go.

Finally, there are days where you need to be in your zone—a quiet place or a loud one—and often you can only achieve that at home. Fair enough: work from home that day. Unlike a traditional office or company, you're not required to be there; just remember that it's your money. If the cost/benefit analysis doesn't work for you, try something else.

Finding the Right Atmosphere

ScribbleSpace is a project developed by a small-business friend of mine, Cynthia. Cynthia's primary business is a creative shop that handles graphic design, advanced public-facing touch-screen applications, animations, and other cool things. Because her work puts her in contact with IT, marketing, and other businesses as well as creative content developers, she developed a space that appeals both to artists and more traditional business professionals. This means ScribbleSpace is a mix of more traditional furniture and fixtures (desks, tables) with the occasional artistic design flourish, as seen below.

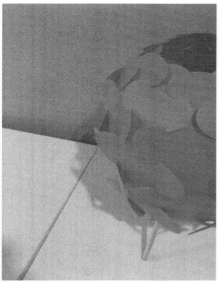 

This is a desk lamp...no, really! Ceiling light, which I call the Death Star...

 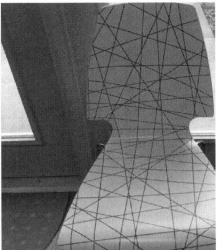

The primary bright color at Scribble-Space is orange–Cynthia is playing that up to the max!

One of several groovy chairs from IKEA.

The goal of this mixed artsy and professional look is to make the place inviting to both types of clients: enough "cool" for the artists to feel at home but enough "normal" that accountants or the more traditional technical writers like me won't think it too weird or messy. A lot of hard thinking and doing went into the place, from deciding the target market to acquiring the facility, a commercial space in the upscale neighborhood of Summerport Village in Windermere, Florida. In addition to being an office-away-from-home, ScribbleSpace was also designed to support classes or other events. The goal is not just to run a well-organized facility, but to help connect the community of freelancers who otherwise would be disconnected from the social whirl of the business world. The place has been open since 2015, so Cynthia's obviously doing something right.

The bottom line is that you have to determine what type of atmosphere works for you and figure out whether you want to create it yourself in your home, visit an existing coworking facility, or start your own space. And if having a lot of people around all the time isn't for you, you don't have to make it a habit. However, I would strongly suggest that you at least try coworking. While not everyone works in the "knowledge economy" and is able to take their work on the road, technical communicators definitely are in that category and should investigate this new form of workplace. It can help relieve some of the loneliness of working from home, and (even if you don't have the loneliness problem) you might make contacts that lead you to new business!

Burning Bridges: Why You Shouldn't and When You Probably Should

Speaking of contacts, I prefer not to burn bridges (end all contact) with professional colleagues in the event of an argument or disagreement. That's not to say I haven't, or that others haven't stopped talking to me. It happens. The point is, where I can, I try to keep my professional relationships going after I leave a workplace. There are a few reasons for this.

It's a Small World

I work in the human spaceflight industry, which is a pretty small community. That also means the odds are often better than even that I will be working with someone again in the future. Getting angry? Backstabbing? Causing a ruckus? Being difficult to work with? None of those responses make life easier if you have to work with certain individuals again. And all that goes back to reputation, which is built over the course of days, months, and years. Would you rather hear someone say, "Oh, good! I get to work with you again!" or "Could we keep it civil this time?"

Friends Are Good to Have

We spend a lot of time at work, sometimes more time than we spend with our families. Given the amount I have spent on the job, it just makes sense to try to be as agreeable and pleasant as I can manage. And really, wouldn't you rather spend the day with friends than people who irritate you?

You Just Never Know

I've had multiple contacts from my professional life circle back and ask me if I would like to work with them again. This is not a primary reason for keeping channels open, or even a secondary reason. Still, I mention it because after 20+ years as a corporate guy, I've now spent over 5 years as a freelancer, and my network has been critical to finding work. In fact, it's been most gratifying that people in my network have sought me out. And yes, on those occasions where work has been a little scarce, I've gone back and looked up previous peers and managers to see if they knew anyone looking for work that a technical writer can do, which (as I noted in the "Cold Calls/Sales Calls" section) is a little different from asking them directly for a job. There is less pain and embarrassment on their part if the answer is no. And if the answer is no and they can't refer me to someone, they at least know I'm looking, right?

When the Bridge Burns Anyway

This section is not about sharing "war stories" or another example of one of my social failures, but I would add some thoughts about how to handle it when you eventually encounter someone with whom you did not part on the best of terms. You might still be angry or hurt. They might still be angry or hurt. Odds are, however, that you'll be in a professional setting and have to put on a good face. Put on that good face. Shake their hand. Say the right things. You might not feel like doing that at all, but for one reason or another your work has put you into a circumstance where you have to work with someone you dislike, and paying the bills requires that you do the work. You're paid to work with them, not like them. That's all part of behaving like a professional.

It's your call as to whether it's worth leaving a job to avoid working with someone unpleasant again, but you have to consider the nature of the unpleasantness (rudeness vs. actual harassment), your long-term reputation, and other circumstances. Is it a permanent arrangement or temporary assignment? Can you shift out soon thereafter? Do you want to be perceived as being immature or unprofessional because you cannot work with a particular person? Or your old animosity might resurface and you'll swear never to work with that person again, in which case you'll learn a professional way to avoid doing so. You might hate it, but sometimes it's worth it to be "the bigger person," and just do the job. You might learn to respect the other person. You might repair that bridge.

And if the previous parting was due to outright unpleasant, unethical, inappropriate, or unlawful behavior on their part, you shouldn't have to force yourself to work with someone who makes you incredibly uncomfortable. Let those bridges burn.

Chapter 7: Maneuvering through Office Politics

I chose "maneuver" specifically because not everyone wants to move up into management. That doesn't mean you can escape office politics; people are people, and they'll behave differently in different types of organizations and situation depending on their role within them. I'll touch on leadership here—for those supporting good and bad leaders—as well as for those who might end up becoming leaders themselves. And because I said the "P word" (politics), there will be some discussion about handling broader political topics in a workplace context.

Large, Medium, or Small: What's Your Best Working Environment?
One of the first things that will draw you to a particular job is the content you will be writing. However, another important consideration when looking at a new job is the size of the company doing the hiring. What follows are my impressions based on supporting organizations of different sizes.

First, some definitions are in order. "Small" businesses can vary in size depending on whom you're talking to or what industry they're in. So, for grins, I checked out the U.S. Government's Small Business Administration (SBA) site.

"Examples of SBA general size standards include the following:

- Manufacturing: Maximum number of employees may range from 500 to 1500, depending on the type of product manufactured;
- Wholesaling: Maximum number of employees may range from 100 to 500 depending on the particular product being provided;
- Services: Annual receipts may not exceed $2.5 to $21.5 million, depending on the particular service being provided;
- Retailing: Annual receipts may not exceed $5.0 to $21.0 million, depending on the particular product being provided;
- General and Heavy Construction: General construction annual receipts may not exceed $13.5 to $17 million, depending on the type of construction;
- Special Trade Construction: Annual receipts may not exceed $7 million; and

- Agriculture: Annual receipts may not exceed $0.5 to $9.0 million, depending on the agricultural product."

It only gets murkier the further you go up the size scale. For instance, a financial website[23] in the United Kingdom set the threshold for "medium-sized businesses" as follows:

> Organizations that are in the startup or growth phase of development and have fewer than 250 employees. This definition of small and medium-sized enterprises is the one adopted by the United Kingdom's Department for Business Enterprise and Regulatory Reform for statistical purposes.

That same site described a large business as:

> An organization that has grown beyond the limits of a medium-sized business and has 250 or more employees. This definition of a large-sized enterprise is the one adopted by the United Kingdom's Department for Business Enterprise and Regulatory Reform for statistical purposes. It is usually from the ranks of large-sized businesses that multinational businesses arise.

So how do you know if you, as a technical writer, are going into a small, medium, or large business? Well, if you do the research online, the company website or job posting might say what sort of business it is, or you can ask during the interview process. Or, given this murkiness across industries and countries, you could try to define the business "size" by the size of the operation in which you, personally, must operate. For example, a Fortune 500 company might have thousands of employees across the country or around the world, but the shop where you work consists of you, your manager, a few writers, and maybe a graphic designer or two. The difference between that operation and an actual small business is that you can probably call on employees in other divisions to help you out if you're busy—in a medium or small business, you might be "it" when it comes to technical communication.

For the technical writer, perhaps the best way to understand the "size" of your employer is simply to understand the scope of resources you can access if you need help. Large business: lots of resources (money,

---

[23] This site has since disappeared. It was QFinance.com.

materials, people) to call upon for help; medium business: a few additional resources; small business: there isn't anyone else, bub—you're it. Okay, so solid definitions are difficult to come by. That said, you can still get a good feel for things after enough on-the-job experience.

Small

Advantages:

- Broader potential range of experiences.
- More creative control over the content because there are not that many people around to second-guess or review what you're doing.
- Good resume-builder due to a broader range of duties; little to no bureaucracy—you can call the owner, walk into his or her office, suggest something, and get immediate feedback.
- More entrepreneurial or creative environment because there are fewer corporate "filters" on bright ideas.
- The excitement of being in on the "ground floor" or part of the core team with the initial "vision."
- More opportunity to work on your own if you're an introvert.
- More of an opportunity to "shape" the job into anything you want.

Disadvantages:

- Few backups if you're sick or need help.
- Fewer resources—financial or human—to call upon if you need help.
- Lots more work because there are fewer of you to do it.
- Because of all of the above, it's more difficult to take a day off.
- More uncertainty about the future.
- You have to be the "institutional memory" for a lot more things because there aren't a lot of other folks on hand to maintain large files—and you still have to keep a close eye on your work and expenditures because money's tighter.
- Benefits could be limited to nonexistent.
- Might have to work awhile before seeing a profit.
- Loneliness if you like working with large groups of people.

- More likelihood of "family politics" and nepotism if it's a family-owned business and you're not a relation.

Coin tosses. Smaller businesses, especially new startups, tend to be run by younger people (less than 50 years old) simply because they have the energy to put in the hours and the freewheeling creativity to try something new. This is not to say you can't find older people creating startups or that entrepreneurship and creativity can't be found in larger organizations—but those would be exceptions, in my opinion. Small businesses are also more informal in dress code, office decorum, and business practices because it's a smaller group of people who all know each other.

Medium
Advantages:
- Still not a lot of people around, so there's room to "grow the job."
- More stability.
- Opportunity for promotions, raises, and paths for advancement, especially if the company has already been around for a while.
- Work includes more than just you and one or two other people—usually at least a graphic designer and maybe a web person—you've got backups and an editor if you need someone else to check your work.
- Benefits more likely a part of the compensation package.

Disadvantages:
- The "heroic" phase of building the team is mostly over (you're an employee, not part of a team starting something new).
- Less creative control: you might have to answer to a manager, lawyer, or committee before your bright ideas can be implemented.
- You might feel understaffed or underappreciated (a large communication staff is often rare in organizations until they find a need for it).

Coin tosses. Processes, dress code, and rules of decorum are still looser than they are in a very large organization, but definitely more formal than a small business where every day can be "Casual Friday."

If you prefer a little more structure and a few more resources to do your job, medium-size businesses might be for you.

Large
Advantages:
- More people and resources to help with large projects (larger budgets, in-house print shop, archives).
- More predictable rules, pay, benefits, and paths for promotion.
- More opportunities for career advancement and development.
- Larger, more ambitious projects.
- Less likelihood of corporate collapse in the event of a major economic event.
- Larger and better facilities with access to day care, exercise rooms, or other amenities.

Disadvantages:
- Lots of bureaucracy, paperwork, formalized processes, and big-group politics.
- Difficult to express your creativity unless it is within very specific boundaries.
- Gossip more likely to flourish with additional layers between front-line staff and upper management.
- Less opportunity for expanding the variety or scope of your job unless you work on cross-division project teams (of course, if you prefer consistency and predictability in your work, this could be an advantage to you).

Coin tosses. Corporate America is organized very much like a factory, with individual tasks broken out by function like a division-of-labor assembly line. This structure requires consistency of, and conformity with, the corporate culture, rules, and behavior on and off the job. A larger organization means more people and more meetings to keep that larger workforce apprised of what's going on. Great if you're an extrovert, not so great if you're an introvert and prefer to deal with only a few people on a daily basis.

These are some general thoughts for your consideration. And yes, I realize they are stereotypes. Newer large companies like Google have made serious efforts to give people a "small-company feel" in a large organization. This can include a looser corporate culture—no neckties, more time for creative outlets, more whimsical corporate décor, or more opportunities for working at home or achieving "work-life balance." Regardless of what improves your personal quality of life, the odds are good that you're going to spend more time there than anywhere else, so in addition to doing up-front research, it is not out of line to ask "cultural questions" during your interview.

Baby Boomers and Generation X have gone a long way toward changing the corporate culture in this country, some of it to the good. Perhaps the most important contribution might be recognizing that, with 30-year job security now the exception rather than the norm, companies and other organizations need to provide other incentives and opportunities to hire motivated employees. Where you work matters, and how you work matters that much more.

Vertical, Horizontal, and Matrixed Organizations (And Why You Should Care)

One aspect of an organization that can affect the technical writer's work "quality of life" is how it is organized. Online, this is by far my most popular topic, so you might want to give this some serious thought before you start job-hunting. First, a few definitions so you understand what I'm talking about.

Vertical Organizations

A "vertical" organization is known for having a large staff of middle managers between the CEO and the front line. In a vertically oriented company—which was the most common business model for organizations in the mid to late 20th century—lines of authority branch from the top down like a tree's roots. Individual vice-presidents direct the activities of the staff below them according to specific activities or lines of business: manufacturing, accounting, human resources, etc. Vertical organizations arose in the 1930s and 1940s to combat the tendency toward cronyism and nepotism in privately held businesses.

Advantages. The advantages of vertical structures are that they have defined chains of command and areas of responsibility; employees (usually) advance through ability and merit based on familiar, clearly defined tasks; and the career path of someone looking to advance "through the ranks" is clearly understood. Also, the longer one stays in a vertical organization the more in-depth knowledge and expertise they gain in that department over the course of time.

Disadvantages. The disadvantages of vertical structures are that they take longer to make decisions; important information does not always filter up or down "the chain" swiftly; and bureaucracy can become rampant as individual lines of business become isolated from each other. This "silo effect" results in separate cultures and procedures; and sometimes company branches try to justify unprofitable lines of business. Another challenge is that one level of a division can be in contact with another, but the "levels" above or below that contact are unaware of those conversations, resulting in lost communications or duplication of effort if someone else at a different level tries to initiate the same conversation. A final challenge with a vertical organization is that communications with other departments can sometimes be actively discouraged or seen as disloyalty below a "certain level"—the idea being all the information you should need to know to do your job comes from your line-of-business managers and no one else.

Horizontal Organizations

In response to the perceived weaknesses of the vertically aligned company, "horizontal" organizations started popping up more often—especially in dot-com companies in the 1990s, where companies were too small to afford large "vertical" staff organizations. Horizontally oriented companies have relatively few layers of management between the CEO and front-line personnel. It is thought that with fewer individuals in the chain of command, decisions can be made more quickly by the people who understand the problem best. As a result of this new management thinking, middle managers in "vertical" organizations saw more layoffs. Much of this "horizontal" thinking was born out of our nation's space program.[24]

Advantages. The goals of horizontal organizations are to speed up decision making; to allow for more management flexibility and cross-training as individuals work more closely with other areas; to eliminate bureaucracy because more people are talking to each other across vertical lines of business instead of creating duplicate functions across

---

[24] If you're really gung-ho to learn about how your space program affected systems management, see: Stephen B. Johnson's The Secret of Apollo: Systems Management in American and European Space Programs. Johns Hopkins University Press, 2006.

organizations; and to increase a company's flexibility when it comes to creating new products or reacting to new market conditions.

Disadvantages. The disadvantages of horizontal organizations include workforce reductions that create a loss of experienced managers (middle managers often make up the "institutional memory" of a company); the breaking up of specialized lines of business, thus reducing the company's ability to innovate; and uncertain career paths for aspiring managers. There can also be a perception that an individual who works in a small, flat organization lacks the necessary expertise in his or her particular specialty to truly excel because effort is diluted—the operative example being a "jack of all trades, master of none."

Matrixed Organizations

Ideally, matrixed organizations integrate the best of both horizontal and vertical structures. The idea is this: a (typically large) company keeps its specific lines-of-business expertise intact—finance, marketing, engineering, and so on—but brings together specialists from each vertical organization to work on temporary projects that develop new products, services, or even lines of business. Individuals working in such a structure would thus have vertical lines of accountability to their immediate line-of-business superiors and horizontal accountability to their project teammates.

Advantages. As stated above, matrixed organizations would keep their vertical lines of business intact to maintain their core competencies while also farming out individuals within those specialties to develop new products and services. The other advantage of this type of organization is that it has more regular and formal contact across disciplines.

Disadvantages. The primary challenges for individuals working in matrixed organizations are accountability, authority, and perceived "loyalty." If a manager is a project team lead or member, she or he must constantly balance which work takes precedence: project work or daily line-of-business work? Next, matrix structures also can impact employee loyalty: if individuals are more interested in doing project work than in doing the specialty work for which they were hired, they might be perceived as "disloyal" by their vertical line-of-business superior. Also, a line-of-business manager might not see their subordinate's work if he or she is heavily involved in project work. There can be a corporate problem of being "out of sight, out of mind," where a project worker misses opportunities for promotion within her or his vertical organization because of a focus on the project. If cooperation does not occur both horizontally and vertically, the company can easily be overrun by politics, as people break into fragmented camps: "Are you a 'project' person or are you an 'institutional' person?"

Why All This Should Matter to You

Opportunities. For the last couple decades, many large organizations have taken on the matrix form of organization (including NASA!). One primary reason is networking: because computers allow us to be connected in more ways than ever before, individual workers expect their companies to behave the same way. More importantly, customers expect that.

Large organizations like Disney spend a great deal of time and money on **Customer Relationship Management** (I believe their internal CRM designation is "Creating Relationship Magic"). CRM is the process of developing information streams that allow multiple parts of an organization to access customer information and use it to better meet customer and organization needs. One example of this CRM-type integration is the Disney **Magic Band, an inexpensive-looking plastic wristband** that is actually a rather complex piece of hardware (and software). The Magic Band serves as a guest's theme park admission, hotel room key, and credit card for making merchandise and food purchases at the parks and resorts. On the spooky side, once you've stayed at the hotel, visited the parks, and made all those purchases, the next marketing letter or email you get from Disney is likely to work like Amazon.com and recommend similar purchases for the next time you visit.

None of that could have happened without a matrixed organization to support it.

And, of course, along the way the company needed technical communicators working alongside the Information Technology people and all the other related organizations (Marketing, Attractions, Resorts) to meet those needs. I shudder to think of what the requirements document looked like for Magic Band, but I've seen it in action, and it does indeed work as advertised. What CRM-based tools mean for technical communicators is that they have plenty of opportunities to work on cross-functional projects, which can last weeks, months, or even years. And at the end of the project, your team has a new product or service to show for its efforts.

Another reason that cross-functional teams are better (and more fun, in my opinion) is that you get the opportunity to work with more customers, more lines of business, and therefore learn a lot more about how the whole organization works, which makes your knowledge much more valuable when you're looking for the next job.

Lastly, project work helps you build your personal network within an organization much better than if you just stayed within one line-of-business team. You might know Finance inside and out, for example, but you might have no idea who works in Marketing, how Public Affairs does its business, or how they affect what you do in your organization. If only out of self-defense, project work is beneficial to someone learning to be valuable to an organization.

Challenges. I'm not going to kid you: matrixed organizations have their challenges. For me, the biggest challenge was the number of meetings I had to attend. As a member of a "vertical" organization (say, the Communications department), you're beholden to that organization's schedule, standards, and meetings and are expected to comply with all three while on the project team. Just because you're "off doing project work" doesn't mean your line-of-business boss doesn't want to see you. She or he does, which means your meeting schedule effectively doubles.

Loyalty and conflicts of management interest. The "loyalty" question was always a puzzler because to me, accountability is pretty straightforward: I'm supposed to provide a good service as a communicator (representing the line-of-business organization) to a project team, regardless of who they are. My boss is in the communications department; my customer is in the project office.

In reality, loyalty doesn't become an issue until your line-of-business manager wants you to support something besides the project you're working on at the moment while the project manager needs you for project work. In such situations, the best thing to do is bring the matter into the open, contact both managers, and let them sort it out between themselves. If necessary, higher managers get involved, and then someone comes back to you and asks you if you can serve both masters in a way that makes everyone happy. It's a challenge, but to me the best way to demonstrate loyalty to the organization is not to show favorites, just let the chain of command sort it out once they realize there's a conflict.

If you're a project manager in a matrixed organization, you might face challenges to your authority. That is, you might be a "Project Manager" on your project, but if one of your attached line-of-business team members is a subject matter expert who outranks you in the vertical chain of command, the SME might not respond to your requests as quickly as you'd like. It's usually good, when setting up a project charter, to lay out clear lines of authority and also to establish a clear understanding that the line-of-business higher-ups will back up your authority with words and deeds. For example, if the higher-ranking SME ignores a project request and decides to do a line-of-business task instead, the project manager needs to have the authority to keep him or her in line...or take it to his superiors if he or she refuses to cooperate. I'm not saying it always happens, just that it can.

Final Thoughts

As I've already noted, I preferred project work in a corporate setting. That suited my somewhat broad (someone once called them flighty) interests. If you're a steady person who likes to become an expert on one topic, appreciates traditions, and wants to know how and why things are done a particular way, you might be a good fit for a vertical or institutional organization. Bills always need to get paid, operations always have to run smoothly, and products always need to come out of the factory working properly. Within those ongoing processes, there is always a need for technical communicators to maintain the institutional memory of How Things Should Be Done and what it means to do something "the company way." Regardless of your preferred type of work, it's good to know what options are available and what structures exist to support them.

It helps to understand how corporate entities are structured, how they can affect your work, and how you can best serve them. As always, the answer to the last item is, "Do good work, and someone will want to hire you."

Is Self-Employment for You?

While I've just discussed working in large, medium, and small businesses, all of those choices assume that you wish to be someone else's employee. Being an individual contractor, con-

sultant, proprietor, or CEO is something else. For simplicity's sake, I'll stick with working on your own as a contractor or consultant (as opposed to starting a company with more than one employee reporting to you).

Advantages. Freedom! I can't stress this enough because it's why I'd rather struggle my way than be content doing it someone else's way. Assuming you're working from home or at a **coworking** site, you can set your own hours, pay rate (subject to negotiation), working hours, sleep time, and dress code.

You can get chores done during regular nine-to-five business hours, when a lot of things are open and the lines aren't as long because other people are at work. You don't have to "ask the boss" if you can take time off for a doctor's appointment. You choose—again, within reason—your days off. You are the boss. Perhaps the most satisfying aspect of working for yourself is choosing the types of work you do and the types of customers you want to serve as your target market.

Disadvantages. It's all on you, buddy: writing, editing, layout, negotiating, bill paying, paying for health insurance (if you can afford it), networking, marketing, and so forth. You might think it's great to take a day off whenever you want, but you're never really off duty: work could come in at any time. If a customer calls, you need to take that call, unless you set hard limits, like office hours or vacations. A day not working is a day money isn't being made.

Yes, you can farm out some things, like going to H&R Block or using TurboTax to do your taxes or hiring a lawyer for any legal issues. And you might find a graphic designer to partner with on more visual pieces. But you'll need to be a lot more conscious about estimating your hours, ensuring cash flows when it should, and that you're bringing in new business (or trying) when other projects end. You need to have cash reserves or backup plans in case work dries up.

Coin Tosses. Actually, both items above—freedom and responsibility—have their ups and downs. When things are going well, you're the one who gets to enjoy it; when things are going awry, you've got to take it on the chin. Also, working alone is not for everyone. You either love it or you don't.

You might find that you feel more comfortable with a large organizational support system around you. (I won't lie—there are times I miss "the bureaucracy.") If you don't, there's always coworking, but again, you have to budget for that. Or, if the money's just not coming in, you might have to beg off freelancing and take a steady job for a while to keep the bills paid.

Other thoughts and issues. Before you go off on your own, it's important to have clients and types of work lined up in advance. You need to have a good network of potential customers, advisers, and references. You need to have a good idea of what your expenses are and how long you'll have to work to make those bills.

And those "financial reserves" I mentioned? You'll need them, especially when starting out because otherwise the odds are maybe 50/50 that you'll have customers the first day you open for business. And even if you are working on day one, you probably won't be invoicing or getting paid that day. You might need to set aside money for a while—6 to 12 months' worth—to cover your expenses if customers are harder to find than you anticipate. (Actually, financial advisors recommend having three to six months' salary in reserve even if you're a full-time employee.)

Lastly: you have to love what you do. As a one-person show, you have to keep yourself motivated to do all the things you need to do to ensure deliverables are produced and bills are paid. If getting up and facing a pile of specific types of work fills you with dread—whether you're on your own or working for corporate America—that's a problem. We all spend too much time at work as it is. If you don't like what you're doing and you're doing it for yourself, you need to seriously rethink what you're doing.

Of course as "an army of one," you're nimbler than a large organization, and you can make a decision that day to look for different work, look for a steady job, change your rates, or whatever. The choices, as an independent contractor, are yours. That's the glory and the hurt of it.

Protocol

I learn a lot of things—scratch that, most things—the hard way. Such was the case with corporate office protocol. I used to work at the front desk of one of the Walt Disney World Resort hotels. I had a guest situation that I have since forgotten. What I do remember is that I had a solution for their situation, but my manager disagreed with me and would not approve it.

I was in my early twenties at the time, and I knew enough about how the system worked to understand that the Big Boss had the authority to overrule my manager. What I did not understand were the consequences of going over the boss's head to try to get my way.

The result (you saw this coming, right?): I did not get my way. In my rather direct manner, I called the Resident Manager, who answered via speaker phone. I explained the situation as I saw it and why I thought my manager was wrong. Not only did I get a "no," but the manager I was trying to overrule was actually in the room as I spoke, and she let me know that she was not pleased with my actions. I still blush thinking about it, and I owed (and probably continue to owe) that manager a serious apology.

I had learned, very much the hard way, how foolish it can be to disrupt the chain of command.

Okay, so if going directly over your boss's head is a Bad Thing, what would be a more appropriate method of handling that situation? My 20-years-later suggestions are below.

- First, think hard about the situation at hand. How important is it that you get your way? Is it a personal matter (say, a leave request)? A matter of content wording or correctness? A problem with following an office procedure? An ethical or legal issue? My first recommendation is that you save your "override" requests for major issues, meaning those issues that have imminent negative impacts for you, the company, or a client, including financial, legal, political, and public relations. You might choose to fight every issue, but that will not make your future professional life easier.

- If you decide to go ahead and move things up the chain ("escalate" is the word I hear most often), start by making your appeal in person, first with your immediate supervisor, and then speak to his or her manager with your immediate supervisor present. Or, if you're uncomfortable with that, at least have the courtesy to inform your immediate supervisor of your concerns and that you would like to take them up with someone further up the chain. Telephone or email communications can very easily be misinterpreted or perceived as passive-aggressive. In any case, if you're going to overrule your boss, you should have the nerve to look him or her in the eye when you do so.
- Maintain your calm. If you raise your voice unnecessarily or get rude or argumentative at any point, you run the risk of being disregarded, being perceived as temperamental, or facing disciplinary action of some sort.
- Argue in a way that will make sense to the system. I am not saying don't fight the system. I am suggesting that you understand how the system works, and for the most part, the system doesn't like troublemakers. However, if you can make a solid case for why your point of view should prevail, you stand a good chance of winning. How does one win an argument with the boss? Usually by showing that their course of action would negatively impact something they care about, like the customer's opinion of the company, the bottom line, or the program schedule. So before you try to make that case, you'll have to ask yourself: can you?

Again, fighting the system is not impossible. Escalation can be successful. I can recall successfully convincing the same manager I previously irritated to change an office procedure because it would have negatively impacted guest operations. However, give the matter some thought before you take something over your boss's head. If your case is good, chances are you won't have to escalate things in the first place because your manager will agree with you and might even become an advocate in your cause.

Speaking Unpleasant Truths Aloud

"Hey, you're wrong!"

"The correct way to contradict a Senator is to say 'That turns out not to be the case'."

–The Mote in God's Eye, by Larry Niven and Jerry Pournelle

"Their decision is stupid! You know it and I know it."

"Yes, but you can't say it that way."

"Why not?"

–Bar conversation between me and a coworker re: management feedback

Once upon a time, I considered a career in the Foreign Service, partly because I was interested in the notion of living and traveling overseas, and partly because I spent an inordinate amount of my time "translating" one form of communication into another or because I spent my time developing more diplomatic ways of phrasing something. The reason this alternate career path is relevant is that if you have some skill in diplomacy, it will go a long way toward smoothing the way when things in your workplace are not so smooth.

Offering Negative Feedback

There comes that moment in every writer's career where someone who is not a professional communicator thinks they can do a better job than you and proceeds to prove otherwise. Sometimes, but not always, this person is at a higher rank in the organization than you. How do you break it to them that their work could use a little rewriting?

Several methods exist for addressing this situation. Not all of them are comfortable, and not all of them will work for you or your particular situation. What follows are a set of tactics for achieving the result you want without anyone getting upset with you even if you're right.

Start with the positive. Compliment your leader on their thinking or content as you see fit. Your goal, remember, should be to help them succeed. Therefore, if you start with positive feedback, they're more likely to listen to you; you can then add, "but I identified some things that could make it even better!"

Offer the feedback privately. One of the easiest ways to irritate the boss is to call out an error in a meeting where they're presenting to others. If you know your supervisor, manager, or customer has spelling or grammar "challenges," the best time to offer that feedback is either before the product is going out the door (especially print or email) or after it has been delivered (as in the case of a presentation). Giving feedback before the presentation or paper is delivered is obviously better in most situations. Calling out the error in front of others is a quick way to embarrass your boss then and endure a long and painful discussion later.

Offer to collaborate, not correct. Yes, it is entirely possible that your intent is to correct the boss's spelling or grammar, and they might know it, too. However, if you've managed to develop a reputation for putting words together well, "collaboration" is still better than "correction." You might offer suggestions that go beyond mechanics and emphasize content, tone, or flow. Just a word of caution: some folks will refuse your edits just because they don't like taking direction from a subordinate. That also goes back to tone. Telling someone in authority over you what to do in a tone that says they're stupid is not a great way to get them to take your suggestions.

Your reputation is on the line, too. There are organizations where a manager will give a presentation they did not write, but which they must present because it's part of their job. That doesn't mean they won't have any input beforehand—they might—but often others in the room know who their ghost writer is, and if something is wrong on the PowerPoint chart, the presenter will take some ribbing from his or her audience...as will you. The bottom line is that any error is a quality issue, and should be a matter of professional pride on your part. The boss deserves your best effort, and if you value your reputation, you need to give it. So yes, that means offering to help put together a customer's presentation or at least performing a quick review prior to delivery.

Two "But, sirs" and a "Yes, sir." I learned this approach from a friend who spent part of her career in the Army. She was a professional communicator as well and would tell her superior officers (often male) when they were about to do something incorrectly. She would try twice to suggest why he should do things her way, and if the colonel, general, whoever, still insisted on doing it his way, she'd salute, say, "Yes, sir!" and let the officer take the consequences. The point being, again using a military turn of phrase, pick your battles. For a briefing involving two or three people inside your company, a "happy" to "glad" wording change isn't worth raising hell about; a full-color, high-quality annual report that goes to thousands of stockholders deserves a little intervention—or escalation.

Disagreeing with a Decision

As kids, if my sister or I asked Mom or Dad (or anyone in authority) for something, the answers were usually yes, no, maybe, or not now. If you heard maybe or not now while growing up, you probably reacted as we did: whine, nag, or throw a temper tantrum until you got what you wanted. Eventually, you learn what form of argument worked best with your particular parent(s). You might even get logical and creative, like the kid on the Microsoft Windows commercial who used a PowerPoint presentation to argue for getting a puppy.[25] Here's the essence of arguing when working to change a manager's mind:

Don't yell, whine, or nag. All the kid stuff? Don't do that. It's a quick way to get on the boss's nerves and hear not just a no, but a "Hell, no!"

Speak their language. This means a couple of things. First, it means communicating in a way that works best for them. It also means framing your argument(s) in terms that match the boss's needs or interests. Example from my Disney life: the room assignment staff had been complaining for a week that reservations coming from one particular organization did not include any guest requests for connecting rooms. The GenX method of using passive-aggressive griping and whining (surprise) was not working. So someone got the bright idea of printing out the full list of guests we had in-house from that organization and showing the manager how many of them requested connecting rooms but didn't receive them because it wasn't noted in their reservation. This the manager understood: it was a service issue, our primary business—and that got her on the phone to the appropriate department to get the problem fixed.

Don't insult them. This should be a no-brainer, but telling someone in authority over you that they're ignorant or stupid for not doing things your way is incredibly ineffective. Yet it still happens.

Understand your supervisor's span of control. There are things you might want on the job that are not feasible for any number of

---

[25] See https://www.youtube.com/watch?v=t7-xoHuX2nc if you're interested.

reasons: they're not company policy; they're too expensive; they're not physically or technically possible; they're unethical or illegal; or they're "above their pay grade." So rather than just get upset about the "no," understand why the boss is denying your request. After that, you might have to change your tactics, change whom you ask, or change your mind about what you want. If it's a straightforward company policy issue, and even your boss is unhappy about it, maybe you can strategize with him or her about how to change the minds of upper management. That's got to beat yelling, whining, and nagging, right?

Concluding Thoughts on Speaking Unpleasant Truths Aloud

I'm always surprised and horrified when I encounter individuals who try to argue their point—any point—while using a whining, nagging, or condescending tone. Their method of argument and the personal reactions the method creates pretty much guarantee no one will take their suggestion seriously even if it is correct because the individual articulating them is so irritating or offensive. And really, if you know a particular method of argument or "persuasion" wouldn't work in a business document, why would you use it in a non-business setting? Again, it happens, but that doesn't mean you have to be that guy or gal.

Five Principles of Good Leadership

These are the attributes that make a good leader for me. Your specific priorities might differ, but regardless of what you do or where you work, leadership matters. If you're a freelance writer, you still have to interact with managers and other individuals that serve in leadership positions. Bad leadership can be demoralizing or emotionally toxic. Forbes magazine even noted that "people leave managers, not companies."[26]

A Sense of Mission

Good leaders, in my experience, have a definite sense of mission and an emotional investment in that mission. Mind you, the "mission" of a particular organization can vary greatly: selling merchandise, checking guests in and out at a hotel, answering guest letters, writing proposals for military hardware, or communicating about space missions.

---

[26] Lipman, Victor. "People Leave Managers, Not Companies." Forbes, August 4, 2015, https://www.forbes.com/sites/victorlipman/2015/08/04/people-leave-managers-not-companies/#3aa9053547a9.

Regardless of the task at hand, a good leader articulates how what you're doing—however lowly or thankless the activity—contributes to some greater, more important enterprise or a greater good.

A Sense of Appreciation

I appreciate leaders who take the time to thank me for my dedication with sincerity. I'm often a sucker for "thank you." Appreciation can take many forms. For example, introverts like me get uncomfortable with public displays of recognition. However, a quiet discussion that explains why an action was appreciated can do wonders. Others, of course, love public recognition in front of peers and leaders. Sometimes the recognition comes in the form of a raise or a bonus. Regardless of how it's done, positive feedback is as necessary as constructive criticism and often rarer because some managers assume if work is being done well, such situations are the norm and don't require thanks. That's a mistake: they do.

An Ability to Inspire Hard Work

The first two abilities—articulating a sense of mission and appreciating employees' efforts—make employees a lot more willing to go the extra mile for a leader when crunch times arise. Leaders of this type often are hard workers themselves and can be found "in the trenches with the troops" when things get busy. If they aren't able to contribute directly to whatever work is being done, they are at least doing what they can to ensure the team has the resources it needs and to reduce any impediments to progress. Donna Shirley, former manager of the Mars Exploration program at NASA's Jet Propulsion Laboratory, referred to her leadership role as acting like a cell wall: "[A] cell wall, what's its function? It's to let nutrients in and to keep bad chemicals and attacking viruses and stuff out."[27] Those efforts by a leader are appreciated.

A Willingness to Respect Employee Expertise

Occasionally, I've encountered individuals who ask me to edit or rewrite their work and then, when I do, they argue against my specific wording or my advice on how to approach a particular communication challenge. This can be particularly vexing when the leader in question specifically confesses ignorance about a subject. Repeated often enough, this behavior eventually creates reluctance to offer any input

---

[27] Shirley, Donna. Managing Martians. Broadway Books, 1999.

or advice whatsoever. After all, if you don't know what you want or how to do something, and then you reject the advice given to you by a person you acknowledge as an expert, why should that expert bother? Respect for an employee's expertise does not mean taking advice without qualification or explanation, though sometimes that happens. A leader might ask why an employee recommends a particular course of action, which is fair in my book, especially if the leader wants to understand the how and why of their thinking. If, after that explanation, the leader decides not to follow the advice, they should explain their reasoning as well. Respect can and should flow in both directions.

A Willingness to Back Up Their Team

I'm not clear on how the term "thrown under the bus" came to be used in place of "blaming someone else for a failure," but I know what it feels like, and I'm certain a lot of people reading this do, too. If something goes awry on the job, and the bad results affect a customer or another organization, the team wants to know their manager will stand up for them, not blame the mishap on their incompetence. Good leaders also maintain the "cell wall" attitude by doing what they can to ensure they get the resources or support they need from other organizations within reasonable constraints. And if the team does not get the resources they need, that leader will go to bat for them and try to obtain relief elsewhere. Good leaders speak well of their team and don't engage in a lot of backstabbing or gossiping with other leaders about the deficiencies of the team.

All of these behaviors engender a sense of trust. If a leader loses their team's trust, they can also expect to lose all of the rest of the attributes described above. But given an environment of vision, sincere appreciation, shared work, mutual respect, and trust, leaders can create high-performing teams who will want to work for them again and again.

Why "Golden Rule" Leadership Doesn't Always Succeed

On a similar topic, one thing I've noticed about effective leadership is that it tends to resemble the Golden Rule: "Treat others as you would wish to be treated." That's great if your leader thinks like you; however, it's not so great if they prefer a different manner of communicating, making requests, providing feedback, or providing recognition.

As an introverted, quiet worker who has confidence in his abilities and prefers to work alone, my leadership habits—on those rare occasions where I've allowed myself to be in a leadership position—reflect my desire to be left alone as much as possible. In practice this means:

- **Providing a minimum of instruction, guidance, and supervision.** This approach assumes that my subordinates have the ability, knowledge, and self-discipline to do what I'm asking them to do without my input, and people prefer to use their creativity as much as possible.
- **Few to no meetings.** Meetings for the sake of meetings are not my favorite things. Time spent in a meeting means time you're not being productive.
- **More communication by email.** Email is asynchronous, meaning it doesn't have to be answered right away. Also, email is quieter and less likely to wander off-topic.

This approach has drawbacks, however. New employees, for example, need more guidance, even if they have the professional skills because they lack experience with the material or an organization's preferred communication methods. In addition, some individuals are not as fully confident in their ability to do something new or unusual and need a lot more hand-holding, support, feedback, or reassurance.

Some people are extroverts and need to do their thinking aloud, among other people. They might have questions not covered by the minimalist guidance given up-front.

Also, some folks find email "cold," unfeeling, and uncaring. They like and prefer social interaction, even—or especially—if the conversation wanders off-topic.

In those situations where I've been in leadership positions, I've fallen prey to all of the above assumptions and misunderstandings. Whatever your particular personality makeup, you need to remember that not everyone thinks about or responds to the world the way you do.

"Bring Me a Rock"

The metaphorical game runs something like this: Someone you work for asks you to bring them a rock—that's all—just a rock. Eager to please, you go out into the yard and find the largest, most promising rock you think might suit your client's tastes—say, a big white one with little sparkling flecks of quartz in it so it has a shiny exterior. You wash off the clots of mud so it seems presentable, and bring it to them.

Your client looks at the rock and says, "What the heck is this? I wanted a red rock!"

So you go back out to the yard and look for a red rock. You end up by the railroad tracks, which have some mighty nice, marble-like rocks that range from pink to a deep purple. You find the one closest to red, a nice hand-sized rock with some tiny veins of white thrown in for style, and you bring that in.

Your client looks at the rock and says, "What's this—railroad bed gravel? I wanted a ruby!"

Frowning slightly, you head back out, at least clearer on what the client wants. Heading for the nearest jewelry store, you strike up a conversation with the owner and explain what you think your client wants. Knowing you're on a budget, the jeweler presents you with a rough-cut ruby, which he says he'll cut to whatever size or shape the client wants. Gleefully, you head back to your client and present them with their requested ruby.

You explain, "I realize this might not quite be what you wanted, but I wanted you to have a look at it before the jeweler went back and shaped it."

"That's very considerate," says the client. "I'd like this to have a Brilliant cut. It looks like you're finally getting somewhere."

Gritting your teeth in a grin, you take the ruby back to the jeweler and say, with an air of frustrated finality, "Make it a brilliant cut!"

The jeweler asks, "57 or 58 facets?"

"Oh, for gosh sakes..." A quick call to the client obtains your answer: 58 facets. The jeweler sets to work, and you relax with a Mylanta smoothie before taking it into the client.

The day you arrive with your brilliant-cut, 58-facet ruby, you see the client has another contractor in the room with them. When you present your ruby, with great fanfare, the client looks at it with only passing interest.

"Oh, that. We decided we didn't need a ruby at the last staff meeting. We brought in Bill here to help us with a bicycle. You two work it out. I've given Bill all the direction he needs. Have fun!"

At which point you have to be restrained from cramming the ruby down your client's throat.

Obviously, reality isn't quite like this—most of the time. Ideally, you're able to speak with your client or boss up-front about what exactly they need so you don't have to keep going back to them for instructions. However, there will be times when she or he just doesn't know. A work situation might call for a simple memo or it might require a full-scale training class that has to be coordinated with Human Resources Compliance.

The object lesson of the Bring Me a Rock game is that you need to work with your customer and have a good enough rapport that you can ask why something is needed and be comfortable enough to suggest something else if you think it will fit the bill. Of course, if you've got a client who likes playing Bring Me a Rock just to watch you jump through hoops, you might want to refer to the section on soft skills. Some days, writing is the easy part of the job.

Handling Political Discussions in the Workplace

My first advice on discussing politics in the office or with clients would be simply: don't. Save it for friends or family—people you know well—or the internet, preferably on a site where your customers aren't used to visiting. You never know which "hot button" you're

going to accidentally push. I understand this is a very American attitude to things. In fact, when I asked a waiter in France what people talked about there if they didn't talk about their jobs or sports, he laughed at me and said, "We talk about sex, politics, and religion."

And some folks are persistent in their desire to talk about politics with you. In which case you can try, politely, to deflect the conversation if you don't wish to engage.

Then again, you might be someone who enjoys initiating political discussions with your clients. Good luck with that if you don't work in the political game for a living. The short version of my advice goes something like this:

- Listen to what the other person has to say.
- Take their comments or thoughts seriously.
- Approach the discussion with an eye toward understanding the other's viewpoint, not forcing your own agenda on the other person.
- Likewise, it's a bad idea to jump right into how you think the world could or should be made better by promoting [X philosophy or policy] and how anyone who disagrees with you is a corrupt, ignorant fool. I've had people do this with me. It's a great way to lose friends and cease influencing people.
- Take the time to explain why you feel a certain way about a particular topic and why it's important to you.
- Try to aim for the best possible outcome, which is to say you should aim for a flow of discussion in which the other person still wants to talk with you when the discussion is over. This means...

- Don't attack, insult, mock, or try to "trap" someone when they don't share your point of view.

I say all this because political discussions are philosophical discussions and philosophy is all about deciding what's important to us. Philosophy is a reflection of who we are, and none of us likes to have who we are or what we care about mocked. Politics is the messy process of trying to balance the conflicting needs, wants, and concerns of multiple free people. And usually not everyone is satisfied with the end result, which is why political "discussions" frequently devolve into arguments. When you have an argument, you cease learning and start attacking (or defending). From there on, you have unhappy people.

So again, I caution you against initiating these sorts of talks with strangers or in a work environment with people you know primarily in a professional capacity. But then I'm a non-confrontational kind of guy. If you want to argue politics, knock yourself out. Just be aware that there's a reason people tell you not to talk religion or politics with strangers. You might just learn the hard way.

Writing about Politics on the Job

I know, I know: I just counseled against talking about politics on the job, but what if your job is political writing? How do you approach the task? What follows are my pragmatic thoughts on the task of writing politically oriented content. By pragmatic I mean simply how to under-stand others' viewpoints—even if you disagree with them—so you can write for any customer, regardless of their political mindset.

There are limits, of course, and you will know what yours are when that moment comes. However, some jobs will simply make political commentary unavoidable, and you might find yourself disagreeing with what you are asked to write. In that case, you have to make a choice: are your political ideals more important than a paycheck? If the answer is yes, you might be better off working for an organization that advocates for a viewpoint matching yours rather than shifting with the political winds. It's not worth the ulcer. That said, if you don't take political writing personally, you can make a reasonably good living.

Government Writing IS Political Writing

Let's start with my background in this: I got a job doing technical, educational, and outreach writing for NASA back in 2006. From then until 2012, I was a contractor creating content on behalf of an agency of the U.S. Government. Any time you are writing on behalf of (or to) a government, you are, by default, engaged in political writing. You could live in a republic, monarchy, socialist democracy, or dictatorship.[28] Regardless of the governmental arrangement, if you are articulating reasons for how public funds are spent, you are engaged in politics because you are arguing that those funds will be or would be better spent your way (or more precisely your employer's way) rather than on some other project. That requires you to incorporate political considerations into the words you use.

Example: Your agency has been actively pursuing a particular program or project. Suddenly, an election brings about a change in the majority party leading the government. The program you were writing prose to support has been canceled. You must now write copy justifying the change even if you believed in the program prior to its cancellation. Can you do this without grinding your mental gears? Honestly, some people can't, and they leave the agency.

The Pragmatics of Government Writing

If you're a little more flexible about such matters, you have to be willing and able to perform the following mental efforts to ensure your continued employment:

- Take the sensitivities of your employer and your audience seriously. This means you have to understand your customer's stated ideals—the reasons they articulate for why they do what they do—and be able to write from and advocate that viewpoint honestly even if you disagree with it.

---

[28] Note: you can face similar "political" issues in a regular business. For example, you might not like the company's official response to a particular situation and have to hash it out with a colleague. As I put it somewhat undiplomatically at the time, "I'm paid to write this ####, I'm not paid to believe it."

- Anticipate what the opposing arguments might be regarding the policy you are advancing and be willing and able to counter those arguments.
- If you are writing in support of a policy change, acknowledge the change and be able to explain why the change was or should be made.
- Expect policy changes if you live in a nation where political fortunes can change fairly regularly. For example, NASA faces political battles every four years when there is a Presidential election, every two years when there is a congressional election, and even every year, when the federal budget is discussed, argued over, and reconciled.
- Know your audience and its "hot buttons." If your primary audience for a piece of writing is a group of elected officials, they will want to know why a new policy is good for their constituents. If your primary audience is "the big boss" (agency administrator, cabinet member, or president/monarch/prime minister), they will want to know how the new policy is advancing their particular plans or agenda. If your audience is the voting public, they will want to know their tax dollars are being spent wisely and what they might, in theory, stand to gain from a particular policy or program.

If you took a speech class or participated in a forensics team in high school or college, you understand how this mindset works. You have to be philosophically flexible enough to recognize arguments other than your own and be willing and able to give as convincing an argument for that position as you would for your own point of view. The goal is to form a cogent argument for the content at hand, not advance your own personal agenda. If you would prefer the latter, again, you might be better off working as an advocate for your favorite cause or as a politician.

Interacting in a Political Workplace

I have one last note on this topic, because it is relevant to "surviving" as a writer in a political environment. If you are working in a highly charged political environment, such as a government agency, it is very much to your benefit to get along with individuals whose points of view differ from yours. If you have a very strong political viewpoint, you have to be able to articulate that viewpoint in a way that will not irritate or offend your employer to the point where they think you're too opinionated to do the work they pay you to do.

I am a philosophical writer by inclination, which by extension includes writing about politics (politics is philosophy put into practice). That is the most interesting sort of writing to me. A while back, I helped an honorable friend with whose politics I disagree reorganize her writing so that she framed her arguments better. I enjoyed the challenge, and she appreciated my input.

Again, I have limits. I had a customer in my senior year of college who contracted with me to edit his book. I found his arguments (and my ability to improve upon them) sufficiently awful that I eventually backed out of the assignment. On the whole, however, I was able to write to and on behalf of government agencies with a minimum of friction. Much like a member of the State Department who must cope with constant changes in administration and policy, a government writer must be willing to serve their customer, whoever that customer happens to be.

Writing for Government Agencies in a Partisan Political Environment
When political passions get heated in a free society, individuals writing for government agencies can find the mere act of posting information challenging. While I'll provide examples below, the short version of my advice is: Write what the party or person in charge says, but don't alienate the opposition. You need to write for everyone.

Doing What the Boss Says
A lot of what elected officials do is allocate dollars in the form of a budget for the federal, state, or municipal government. Different political parties have different funding priorities, to the extent that a program highly touted by one party can be cut or canceled when the opposition comes into power. You can debate whether this is "good" or "evil" if you like, but it is one of the realities of representative government. For the technical writer, this change in party can become challenging if one of your jobs is to write public outreach content for a government agency website or publication. How do you handle it when a prominent program is canceled?

This happened to me at NASA when the Obama administration canceled the Constellation Program in 2010, and it would've happened to me again had I stayed around for the Trump administration's cancellation of Obama's mission to an asteroid in 2018. Again, it's a fact of life, and if you're a partisan of one particular party or simply a fan of a particular type of program, it can be hard on the morale when one of your favorites gets axed.

You still have a job to do.

Often, the direction for what to say about a policy change will come from the top of the agency. And if the direction is, "Stop writing, pencils down," then that's what you do. This became a challenge when Constellation was undergoing review and, eventually, budgetary constraints. The work was still going on—slowly, quietly, but still purposefully—until the official order to cease and desist finally came down. So what are you expected to write about X hardware or program review, knowing the program might go away soon? This is where you stick to the Dragnet approach of "Just the facts." You explain what the story is, what the hardware is doing, and what progress has been made to date, and that's it. You don't talk about future work or what happens next. The in-house term of art was "not getting ahead of the administration."

Finally, the announcement came down that Constellation was to be shuttered. That announcement came from the top: the NASA Administrator. There would be some political wrangling on Capitol Hill, which eventually led to parts of the program being preserved, such as the Orion spacecraft and the heavy-lift launch vehicle now known as the Space Launch System (SLS). However, what happened in the meantime is that the outreach team—along with a lot of other contractors—got downsized or, in some cases, relocated elsewhere within the NASA system. The websites we'd been populating remained up for a while, then went into archive mode, removing them as primary links and making them a little harder to find. Then the new mission focusing on SLS and Orion was announced, and the outreach work ramped up again.

The agency continued, hardware was abandoned in place or repurposed for the new mission; some of us moved from wherever we'd been relocated back into human spaceflight; and we had a new mission to promote for a new administration. The education and outreach work continued.

Not Alienating the Opposition

Barring the occasion of a continuing resolution, which happens more and more often, most U.S. federal budgets are passed through a majority vote in Congress, with the majority party comprising the bulk of the votes that control the outcome, and some of the non-majority parties signing on occasionally for reasons related to their own constituencies. If you're writing policy documents in a partisan political environment, it is good to identify bipartisan cooperation on the agency's goals or programs.

The NASA Authorization Act of 2010 was one such example, as it was passed and reaffirmed by individuals from both major parties across multiple congresses since it was first passed. Bipartisan activities are important to note when you want to demonstrate that a program or mission is continuing an ongoing policy and has broad political support from "both sides of the aisle" in the legislature.

If you're in a position to quote people from multiple political parties in favor of a particular policy, so much the better. Otherwise, if a new policy is in the offing and it faces strong opposition, you sometimes have to toe the line and restate the declared goals of the policy or program, emphasizing how it meets the needs of the public as a whole (as seen from the originators' point of view).

Bottom Line

Government agencies in free societies have a certain amount of latitude when it comes to executing their specific mandates. However, they can't say things their duly elected or appointed leadership does not want them to say. Therefore, as I said before, if you find the back-and-forth of changing parties and priorities disorienting or unpleasant, you might be better off working for a business or advocacy group with one goal (profit or specific policy outcomes) in mind. Otherwise, it's important to remember that, whether you're a civil servant or a government contractor, the content you create—like the agency you serve—is meant to serve all of the people, not just the ones elected to office.

Part IV: Professionalism

Chapter 8: Doing a Good Job for Others—Attitudes and Behaviors

This might seem like a light, "fluffy" chapter as it's not talking about writing. However, please consider this to be one of the most important chapters in the book because it touches on your attitude. It's not just about what you know or how well you do your work but on how you interact with other people. How do you relate to your work? To your position as a writer among technical people? How ethical are you? How hard do you work? How do you handle yourself when things go wrong? How do you improve yourself and make yourself more useful and marketable in the future? How should you dress on the job? How should you behave on social media? These are the most important lessons I had to learn the hard way in my 20s and 30s. With any luck, you can read this chapter and learn from my mistakes.

The Attitude of the Technical Writer

> "We can say that Maud'Dib learned rapidly because his first training was in how to learn. And the first lesson of all was the basic trust that he could learn."
> –Frank Herbert, Dune

When I was in grad school, I encountered a curious attitude among some of my fellow English majors: specifically, some of them feared or refused to go into technical writing because they felt "I'll never be able to learn X. That's why I'm an English major in the first place." I found that attitude somewhat surprising. Believing you can't learn something is a serious barrier to learning anything. If your concern is about doing math, then perhaps they have a point. I ended up in the technical writing grad program because I was reaching the limits of my capability (and interest) in "doing the math" while pursuing a B.S. in engineering.

Here's a dirty little secret, though: there isn't a whole lot of math required to be a technical writer. Mind you, I could name a couple of big-name aerospace companies that would prefer to hire engineers who can write—okay, stop snickering, it happens—but the primary reason a technology-based company hires you in the first place is for your writing ability, not your ability to correct the engineers' or scientists' math. To some extent you have to take it on faith they know what they're doing. And even if you don't know calculus, trigonometry, or Eigen vectors, your editor's eye might still catch things such as discrepancies in a document ("The rocket produces 10,000 pounds of thrust on page 7 and 100,000 pounds of thrust on page 31. Which is it?"). Basic arithmetic should be a minimum skill. If not, you can at least keep a calculator handy.

However, I want to get back to this notion that an English major can't learn "this stuff," whatever the stuff is. I've had a rather odd and diverse career, but that doesn't mean I'm some sort of genius. I do, however, have an abiding belief that I can learn my subject matter, given time and resources. You've got the internet, you've got the dead-tree-book library, you've got Amazon.com or your local book store, and you've got SMEs around who can explain things to you. Businesses have a vested interest in helping you succeed, but so do you. Employers do not want writers who can't at least pick up the rudiments of their business. If you don't know what's being said, ask.

I surprised a techie friend years ago because she caught me at my desk reading a textbook on object-oriented programming. She asked me why I was reading the book, and I explained that I wanted to know what was going on around me. She explained that not every tech writer does this. Good grief, why not?!?? Taking an interest in the subject matter makes you a more valued member of the team because the SMEs know you will "get it right" when it comes to explaining their work. Another way you can add value through product knowledge comes at proposal-writing time. If you understand how a particular widget works, you can help the SMEs identify the most marketable aspects of the organization's product or service and the best way to present them to a specific customer.

I have encountered individuals in my career who quite frankly dismissed me because of my English degrees. It's not my mission in life to convince people who have that attitude to like me, but it is important they respect me and my knowledge or skills enough to let me do my job with a minimum of fuss or condescension. The best way to do that is to know their business. If you work with multiple parts of an organization, you might understand their work in a broader context than they do simply because you see how it fits into the system as a whole.

You can do this—don't let anyone tell you differently! And if they do tell you that, don't believe them.

How a Liberal Arts Major Can Relate to the Techie World

If you spent your university time as an English, journalism, history, or other liberal arts major, you might have noticed the vast difference in priorities between yourself and your friends working in the sciences, engineering, or accounting. For one thing, they were (and, once they get  into the professional world, are) focused on activities that involve math. Or they were studying the inhuman activities of geology, meteorology, or physics. Or they were into designing gadgets or coding software. Perhaps you might have felt the not-so-subtle snobbery that comes from your own major: "They're dealing with things, I'm writing about people!"

Take a breath there, English major. Yes, indeed: your work does involve people. But before you go getting all high-and-mighty about the enlightened concerns about your discipline, take a moment or two to realize human beings don't necessarily study "inhuman" things because they hate people or have no interest in other people's concerns.

Why do people study accounting? So the financial transactions of businesses providing the public (people) with goods and services are in balance, profitable, legal, and sustainable.

Why do people study geology? To understand which types of landforms might be suitable or unsuitable for people to live due to earthquakes, volcanoes, or other seismic disturbances. To determine the most likely places to find useful metals and minerals that build our cities, transportation systems, and gadgets.

Why do people study science? To understand how the universe works, from the cosmic scale (stars and galaxies) to the infinitesimally small (quarks and atoms). To better understand humanity's place in that universe, how we function within it (biology, medicine), and what we can or maybe shouldn't do in it.

Why do people study engineering? So they can learn how to build useful structures, devices, or tools that allow us to live and work better, more efficiently, or in a more environmentally friendly way.

Those numbers-based disciplines are serving human interests just as much as political science or poetry, just in a more indirect and tangible way. So perhaps the first lesson a liberal arts major needs to understand when approaching technical writing is that they are not writing about some inhuman machinery or confusing scientific curiosity: they are talking about acquiring machinery or knowledge to meet human needs.

Meeting Public Needs

Next: You are not writing to serve "the machinery" (at least I hope not). Anything you work on in a business context has a specific human audience or customer in mind who must use the information you're imparting in a specific way to enable them to perform some specific human action.

Translating English into Engineerish and Vice Versa

Once you've accepted the notion of science, technology, engineering, and math (STEM) activities as human activities, you can start putting STEM-related actions into terms you understand—at least to help you think through the problems of "translating" Engineerish into English. The audience for your work is like any other in that you're hoping to get them to react in a particular way. Instead of moods, however, you're engaging their minds and, in some cases, their senses to get them to use your information appropriately, as in the case of instructions, for example.

What does this mean in practical terms? Your work needs to be correct and precise in a way that allows people operating in different locations or circumstances to complete the same task in approximately or exactly the same way to get the same outcome. Despite what your Postmodern Theory professor might have told you, it is possible for two people to have approximately the same level of understanding on the same topic to arrive at the same conclusion (i.e., practical outcome). If that were not the case, a lot of very complicated hardware in our world would never function and there would be a lot more things going BOOM!

STEM Has a History, Too

Many documents require you to provide some sort of background or history of the product or service you are describing. However, instead of progressions of monarchies or "great person" stories, the "histories" you're sharing in proposals or white papers are tales about the progression of your organization's science or engineering field. What was discovered when? How were certain tools developed? What set of ideas combined to set Advanced Program X into motion so your organization could capitalize on it?

This sort of history requires the same sort of research you would conduct in a history, English, or political science paper. The "actors" in said histories might be more idea- or machinery-focused than people-focused, but those histories were still set in motion by people with very human interests (performing X action to advance human interest Y).

Using Words Rather Than Equations

I am only so-so on math, algebra, trigonometry, what have you. However, to repeat: organizations don't hire writers to write equations or develop engineering processes. They do hire us to explain what those equations and processes mean in practical, human terms. As one manager told me, "I've got plenty of engineers, what I need is a writer!" So, again, you are getting paid for your ability to explain how a scientific process affects the world around us or an engineering activity advances a human need. Leave the engineering to the engineers and the science to the scientists. Your job, in the end, is to help non-scientists and non-engineers understand the implications of whatever the STEM geniuses have discovered or built. The advantage of being the writer is that you can write things so you understand them. In your own way, you get to become a subject matter expert.

Because the state of scientific knowledge or the technological state of the art is always changing, that means science and engineering are always finding something new to discover or build. No, you're not helping "make" the big discovery or building the Next Big Thing, but you are in some way helping the rest of the world relate to whatever the scientists or engineers are doing—and that's a pretty nifty and very human thing to do.

Basic Ethics for the Technical Writer

Regardless of what you are writing about, ethics are central to a writer's trade because if we are not ethical in how we handle ourselves and the information entrusted to us, we are unlikely to remain employed for long. I'm a bit of a stick in the mud on some things, but being picky about my behavior keeps me employed in high-competence, high-trust organizations. I recall telling a college buddy that I wouldn't go along with some harebrained scheme of his because I didn't want to screw up my chances for getting a security clearance. The guy thought I was nuts, but I stayed out of trouble.

That said, here are my suggestions when working out the minefield known as corporate ethics.

1. Don't knowingly lie. You can't help it if you are operating with blatantly wrong information, but once you discover it, correct it (see #5 below).
2. Don't divulge corporate or technical secrets unless someone's on a need-to-know basis like, say, your manager, and even then you might be told to keep something to yourself by another, higher authority. If someone asks you about a sensitive topic and you know you're not supposed to share the information, say that. (See #1 for clarification.) If you're in a position of trust, have undergone a background check, or have a security clearance of any kind, this should be obvious because it's explained to you.
3. If you're in doubt about sharing a particular piece of information, don't.
4. If you find someone divulging sensitive information to people who do not need-to-know, report them. The U.S. Military Academies have honor codes that address this sort of thing. There's also that motto from World War II: "Loose lips sink ships."
5. Admit it when you're wrong or have made a technical error. Don't throw people under the bus (i.e., blame them for something that was your responsibility). That behavior doesn't make you look any better and the person you've blamed will remember the gesture next time you need a favor from them.
6. Keep your promises.

7. Use good sources, cite them appropriately, and don't plagiarize your work. (I'll caveat the last item, as I feel you're free to plagiarize your own work all you want if everything's under your name.)

8. Only bill for hours worked or work produced.

9. Don't air office politics ("dirty laundry") on the internet. Heck, that's not just good ethics, that's good manners! In general, don't gossip or traffic in corporate rumors, unless you're in the position of trying to dispel them. I've had that job and it's not fun, but the goal is to prevent problems, not conceal them.

10. This hasn't happened to me, but I'd like to think I could do this: if you find that the ethics of your organization are compromised, be willing to go through proper channels as far up the chain as necessary, within the system first, to address the issue. If you still can't get your well-documented case heard, be willing to be a whistleblower. That, perhaps, is the ultimate example of "heroic technical communication." It might not make you a lot of friends, but jeez, you have to look yourself in the mirror, right? Or, if you don't have the stomach for the whistleblowing track, get out of the organization. No sense in you going to prison, too. When the malfeasance comes to light, you can always say, "I told you so." But there's no reason to associate yourself with bad people or a bad situation.

Okay, those are my "Top Ten" ethical reminders. You might have different priorities, but your reputation is closely associated (engineers would say "closely coupled") with your ethics, so they're worth considering. If you're interested in the topic of ethics in technical communication, I highly recommend a book by one of my University of Central Florida professors, Paul Dombrowski: Ethics in Technical Communication.[29] The book provides the reader with several different challenging ethical situations that involve tech comm and reviews those situations through several different ethical perspectives, including Aristotelian, Kantian, Utilitarian, and the ethics of care. They all say pretty much the same thing: "Do the right thing, don't be evil."

Just some food for thought.

---

[29] Allyn and Bacon Series in Technical Communication, Pearson, 1999.

Reputation Maintenance

This is sort of a hot button with me, hot enough that I've dedicated much of this chapter to it. What you do and what you accomplish are important. But there's still that extra little bit—how you do it—that can make the difference between whether you get and stay hired or not. Your reputation rests upon your personality and work habits: are you pleasant to be around? Are you known for the quality of your writing? Your attention to detail? Your ability to hire and lead good people? Are you a hard worker?

Again, these are things you don't necessarily put on your resume (though you could!), but they are the things peers and leaders notice. If I had to guess, I'd say my personal rep includes things like being a hard and quick worker. I can also kick out decent prose on a deadline, regardless of topic or document format. For the most part, I'm perceived to be a decent, funny guy to be around. On the other hand, I'm not always the most detail-minded person in the room (I could name two or three people who are much better editors than me, for example, and I happily recommended them). I also get flustered when I've got too many things happening at one time. I spend a great deal of time on my own, and while I'm a good talker for an introvert, I keep my distance from new people for a while until I get to know them. I can get a little cranky if I think I'm being accused of something falsely.

But then that's my impression of my reputation, which will obviously differ from what people say behind my back, good or bad.

Why Should You Care?

The thing is, how others respond to what you do and how you do it is where your reputation really resides. That can be vexing for some who think, "Who the heck cares what other people say about me? I do good work!" And the truth is you can't control what other people will think or say about you. That's a hard lesson to learn; however, you can influence others' opinions of you, and that requires you to pay attention to what you do and how you do it. If you're not sure what your reputation is, and you're willing to accept honest feedback, you'll get it. If there are things you don't like about your reputation, you can make efforts to fix them. A bad reputation can cost you relationships or even jobs.

One major challenge with reputation-building is that it can take years to build and a moment to completely shatter. Keep someone's books honestly for 20 years but then get caught embezzling once? You lose your reputation instantly, along with your job, and quite possibly your freedom. Yet even something simple like having a reputation for an even temper can be blown away if you spend one whole day yelling at people. Or a normally kind person stabs a coworker in the back (figuratively, not literally). Political campaigns can hinge as much on reputation as someone's voting record. Or, conversely, a renowned curmudgeon is suddenly discovered to be tutoring an immigrant in English and becomes a beloved figure.

But, again, reputations can be made or broken through single incidents...and they don't always have to be in person, either. I'm sure if you take a look through the news or your local divorce proceedings, you'll find any number of reputations that have been destroyed by personal behavior on the internet.

Building Your Reputation "Account"

Another approach would be to treat your reputation like a bank account, and all the good things you do day by day amount to "deposits." If you do something awful to someone you barely know, you won't have built up enough "deposits" for them to want to forgive you. On the other hand, if you've known someone for a long time and have done a lot of good things for them over the years, they are likely to be more forgiving when you have anything from a bad mood to a meltdown. After that moment, however, you need to get back to building up your account with them again to restore your goodwill.

The bad news, again, is that you have little to no control over what other people think of you. You do, however, have control over the behaviors you exhibit and what others observe. So if you crash your reputation with a large segment of your acquaintances, you have the ability to take action on the things that caused you to lose it; just be aware that it's a very long process requiring a great deal of patience. You might not win back your rep with everyone, but you can with a few, and they can spread the word from there.

Identifying Your Preferred Work Load

Everyone has a certain operational tempo or workload they're comfortable with. How many tasks need to be on your list for you to feel restless? Comfortable? Stressed out? Some of this is a function of the work you do and the documents you produce. My buddy Doc once had an entire

book he had to write and deliver by the end of a single business quarter. There are lots of sub-items under that one task, but it was still only one deliverable. Another coworker had anywhere from 6 to 12 speeches or presentations on his pile at any given time. When I worked at NASA, my active workload hovered anywhere from 1 to 20 items, but I was usually happiest in the 4 to 6 range if those 4 to 6 items were all due within a month.

Again, your workload is a function of what you're producing. When I was checking in guests at one of the Walt Disney World Resort hotels, I might have checked in anywhere from 1 to 30 guests, depending on the day. When I was writing training scripts for the Disney University, I had something like two products due at once, and three was pushing it because each product was several dozen pages in length.

The most important things to know about your workload are:

- What can you expect?
- What can you handle?

The first bullet can be answered by having regular discussions (weekly or however it seems warranted) with your immediate supervisor (starting with your interview), tasker, or customer, during which you ask what the workload looks like, how you're doing with what you have, and what's on the horizon.

The second bullet can only be answered through experience and, again, through the type of work you do. Proposal writing for the government, for example, tends to peak March through May and September through November, with occasional surprises thrown in along the way. Newspapers are constantly humming, with assignments coming in and going out daily. When I answered Disney guest letters, I could usually kick out 40 a week, or one an hour (and before you think I'm slacking there, you've obviously never researched guest complaints). Let us also not forget that your "work" will include meetings of various sorts, which can either contribute to, or distract from, the products you need to produce.

The newer you are to a position (or the work), the more likely the workplace is to give you assignments gradually until they understand your work pace and quality. The first time I worked for the NASA human spaceflight business, I was tasked with writing conference papers for the manager of one element, the J-2X engine. As my understanding and writing velocity picked up, so too did my number of clients and workload, with two other groups being added to my plate. A reorganization of duties shifted me to the Ares I-X flight test and supporting the project manager, his deputy, the outreach manager, and his deputy. Running flat-out, I was writing conference papers and presentations for around half a dozen people, at which point I cried "Uncle!" and asked for a little relief.

But really, until you test your limits and then go beyond them, you won't really know how much work you can handle (and like to have) until it hits you. And if you're underworked, which happens occasionally, you can always go scouting for more.

(Side note: My military buddies tried to explain to me the cardinal rules of the service, but it didn't work. "Don't be the first to do something. Don't be the last one to do something. Don't volunteer for anything. And never tell the sergeant or commanding officer you have nothing to do." I've managed to violate pretty much all of those "rules," but I've gotten some interesting work as a result.)

The most important thing you can do with your workload is monitor your tasks carefully so nothing falls through the cracks and then be willing to ask for help if things are going awry through under- or overwork. You want to succeed, and so do your peers and leaders. Moving at the wrong pace helps nobody, least of all you.

What Competence Looks Like
It might appear that I make a lot of mistakes, given some of what you read here or on my blog. You might wonder, given the various hiccups

I write about, whether I'm able to perform my job adequately. I imagine some professional tech writers among you might read my blog occasionally and shout, "You can't keep sharing these stories! You'll make us look incompetent!" Very well. I'll explain how I manage to keep my job.

Let's start with something obvious: I have had a fun and diverse tech writing career, which allows me to write about many different types of experiences from multiple perspectives. And while I try not to brag here, my diverse skill set and specialized technical knowledge (aerospace) have ensured that I have people contacting me for writing or editorial assistance; I don't have to market my services very often.

More to the point, I can deliver good work. "Good" in this case includes some of the following attributes:

- Is delivered on time or **early**.
- Includes few to no **spelling**, grammatical, or punctuation errors.
- Makes the point(s) that the customer wants made.
- Is **organized** in a way that the content flows logically.
- Is technically correct or, where I have doubts, is flagged to ensure that a subject matter expert confirms its accuracy.
- Is presented in an orderly, aesthetically pleasing fashion, with no more than two fonts on the page and effective **graphics** or other visual aids presented in an appropriate fashion.
- Is communicated properly to the individuals who need it, along with any pending questions or concerns.
- Is written in a style appropriate to the audience, content, and delivery format.
- Is written clearly and directly (unless murkiness is called for).
- Is provided in a spirit of politeness, professionalism, and (usually) good humor.

So Why Do I Write about All My Screw-ups?

From the beginning of writing the blog (2011), I wanted to share my insights and observations about the world of work, specifically the business realities of being a professional technical writer, warts and all. Sharing my little foibles with you is partly an effort to make my writing somewhat entertaining, partly a reality check for someone who thinks X career is "perfect," and partly used as an opportunity to show that even full-time technical writers can make mistakes and recover from them. My theory is that you can go anywhere for advice on how to write a resume or format a white paper, from books to other blogs. The times we really need advice, though, are for those situations that aren't in the textbooks. In those situations, I'm here to help.

Doing Your Best

"What do you mean, you don't like proposals? You're so good at them!"

–Former manager to me, 2006

My work tastes have changed over the years. For example, I actually like proposal writing now, but my manager's question at the time provided me some insight into how I work: even if I don't like what I'm doing, I try to do a good job. This is a fundamental success behavior wherever you work.

You might not enjoy proofreading, meeting minutes, proposal writing, or some other task your job requires. You're not required to enjoy them all (sorry, managers, but it's true). Still, it behooves you to do all of those thankless tasks well. The ability to take something mundane and kick it up a notch will be noticed. As a side benefit, you can find yourself being asked to do other, cooler things unrelated to said thankless tasks simply because you did well on them.

If you're starting a new job (and this happens to people in mid-career, not just those fresh out of college), you usually find that you're assigned a lot of boring, routine, or low-skill work—small tasks no one else wants—before you get to do the cool stuff you interviewed for in the first place. It's a test, naturally: if you can handle the small stuff skillfully and with a good attitude, you're more likely to be trusted with the big stuff. Do the small stuff halfheartedly or with a bad attitude, and you'll soon find yourself going nowhere fast.

The tasks will always be what they are. You're unlikely to change their level of challenge. Or, to throw in another Star Trek quotation, "There's no correct resolution, it's a test of character."

Dealing with Proposal Losing Streaks

I'm a Chicago Cubs fan. As you might imagine, that has made for a vexing sports entertainment experience through most of my life, at least until a few years ago. However, rooting for the Cubs taught me the value of optimism in the face of long-running challenges. "Anyone can have a bad century," as one Cubs manager put it. That doesn't mean I learned to like losing.

In 2016, a proposal I helped a customer write won the bid. This was a moment of joy for the customer and a great relief to me. I'd worked on a lot of proposals over the previous three to four years, during which, to the best of my recollection, I lost nearly every single one, going back to 2012.

It Isn't Personal, Sonny, It's Just Business

Note the "I" there. That was my first mistake: an understandable one, but a mistake nevertheless. A proposal has many contributors, from the technical SMEs to the people providing the cost figures to the graphic designers doing the graphics. Still, it's the writer, book boss, or proposal manager who typically has responsibility for the final product. To not win a proposal means the potential revenue from that opportunity won't be coming in, so there's ownership and pressure there.

Ownership and pressure are inevitable side effects of proposal writing. Winning isn't inevitable, however, so you will lose a few. Or in my case, several of them scattered over multiple customers and years.

The important lesson here, as noted in the quotation from The Godfather above, is: don't take it personally. That's not to say you didn't have a role in some of the losses, you're also overlooking the realities of requests for proposals (RFPs).

Some Reasons Why It Might Be Your Fault

Okay, let me get this part over with so I can move on to the more optimistic angles. There are, in fact, a few things a proposal writer or manager can do to torpedo the success of a proposal. You're just asking for trouble that way, like Charlie Brown repeatedly accepting Lucy's challenge to hold the football for him. There are some things you should just learn not to do.

Don't turn it in late. No excuses: you've got to make the deadline, not just the date, but the designated time. One proposal I worked on was submitted in parts. Three-fourths of it was submitted before the deadline. The last part—the cost volume, not my area, I hasten to add—was still being worked on up to the last minute and then some. It was submitted some seven minutes late. Proposal: rejected. X millions of dollars in potential revenue: gone. It's not just college professors: the government takes its deadlines seriously. You should, too.

Don't submit a proposal doesn't comply with the instructions. Aside from the obvious deadline, government solicitations especially will prescribe the specific order of a proposal, including the section headings, along with the page margins, fonts, and font sizes. There might be other reasons a proposal gets bounced, which I'll get into in a moment, but noncompliance with the instructions is an easy way for a reviewer to get your proposal off their pile and reduce their workload. Read and follow the directions.

Don't misspell obvious, visible, glaring things. These are items such as the name of the customer, the name of your company or product, or other words in the title. English majors know this better than anyone: people judge you based on the quality of your spelling. Those are the same people picking on you for typing in Twitter-speak. They're out there, and they're not all proposal writers. The proposal reviewers will think, "If they can't even spell X product correctly, how am I supposed to believe that they'll do the work well?" Spell checking is important, but reading is also important.[30]

Don't get the technology wrong. Suppose a SME gives you an explanation of the XYZ Widget. You think you translated the technobabble into proper English but neglect (or run out of time) to ask the SME to provide a technical review. Your work ends up in front of the technical reviewer, who takes one look at your prose and says, "These guys are full of BS" or "That violates the laws of physics" or, more likely, "These guys don't know what they're talking about." Make sure your technical write-ups make sense.

Some Reasons a Proposal Loss Was Most Likely NOT Your Fault
Unless your company is writing a task order proposal under a sole-source contract, the odds are good your proposal went up against at least one other competitor. The other thing you have to consider is the

---

[30] If you get a chance, look up "Spell Checker Poem" online.

customer(s) and what might be going through their mind. Let's look at the factors that are beyond your control.

The competition had the lowest bid. Your company might have the best left-handed widget in the industry, but ABC Company down the street, which is almost as good, is bidding their widget for half a million dollars less than yours. If price is the most important criteria (and quite often the customer will tell you that if you request an after-action briefing), your company is going to lose, plain and simple.

The competition had a better product or service. Sometimes a customer is looking for the best left-handed widget, and ABC Company down the street is famous for designing and building left-handed widgets because they invented them and have stayed on top of the game ever since then. Or maybe you are the ABC Company and the customer is looking for something new and radical rather than something that's been around for 50 years.

The competition has what the customer is looking for right now. I've seen this problem occur with both government technology opportunities and nonprofit foundations. The U.S. Government's SBIR opportunities and the NASA Institute for Advanced Concepts (NIAC) solicitations are annual, open invitations to businesses to submit bright ideas that could help the government solve a particular problem. The RFPs frequently feature a range of topics or technology areas. Your company might have a bright idea for a right-handed widget that is just perfect to solve Problem Y. However, when the Source Selection Evaluation Board finishes going over all the proposals, they might decide that while your right-handed widget is quite clever, it doesn't meet their needs because they're really more focused on Problem Z this year, and the ABC Company has exactly what they want. In the nonprofit sector, foundations face similar constraints. They have particular types of organizations or projects in mind when they're handing out grants. Sometimes other organizations just fit the objectives better.

Things You Can Do to Improve Your Odds in the Future
Ask for a debrief. This is a fairly common practice in government contracting. Contractors can request a one-on-one session or just an email or letter from the contracting officer for feedback on the proposal. This is often a good idea whether you've won or lost so you

know your strengths and weaknesses. The loss discussion, while not fun, is absolutely vital for helping you and your company learn how to do better in the future. A win discussion is a good idea, less painful, and much simpler. In that case, you can ask the customer directly or send an email asking, "What were the key differentiators in accepting our bid?"

Up your game. Are you saying the same things in the same old ways? When was the last time you took a refresher course in proposal writing? If you don't have the money or time to upgrade your skills, you can always go online and look for pointers. You can also read Heroic Technical Writing—this book or the blog, among others.

Get some help. Some proposals—especially the big-money, sink-or-swim proposals the whole company is counting on to win—have the attention of upper management. Knowing the importance of the opportunity, you can request additional help to ensure perfection: editorial, graphical, technical, financial, or legal. However, sometimes a proposal is not that important, but you feel could use the help anyway. Ask for it.

Improve your business intelligence ground game. You might or might not be part of the business development team that goes out and talks to customers, but you can encourage those who do talk to customers to get a better idea of what their current needs truly are so that future proposals are geared to meet those needs. Those discussions are easier if you already have a relationship with a customer, but there are other opportunities to reach potential customers, including conferences, where your business development team can have meaningful conversations that guide your future proposal efforts.

Shake it off, try again. Like I said, losing streaks can happen, but you can't let it affect your confidence in your ability to do the work. You have written winning proposals, you will do so again. You have to believe that as a simple survival mechanism and for the good of your own mental health. Oh, yeah: and your paycheck.

Note: In 2016, Chicago Cubs had not won a World Series since Theodore Roosevelt was President of the United States. That didn't stop me from cheering them on when they lost in the playoffs the previous year or all those many years that they haven't even made the playoffs.

However, that was the year I was lucky to see them win the World Series. Hope springs eternal.

How to Stand Out in Your Profession

Before anyone gets a chance to learn about your reputation or attitude, it's quite possible their first contact with you will be your resume. Whether you're networking somewhere or laying out your work history in a resume, you need to be able to talk about your differences— the highlights of your skills and career. This is all about "playing to your strengths."

Numbers

These are the accomplishments that can be measured: grade point average (this one has limited shelf life, like maybe one year after college), sales made, customers brought in, money or time saved, documents created, and anything else you can count.

Awards

What sort of recognition have you received over the course of your career? Are those awards relevant to the job you're pursuing? Have you been recognized by managers? Peers? Subordinates? Members of the community?

Processes

While you were at a job, did you create a process that improved an operation's profitability? Improved efficiency? Reduced losses or fraud (are there numbers attached)? Did you create a recognition program? Did you eliminate processes or paperwork?

Documents

Have you helped develop large documents or projects that had a huge impact on your organization? Have you helped write policies or training programs? Have you worked on products that got a lot of attention outside your organization? Did you work on "conversation starting" or "paradigm shifting" documents?

Customers

Have you worked for high-visibility organizations or individuals? Have you worked in environments with high traffic, high prestige, or high name recognition? Have you worked for nonprofit organizations related to the industry you're trying to enter?

Situations

Sometimes we're known by our workplace "war wounds." Did you get your organization caught up on their payments? Do you work in a high-hazard workplace? Have you helped a company work through a massive layoff? Have you saved lives as a direct result of your work? Have you rebuilt a business after a natural or man-made disaster? Did you help build an organization in a high-crime or economically depressed area?

All of these topics offer opportunities for you to stand out to a prospective employer or customer. These are the sorts of factoids that you need to include as part of your marketing materials or networking talking points. The point isn't to brag, though it does require you to share your accomplishments, especially if someone asks, "So what do you do?" or "What have you done?" Accomplishments and unique situations are more interesting than job descriptions. Stand out—in a good way!

Upgrading Your Skills

Do you ever have moments where you have too much time on your hands? After a period of enjoying the sloth, eventually you can get to the point where you realize you should probably be doing something constructive. One thing you can use the time for is to add to or improve your current skill set. There are a few ways you can go about upgrading your skills, including traditional academia, seminars and conferences, and online learning.

Traditional Academia

I took this route back in 1999, when I decided to get serious about finding a job in the space business. I pursued a master's degree in technical writing through University of Central Florida (UCF). At the time, my educational background consisted of a B.A. in English Literature, while my work experience was all service industry-related (retail + Disney front desk, and guest letters). The time and money invested in my degree were, for me, absolutely worth it because I had only taken a single course in technical writing while pursuing the B.A. and so was mostly unfamiliar with the discipline. The extra degree opened the door to technical writing positions within Disney, a defense proposal writing job in the DC area, and then additional roles after that. I think my whole grad school program cost U.S. $10–

15,000. In-state, per-credit-hour costs at UCF are about the same as they were then (approximately $330), so if you don't feel the need to attend Stanford or something in the Ivy League, you can probably get away with a less painful student loan to pay off if you attend a state school. If you're over 40, a certificate program requiring fewer credit hours might be a more efficient use of your time and money. And if you land the better-paying you job you want, the debt can be paid off that much more quickly.

Seminars and Conferences

Seminars and conferences are a lower-cost, less time-intensive alternative to a full academic program. For instance, I took a five-day course in grant writing from **The Grantsmanship Center** and found that worthwhile. I'd already done proposal writing professionally for several years by the time I took that course, so the seminar helped me understand the details and nuances of the nonprofit world. Total cost of that program was around $1,000.

On occasion I've also attended conferences that matched either my professional skill interests (technical writing, instructional design) or my content or customer preferences (aerospace, engineering). Conferences are usually three to five days of networking while also attending seminars on topics of interest to the given audience. Between hotel, air, and registration fees, most of which you can write off if you're a freelancer or an employer will pay for if you can show a return on investment for them, conferences can run you anywhere from $1,000 to $5,000 or more depending on your field.

Online Learning

Often I'm looking for something quick to pick up specific skills. The internet's resources along these lines have vastly improved. In consultation with my mentor D2, I was referred to several different Massive Open Online Course (MOOC) sites, including:

https://www.mooc-list.com/tags/instructional-design
https://www.edx.org
https://www.coursera.org
https://ocw.mit.edu/

These are courses conducted online, live or asynchronously, by actual university professors. For an additional $50 or so, sites like EDx.org will provide you with a **certificate** showing that you actually completed the course. The courses themselves are often free, and so can be your best bang for the buck if you just want to get smart quickly about a topic.

At any rate, I suggest keeping your skills or knowledge fresh one way or another, even if you aren't looking to change careers. Thanks to the internet, there has never been a better time to acquire high-quality information and education. When you're done, you can go back to posting pictures of cats.

Developing Your Own Personal Writing Style

What do we mean when we talk about writing style? Is such a thing even permissible in "technical" writing? Let's take on the first question first.

The Bartish definition of writing style encompasses the words writers choose when communicating their thoughts. Of course it's more than just words—it's the order they use them, as well as their diction, punctuation habits, range of vocabulary, emotional tone, and favorite turns of phrase. If you've read my blog or made it this far in the book, for instance, you might already be aware of some of my stylistic "tics," such as my use of long dashes and parentheses, personal storytelling, meandering prose, and occasionally a sarcastic tone to keep the content (hopefully) humorous and accessible. My informal writing style is a text-only version of how I tend to speak, minus some extraneous cussing and with undoubtedly better grammar.

Of course that's just my blogging style.

I've had to develop different styles for proposal writing, official correspondence, marketing materials, white papers, letters to Congress, and emails and blog entries for the Science Cheerleaders. Occasionally I even write fiction, though you will note that I pay my bills writing nonfiction.

If you're a technical writer, you've no doubt noticed your style has had to vary by circumstance as well. The usual circumstances that affect my writing style are audience, situation, and outcome.

How Your Audience Affects Your Style

Just as the person you want to communicate with greatly affects how you will speak to them, so too it will (and should) affect how you write. A personal thank-you note to a dear friend or close family member will read differently from a formal letter to a senator you've never met requesting an official appointment. Why is that? One reason is simple familiarity. Unless your close relative is a senator, you're unlikely to use the same casual language as you would with someone you've never met. Familiarity or lack thereof affects your level of formality.

Are you writing to one person or multiple? Family members? Friends? Coworkers? Members of the general public via a letter to the editor? The larger the audience, the more distant you are from them and the more general your tone needs to be. Lots of other little things about an audience can affect your writing as well, such as their average age, their political or religious affiliations, their level of education, and their gender mix. This doesn't mean pandering, but it does mean being conscious of how you phrase things to ensure your audience feels included and receptive to your message.

How Situation Affects Your Style

After you settle on your audience, you need to consider the circumstances of what you need to write: is it good news? Bad news? A request from a stranger? A reminder of a favor? Simple information? Is the information you need to share new or familiar? Does what you say or write affect someone's (or many someones') job or financial security? A lot of these questions amount to your audience's potential reaction to the information. How you share the announcement of the early arrival of an expected bonus will be quite different from how you announce an unexpected layoff.

How Your Intended Outcome Affects Your Style

"Outcome" is simply how you want your audience to react after receiving the information you impart. Maybe you just want them to be aware. Maybe you need them to check a box or fill out a form. Maybe you want them excited and happy (which is easier when there's a bonus involved). Maybe you want them calm and receptive (tougher when there's a layoff). Maybe you want them angry or outraged and ready to take action.

How Audience, Situation, and Outcome Combine to Affect Style

Now you see how the circumstances of a piece of communication will greatly affect what and how you write:

- A short thank-you note to your parents for taking you to dinner can be as warm and fuzzy as you like because you know them well and want them to come away from the note with a good feeling.
- An engineering proposal to a government agency is going to be a lot more formal but can include more dynamic language about your product or service to get your potential customer interested in buying it.
- A speech announcing a massive layoff is going to be carefully worded (perhaps with help from the Legal or Human Resources Department) to explain the how and why while requesting calm and professionalism as well as expressing sadness and inevitability. You don't want to sound so sad that people respond with, "If you're so sad about it, why are you letting us go?"
- A letter to a member of Congress or Parliament making a specific request of the government is going to be polite, formal, and deferential without being too obsequious.

And so forth. Time, experience, and the input of others will help you shape your communication outputs to ensure that you use the right words to achieve the ends you desire. The more writing situations you encounter, the better you will know and use words that make for effective professional and technical communication.

Continuous Improvement for the Writer

I was rambling on in my personal blog awhile back about self-improvement[31], and after some thought I realized that I could find a way to tie that blog to tech writing. Businesses talk a lot about "continuous

---

[31] BartLeahy.com, "Continuous Improvement Starts from Inside," https://bartleahy.com/2017/05/23/continuous-improvement-starts-from-inside

improvement," but it's often difficult for the tech writer to crystallize what that means for him or her. I'll take a shot here.

Continuous Improvement in manufacturing organizations usually focuses on quality: faster output, fewer defects, at lower cost (as my engineering friends like to say: "Faster, Better, Cheaper—Pick Two!"). Can such standards be applied to our lofty literary efforts? Aye.

Faster!

Does your department produce a lot of documents that have to get out the door "as soon as possible?" Or do you have occasional situations where a specific type of document (say, a press release) needs to get out the door faster to respond to real-time events?

Reusing content. There are a few ways to speed up the process of responding to demands for "faster" writing. One of them is to repurpose content. I recall hearing at the STC conference in 2000 that advanced markup languages like XML were supposed to make content like corporate messaging much easier. You write a paragraph once and are then able to apply that message in other documents. This would be things like corporate mission statements, company business overviews, and executive biographies. One person would be responsible for maintaining the original, and everyone else would use the existing verbiage. One department I worked for had a Word doc full of paragraphs that functioned that way (we called it the "junk file"). It saves having to reinvent the wheel every time a new situation arises.

Simplifying processes and approvals. This approach tends to make some managers uncomfortable because it usually means fewer people have the authority to change a "happy" to "glad." And some folks really like having that authority. However, if the chief executive or other senior managers want content out the door sooner and you have five people approving a document, that process just might require some reworking. I once spent three August days in a non-air-conditioned trailer in Alabama participating in a **Lean Six Sigma** exercise to simplify an export control approval process for conference papers. While definitely an exercise in heat endurance as well as patience, when we came out of that hot trailer, we had a system that could be executed in a week vs. two or three. And yes, one person no longer needed to be included in the loop. A small victory, but worth it.

Contingency planning. While managers often don't like to dwell on such things, humans being what we are, things are going to go wrong. A sensible contingency plan can include having failure-related content already written should Bad Event X occur. How do you do this? One way is to embed a technical writer with the engineers working on risk management to keep track of the top risks of a given project. Writers might not know all of the ways a risk could manifest itself, but they can at least have text ready that explains the root cause of a problem so they know what to say when something goes awry.

Cheaper!

Often the biggest-cost items for documents or other products are not within the control of the individual technical writer. That doesn't mean you can't provide input.

Spending money wisely. It's amazing how much waste occurs due to errors caught only in the print cycle. Most quality control issues such as misspellings, bad capitalization or punctuation, backwards or outdated illustrations, can and should be caught before anything goes to print. This might require more labor hours to ensure an editor looks at a document, poster, or proposal, but if the alternatives are reprinting several thousand flyers or millions of dollars in lost business, an additional set of eyes might be worth the overtime. Of course, an additional review takes more time, which conflicts with "faster," but that's a decision that would need to be made based on your circumstances. If you want documents done right, "better" is cheaper.

If you must print... Printer cartridges and paper can eat up a budget. Try to edit on the screen first (if you're under 30 and reading this, you probably think I'm crazy, but some folks really prefer to proofread on a hard copy). If you insist on printing, print in "draft" mode, which is not quite as high-quality and doesn't eat up as much toner, and use the duplex feature to print on both sides of the paper.

Better!

I've already covered one quality issue: mechanics. There are other ways content can be made better, though that depends on how you choose to measure it. In a class I wrote, I included the comment, "What gets measured gets done."

Improving access. Depending on what you're creating and whom you're writing for, "accessibility" can mean many things, from writing in multiple languages to including closed-captioning on videos. Are you writing for the general public? For younger people? For people for whom English is a second language? For international audiences? Improving readability might include simplifying your language to reach your target audience.

More depth. When I worked for Disney Information Technology, I picked up and read some books on object-oriented programming so I'd know what the programmers were doing and to get myself smarter about what I was actually saying. In similar fashion, when I started working for a defense contractor and later NASA, I had to educate myself on the intricacies of petroleum and water pumping systems or rocket propulsion systems so that I could write accurately to the level of precision my customers required.

Bottom Line

While it might be impossible to achieve "faster, better, cheaper" all at once, it helps to have a mindset that's open to continuous improvement. Much of it starts with a willingness to ask yourself, "Is this the best I could be doing? What is getting in the way of my doing better?"

Secrets of Being a "Miracle Worker"

In the Star Trek universe, Montgomery Scott ("Scotty") is the quintessential competent engineer. He might gripe and complain in his Scottish burr, but you know in the end that he'll do what it takes to get the job done and save the Enterprise, whether it's restarting the warp drive or ridding the ship of a Tribble infestation. By the time the movies came out in the '70s and '80s, Scotty's legend was all but a given, to the point where even his long-time commanding officer, James T. Kirk, had the following exchange with him in Star Trek IV: The Voyage Home:

> Kirk: How much refit time until we can take her [the Enterprise] out again?
>
> Scotty: Eight weeks, sir. But you don't have eight weeks, so I'll do it for ye in two.
>
> Kirk: Mr. Scott, have you always multiplied your repair estimates by a factor of four?

Scotty: Certainly, sir. How else can I keep my reputation as a miracle worker?

I've got some folks convinced that I'm a literary "Scotty." Yes, there is some skill and speed involved, but much of my working success comes from processes anyone can follow.

Give Yourself More Time Than You Think You'll Need

Last-minute-itis drives me crazy. I used to have the habit in college. I grew out of it after learning the hard way that things can and do go wrong (I'll cover that in a bit). The first priority, however, is to give yourself enough time to think clearly and do the job well.

People under stress miss things. For instance, even if you remember to use spell check under deadline, that's not to say that the wrong word won't show up in your prose. People under pressure can say or type the wrong things.

Scotty's little trick of multiplying repair estimates by a factor of four, while not 100 percent realistic, has several grains of truth in it. Much of what I do is deadline-driven, so regardless of my "estimates" of the time needed to get work done, the due date is the due date and the due time is the due time.

Given a deadline, there are still ways I can arrange my workload so that I am not doing things at the last minute. Also, yes, I do add time to my estimates, depending on the task at hand, other tasks I have pending, and the likelihood that I will be interrupted while trying to meet said deadline.

Start As Soon As Possible

One of the things I try to do when I get a new assignment is jump in right away and start working. One good reason to do this is because the information and parameters of the task are still fresh in my brain. If I just listen to the request or write down a note and then don't come back to it for several hours (or days), inevitably data is lost. Your brain can only recall five to seven bits of data at a time. You might be lucky and be one of those people with an eidetic memory. However, if you don't remember everything after a long delay, you'd better take good notes. Or, like I said, start the task right away.

By starting the task right away, I should clarify that I don't always mean doing the whole thing—unless that's required or feasible and you've got the time. Sometimes, at the very least, I'll set up a document outline or structure in my head and then set it up in a file somewhere. Maybe I'll just set up a table in Excel or put together a proposal "shell" (i.e., a proposal document that's formatted, includes all of the relevant headings, titles, and other formatting styles, but doesn't have any content) just to get the process rolling.

Again, this was a learned behavior, but it was one well worth learning because you need to…

Prepare for Things to Go Wrong

I have a dear friend who is wicked-smart and great at her work, but she is fundamentally unable to arrive at an airport early. I can recall multiple instances where, due to traffic hiccups or other unexpected issues, she missed a train or airplane and had to wait for the next one.

Travel and technical writing actually have some similar requirements.

- They are both deadline driven.
- You need to have everything on hand at the time of the deadline (luggage, tickets, people).
- If you don't show up on time, the train, plane, or ship will depart without you, your stuff, or both.

I try to get to the airport the recommended 90–120 minutes before flight time. Mind you, I don't always arrive that early, but I plan to arrive at that time just in case things go wrong. And if I've eaten into my fudge-factor time but arrive on time for the flight, I'm still ahead. Scotty's 21st-century engineering progenitors call this "schedule margin."

On a vacation, a missed flight might cost you a few hours and maybe some hefty ticket change fees. In a professional environment, you or your employer can lose out on thousands—nay, millions—of dollars.

What could possibly go wrong when creating a document? Oh, let me count the ways:

- Printer jammed or out of toner.
- Last-minute meeting with the CEO or program manager.
- Power outage.
- Tornado warning (others: hurricane, earthquake, fire drill, security scare).

- Team member stuck in traffic or unable to deliver content when you need it.
- Someone spills coffee on your keyboard.

You get the picture. Accidents happen. Life happens. You don't need to expect World War III to break out at any minute every time you do an estimate, but you need to give yourself some flexibility to be prepared when things go awry. People who are stressed out under deadlines tend to get sloppy or clumsy. I do, anyway. This opens the door for your own self-sabotage. Any job goes a lot more smoothly if you've got the time to do it right, and the more work you do early, the less work you have to do at the last minute.

Estimate Honestly

The last point I'd make here is not to sandbag people with your work time estimates just to make yourself look good or to pad your hours. Multiplying your work times by a factor of four might make you seem like a "miracle worker" once or twice, but if you keep doing that, eventually people are going to want to know "how long will it really take." The best way I know to do that is to be mindful of how long it takes you to produce, say, one page of high-quality text under ideal conditions and then how long it takes under not-so-ideal conditions and find an average of the two; after that, multiply by the number of pages. You also might want to factor in your familiarity with the content or the specific task at hand and adjust your scale accordingly.

I underestimated my time on a big job once and ran over budget, specifically because the content was new and the task unfamiliar. I estimated my time based on my aerospace performance, which was a mistake because my topic was not anywhere near space. I needed ramp-up time, which I didn't factor into my estimate. Fortunately, my employer still covered my hours, but I was prepared to absorb a significant amount of unpaid work due to my own misjudgment.

The last factor in your "padding" should be the "things-going-wrong" number, which will vary from person to person. It could be 5 minutes per hour or 15. Just be prepared for the warp drive to have a hiccup now and then. Having that extra margin allows you to remain calm when things really do go awry. If you appear calm when chaos ensues, others are more likely to remain calm as well. It took me 20 years to learn that. With any luck, you'll learn more quickly than I did.

What to Do When You Miss a Deadline

There have been occasions when I don't post a blog entry at my usual time of 9 a.m. U.S. Eastern Time. I could blame the switch to Daylight Saving Time. I could tell you I just got distracted because my family was visiting, which was true in one case. I could blame busy-ness, stress, or any number of issues that regularly afflict the freelance writer. However, the truth is often that I just plain forgot. As that former general I mentioned earlier put it, "The proper response if you drop the ball is, 'No excuse, sir'." Just own the oversight, apologize, and get it in gear to fix the problem created by your oversight as soon as possible.

Dressing for Success

Whether we like it or not, people judge us by the clothing we wear. While I tend to wear a Hawaiian shirt, jeans or shorts, and gym shoes when I work from home or on my days off, I make an effort to dress more formally if I'm en-

tering a professional office environment. Sometimes I've learned the hard way by not dressing appropriately, so maybe you can learn from my mistakes. If you're not a conformist, this section isn't for you. However, this is advice I wish I'd paid attention to when I was younger.

I have a couple of rather long blog entries[32] on this subject—one for men, one for women—but I'll keep things short and simple here.

Interviewing

This is where you wear your best business attire to make a solid first impression: a jacket, tie, matching or complementary-colored trousers, leather dress shoes, conservatively colored shirt for men; a similar suit-type look for women with (potentially) a conservative, knee-length or longer dress or skirt, conservative flat or low-heeled dress shoes. Other details that work for both would include minimal or no

---

[32] "Dressing for Success—Male Tech Writer Edition" https://heroictechwriting.com/2015/01/27/dressing-for-success-male-tech-writer-edition/ and "Dressing for Success—Female Tech Writer Edition" https://heroictechwriting.com/2018/05/03/dressing-for-success-female-tech-writer-edition/

perfume or cologne; orderly, conservative, single-color or natural-looking hair; and minimal, unobtrusive jewelry.

Yes, there are exceptions. If you're going into an artsy, fashion-focused, or "dramatic" environment where people expect you to stand out, feel free to wear the wild colors or eye-catching attire. However, in most businesses that hire technical communicators, the focus is on you, your accomplishments and resume, and your brain, not your fashion sense. Sensible business attire ensures that you look the part.

On the Job
This will vary with the job. If you're in an environment where you're always in an office that doesn't see a lot of customers and the dress code is a bit more relaxed, you might get away with a golf shirt, blue jeans, and flip flops. If you're in a high-visibility administrative area, suits or dresses might be the order of the day. If you work in an environment where you have to be on a shop floor, you'll be wearing close-toed, steel-toe shoes; functional clothing or a short haircut that you won't snag on machinery or mind getting oil or grease on; and possibly even safety glasses or goggles.

Social Events
Social occasions in the U.S. can range from office outings at the movie theater to in-office "pot luck" lunches to formal banquets. The clothing could range anywhere from the aforementioned jeans and flip flops to tuxedos and dresses.

Bottom line: if you're uncertain, ask! I once showed up at a NASA meeting in a golf shirt and khaki pants only to discover everyone else in jackets and ties or dresses. I'd have known to pack the right outfit if I'd thought to ask.

What Should You Share on Social Media?
This topic comes up occasionally, but it's still worth discussing. Being a cranky Gen-Xer who spent his formative experiences working on the early internet at Walt Disney World, I developed a healthy respect for and paranoia about the wide reach of social media: email, blogging, and all the rest. It probably also helped that I worked for a very image-conscious company.

I have friends and family members who absolutely refuse to use social media, and I have some who share way, way too much information for my tastes. Your level of comfort with social media might vary, as might your use of it. Let's cover the basics of your online "persona" and how that can affect the way you are perceived in the job market and workplace.

The Basics

It's probably not a big shock to you, but the content you post on the internet can reach nearly anywhere in the world. This is a blessing and a curse, depending on how you wish to express yourself.

In a business context, you might find that you can easily separate what you do for work from what you do in your free time—accountant by day, Manga or country music fan by night—and never the twain shall meet. Or shall they?

Big Brother Is Watching

The long, wide reach of the internet is important for your professional prospects. How you conduct yourself and what you post can and will be judged by current and future employers, and you just never know when one or both might be seeking information about you online. So as you think about what you post online on a regular basis, whether it's on Facebook, Twitter, your blog, Snapchat, or wherever, consider how a current or potential employer might react if they see your "private life" posts.

- Do you use a lot of profanity or bad grammar?
- Do you post pictures of yourself getting obnoxious and drunk out with your friends?
- Do you complain about or insult your boss, coworkers, or customers?
- Do you share company secrets (either inside gossip or actual intellectual property)?

I can imagine some of my younger readers rolling their eyes at this point and thinking, "What does that matter? That's my personal business!" Except that it's not, especially if you're divulging inside information about where you work. The internet, for better or worse, has caused our personal and professional lives to overlap to a considerable degree. Conduct performed in a "personal" context can now be observed (if you're foolish enough to post it) by your professional audience, and that audience can and will judge you for it. Companies and customers who see your name attached to them don't want to be seen as hiring party-animal derelicts. If you're public about representing yourself as employee of Company X, then there's an unspoken assumption out there that you "represent" Company X. It's no use complaining about your private life being intruded upon when you're sharing it with the world.

Balancing Your Personal and Professional Identities

This is not to say you cannot express yourself. You have interests, opinions, ideas, and perhaps a sense of humor, and any or all of those can be incorporated into your online activities. Just be aware that others will be watching.

As it happens, my work has put me out in front of the public quite a bit because I've written articles about space exploration, organized events for the Science Cheerleaders, and maintained connections with personal and professional friends on Facebook and Twitter. My personal and professional accounts cannot help but overlap. As a result, I reduce the level of salty language from my posts or the various internet memes. While I have some very definite political opinions, I find it's better for the sake of amity among my friends and sanity in my own mind not to get into extended "flaming" wars about the various issues of the day. One thing I include in my Twitter feed profile occasionally is a simple note saying, "Opinions are my own." Also, I try to maintain a "PG-13" rating on my posts. Not sure what that means? Check out the Motion Picture Association of America (MPAA) guidelines and resources for what sorts of things are and are not acceptable for broadcast TV or movies.

Politeness and good manners also go a long way toward helping with your online postings, as do common-sense behaviors like not libeling someone. And if you're ever in doubt about whether you should post something, you can always use the rubric of "Would I want my boss, customer, or parents to see this?" If the answer is no, don't post it.

Why I Don't Talk About Work on my Blog

I was at an entrepreneurs' meeting a while back, during which we learned about blog contents from a professional marketing expert (@TheChefKatrina). Her talk was instructive because she pointed out new things I could try to improve the quality and success of my site.

One obvious hole I had on my page, despite my passion for and employment by the aerospace industry, is a regular sharing of writing samples. This hole became obvious to me after the talk, when one of the participants (**Eriq**) wanted to read some.

Proprietary or Other Sensitive Information

I might have explained this before, but quite frankly a lot of what I write is not for the general public. That doesn't mean I'm writing for secretive, three-letter agencies in Northern Virginia or James Bond villains. It does mean that much of my work is tied up in proposals, where my employer is pitching a particular widget or "secret sauce" they built to help the government solve a problem. Many proposals have a notice on the cover informing the receiving agency that the contents are proprietary and thus not to be shared beyond the agency personnel reviewing the proposal.

Some proposal work also can be subject to the **International Traffic in Arms Regulations** (ITAR)[33]. These are regulations dictated by Congress and enforced by the State Department that keep sensitive or strategic technologies made in the U.S. out of the hands of foreign governments. This happens a lot when you're working with rockets, missiles, and things that can go boom. The U.S. Government takes a dim view of sharing those types of secrets with the rest of the world. Penalties for violations are stiff, and can include losing your job, paying hefty fines, and even facing imprisonment. So no, I don't share that stuff, either.

Even the public conference papers I wrote for NASA went through an internal export control review before being published.

Content Fatigue

Blogging, for me, is a leisure activity, albeit with a serious purpose (I hope people learn from it). After writing about rockets or spacecraft for several hours each day, it often happens that I'm "spaced out" at the end of the day and don't feel like writing about them in my free time. That's why I write about the business of technical writing—

---

[33] U.S. Government. "International Traffic in Arms Regulations: U.S. Munitions List Categories I, II, and III." Federal Register. https://www.federalregis-ter.gov/documents/2020/01/23/2020-00574/international-traffic-in-arms-regula-tions-us-munitions-list-categories-i-ii-and-iii.

something that I know and am passionate about but is still sufficiently different from my day job that I don't get burned out in my free time.

The Space Blogging Business Is Getting Crowded

There are already some first-rate bloggers out there who share their better-informed opinions about specific aspects of space, including defense, NASA human spaceflight, NASA robotic explorers, and commercial space. There's a guy out there whose entire schtick is to criticize everything NASA does. Others are defenders of NASA and harsh critics of commercial space. And so forth.

I started writing a space-related blog for a while, but the problem was that I'm a "space moderate," which means that I'm fascinated by all military, civil, and commercial space efforts and am unlikely to criticize the fundamental basis of specific programs out of sheer ideological pique. For instance, I was once called a "socialist" because I dared say nice things about NASA. And there are some NASA people who thought I was not quite trustworthy because I get along with "those [commercial space] people."

I'm not here to offend people, I'm here to make a buck. There's more and steadier money to be made writing for and getting along with the various players in the space business than there is writing opinions about them…at least that's been my experience. Which leads me to the final, and perhaps most important reason why I don't write about space on my blog very often.

I Need to Eat

When I interviewed for my first "space writing job" with NASA Marshall Space Flight Center, I needed to bring along my portfolio, which included samples of my space-related writings to that point. Many of those samples were letters to the Orlando Sentinel critical of NASA and its handling of the space program. I decided to take the risk anyway because they were on topic and they showed that I could advocate for a point of view. Rather than me asking if my letters would keep NASA from hiring me, I was surprised when one of my interviewers asked, "Given your opinions, are you sure you want to work for NASA?" The answer, obviously, was Yes! Again, I'm interested in human space exploration, regardless of who does it. Yes, there are things I think could be done better by the commercial sector vs. the government, but I don't want to see NASA shoved out of the business entirely. Perhaps I'll just leave it at that.

The lesson of the letter-to-the-editor writing example should be obvious: if I write opinions that are too sharply critical of a specific organization (agency or company), program managers and corporate CEOs in those organizations can take criticism personally. People are people. They can get defensive about the programs they lead. They can hold grudges. Those responses can interfere with my ability to obtain future work.

The aerospace business is surprisingly small, and the aerospace writing business is small enough that I know the names of or have met many of the practitioners in the field. I'm more interested in contributing to projects that advance the cause of space exploration than I am in criticizing failures. And like I said, I've got to eat.

How to Make a Good Last Impression

We put a lot of work into getting jobs: picking the right clothing, speaking politely with our potential employer, and showing off our best stuff in our portfolio. And since we like pay raises and recognition, we try to do good work once we're on the job. However, what do we do when we leave a job?

Why Are You Leaving?

This is tricky, because there are any number of things that could result in you losing your job in the first place:

- Laid off
- Downsized (job eliminated)
- Fired for cause (poor performance, bad behavior, etc.)
- Found a better position elsewhere
- Quit because you're miserable where you are

Let's assume, for our purposes, that you have not died or been fired, and you have some time between knowing your job is finished and actually leaving the organization.

What You Can Do about It

Leave your ego at the door. You might have some very hard feelings about your departure toward your management, peers, or the job itself. Try to leave those feelings at the door. Coworkers are often well aware of your circumstances. Showing up at the office grumpy, angry, or depressed doesn't make things easier. You still need to talk to people and get things done. Which leads me to my second point…

Finish your work. There will, in fact, be some things you can or should get done before you leave. You need to deliver those items on time with the same quality (or better) that you have demonstrated since you got the job.

Ensure an orderly handoff of tasks you won't or can't complete. For the tasks you have on your plate, you need to take the time to hand them off to whoever is going to handle them. This includes sharing your current progress, what remains to be done, who you're working with, who needs to receive it, when it's due, and what its priority level is.

Train your replacement. It is entirely possible you will have to educate the fresh-out-of-college trainee who is replacing you. You owe it to yourself (not the trainee, not the company) to pass on whatever useful knowledge others will need to do the job effectively. Legally, I'm not certain companies are even allowed to ask you to help after you leave a job. Assume they don't and you need to pass on whatever useful, critical knowledge you have to the person or people following you.

Secure a reference or two. I'm guessing you don't work at Initech (the fictional company in the movie comedy Office Space) or a crime syndicate. Therefore, there should be a couple of people you can count on to speak well of you when a future employer does a reference check. That could be a supervisor or a coworker; regardless, assuming you're keeping things cordial as you leave, there's no harm in seeking that support as you leave.

Don't sabotage anything or anybody. This behavior can take many forms: training your replacement incorrectly, destroying company files or materials in your possession, badmouthing your employer to customers (or on social media) while still on the job, or stealing the keys off of company computers. I get it: you're angry. The Very Large Corporation of America has just screwed you out of a job you loved. You'll be tempted to take out that anger on the company or your managers. You might even have some just cause. Don't do it.

The short answer here is: it demonstrates class. You want (and you want others) to take yourself seriously as a professional. Of course you demonstrate that when you're trying to make a first impression.

The tougher part can be demonstrating the same level of professionalism on the way out the door.

You will have to find the next job after you leave the one you're at now, and you want to make the transition as professionally and painlessly as possible. Again, if you weren't terminated for cause, your behavior on the way out the door can make a big difference as to whether you will be able to get a good reference from that employer once you're gone.

Part V: Pursuing Work

Chapter 9: Looking for Work

This chapter is also important: you want to find a job, don't you? It's not just a matter of having a neat resume or portfolio or having the right network, though all of those are useful. You'll also find advice on how to tailor your job hunt to meet your personal and professional needs, whether you're a college student new to the job market or in the middle of your career and looking to make a change. Again there will be some talk about attitude, which is definitely important, especially when you've been unemployed for a while or you don't get the job you wanted. You'll also learn about planning out your approach to interviewing, seeking opportunities, and setting a proper value for your services.

Goal Setting for the Future

We always have crazy dreams as kids—I want to be an astronaut, I want to be president, and so on—but eventually adult reality creeps up on us and we grow up to do that which most suits us…or just what's available. Some of us are lucky enough to get paid for what we love to do. I happen to enjoy writing about space, science, and technology. However, I have many friends who are well into their thirties or beyond and still don't know "what they want to do when they grow up."

Below is a suggested extended exercise based on the advice I've offered up previously:

1. List your current skills—all of them—whether they be work-related, domestic, or other.
2. List your current interests.
3. Take inventory of who you are as a person. Yes, it is possible to go overboard with "personality tests" or career assessments, but if you are honest with yourself about who you are and what motivates you, some lines of work will automatically suggest themselves while others drop off the list completely.
4. List your primary motivators for working or for changing your current circumstances: money, idealism, work location, coworkers, commute, or others.
5. Pick your favorites from the above.
6. Take some time to describe your "ideal state" work environment. This includes:

a. Where is it geographically?
b. Where is it environmentally (city, suburbs, rural)?
c. How large is the **company** or team?
d. What sort of money or benefits do you want or expect? Side discussion: what are your wants and needs and what do they cost?
e. What sort of work environment makes you most comfortable: office, workshop, traveling sales calls?
f. What sort of team or social environment makes you most comfortable: formal, informal, wild and crazy?
g. Does the work you want to do require you to work alone, in a small group, or on a large team?

7. Do you have or want a spouse/family? How do you want your "work/life balance" to look?
8. How often and when do you want to work?

At this point, you've got quite a pile of information about yourself, what motivates you, and where you want to work. This self-awareness is helpful and necessary if you're going to apply for your first job, make a career plan, or plan a career change. Of course, once you know what you want, you have to start hunting for it. It will take longer than a few weeks to find an ideal fit, so this approach is not good for people who need a job now to pay the bills. You might have to take a job that pays the bills until you figure out what you want, unless you're fortunate enough to have time, space, or money not to need that job immediately.

The other great advantage of taking this personal inventory is that it will focus your interview questions and answers because you know what you want. If your attitude and behavior are in the right place, the interview can be a mere formality. I can attest to this through personal experience. I've never had a cool job come out of a boring interview.

Job-Hunting Advice (The Short Version)
Job- or career-hunting need not be painful or difficult. Mind you, I have no control over the employment market or how individual companies choose to hire. What I can offer are some basic tips to help you determine what type of job you should pursue and how. My buddy Jason at **Zero Point Frontiers** Corporation liked to keep ideas to no more than five points, so here's my five-step approach to job-hunting:

- Determine what you enjoy doing and what you're good at doing; ideally you can find a line of work that allows you to do both.
- Identify the required skill sets, requirements, or qualifications for that particular line of work and evaluate your experience and education vs. those requirements.
- Identify any gaps, determine whether you have related or alternative experience that addresses the gaps, or take active steps to fill the gaps through education or other experience.
- Organize your resume and portfolio to highlight your experience to its best effect (i.e., so that it matches what your prospective employer customer is looking for).
- Communicate with your network, let them know specifics about what type of work you're looking for, and ask if they know who's hiring (rather than asking someone directly for a job).

Job-Hunting Advice (The Long Version)

Generally, the questions I've heard over the years fall into a couple of categories:

- I want to get a job doing X in Y industry. What do I need to do, learn, or know to get there?
- I'm unhappy doing X, but I don't know what to do next.

I'll take these one at a time and see if I can provide some more generalized advice (realizing that not all of you want to be writers in the space business).

I Want to Get a Job Doing X in Y Industry. What Do I Need to Do, Learn, or Know to Get There?

The people asking the first question are often asking how to get my job or something similar. Say you have no interest in working in aerospace. You want to work in the automotive industry, or medical, or (Deus protect you) banking regulations. The approach, I would argue, is similar regardless. Your first step, of course, is to learn about the job.

Research. Before you dive into a new field, you might want to get a better look at what the job actually entails and how healthy the market is. The Occupational Outlook Handbook assembled yearly by the

U.S. Department of Labor's Bureau of Labor Statistics is a great starting point. The OOH might or might not have your specific title in mind, but you might find something similar.

Check the want ads. Try Indeed.com, Monster.com, your local newspaper—whatever job site suits you. The job descriptions, experience qualifications, and other background are usually all right there.

Talk to people in the field. There are a few ways you can go about this, from face-to-face interviews or discussion to email to going to conferences and speaking with people there.

Your next step in the process is to determine your best angle for getting where you want to be. Is your gap degree-focused (i.e., do you need a specific type of degree to get the job)?

See what you can do or learn to minimize transition costs. Given the ridiculous cost of colleges and universities these days, it's better to seek the path that requires the least time, effort, and money so you can get into your chosen field as quickly as possible. If you have a comparable degree, for instance, you might be able to get smart on the subject through online research, reading, or short (free) classes (see the section on "Upgrading Your Skills" in Chapter 8).

Do volunteer work related to your chosen path. In my case, I did a lot of writing for the citizen space advocacy community, doing letter-writing campaigns, running conferences, and writing policy papers related to space exploration. Yes, I did this in my free time, and no, I didn't get paid (hence "volunteer"). However, I did get that marvelous addition for the resume: experience. As a bonus, that experience demonstrated my interest in and commitment to the industry. This unpaid option is easier if you're younger, still working, and able to devote the free time.

Get smart about the industry. Again, regardless of your chosen path, you can find any number of industry news resources online or in your local public library to help you learn what's going on and what the big issues are in your preferred industry or line of work. Take the time to read what's being said in trade publications, traditional news outlets, and blogs so you can be up to speed.

Blog about your topic. This approach allows you to demonstrate your knowledge of and enthusiasm for the industry as well as your writing style.

Swing for the fences. If you're passionate about working in a particular industry and your resume doesn't quite match the requirements (yet), you might at least try writing a really snappy cover letter sharing your enthusiasm for the work. You might get an interview anyway.

I'm Unhappy Doing X, But I Don't Know What to Do Next

This will delve a little bit into personal self-analysis (a subject, again, in which I am not a licensed professional), but experience still counts for something, so people ask my opinion. Often, you have to start with the basics, which includes healthy doses of honesty and introspection.

Figure out why you are unhappy. Ask yourself what is making you unhappy. Are there other problems in your life outside work causing you stress or frustration? Is the problem your work environment? Problems at home? Your chair? Your boss? Your office culture? Your work content? Your working hours? Your lack of promotion or career development opportunities? Your benefits? Your work-life balance? Your location? Your pay? Your commute? Because we spend so much of our time at work, it engages many parts of our lives. You might try listing out each of the items above and rating them from one to ten and see if you can identify your "pain points."

Take action where you can. You might find that, overall, your job is pretty good, but the two-hour commute every day is kicking you in the rear and draining your energy. Maybe you just need to ask your boss if you can telecommute or work in a location closer to home. The point is, if there are little or big things in your job that would greatly increase your quality of life, take those steps first before throwing your life into upheaval.

Find help. If the problems you're facing are moral or ethical, you might need to speak with a mentor, spiritual advisor, or even a lawyer. If they are cultural, you might talk with friends inside or outside of work. If they are management-related, well, given our litigious society, you might want to think through any formal complaints very carefully…again, perhaps by consulting a lawyer. If the problems are related to violence or illegal activity, you need to talk to law enforcement, lawyers, and maybe a counselor for yourself and anyone involved. Your level of assistance should reflect the realistic nature of your problem.

The little things are fixed, but you're still unhappy. Let's say you've taken what steps you can to improve your work situation. You got a new chair for the office, your computer got upgraded, you've been given permission to telecommute, and the office culture is on the whole friendly and supportive...and you're still unhappy with what you're doing. In other words, let's say you've got a good thing going and you just don't like your job. Now what? It's at this stage you need to start looking at the specifics of your work rather than the circumstances surrounding your work, as noted above. Is it the level of detail you're asked to handle? Do you dislike working in large groups of boisterous people who might be typical of your industry? Does the content bore or offend you? Do you seek more autonomy?

Identify what you want. This is sometimes trickier for people than identifying what they dislike. It's like you're hard-wired to complain but speechless when it comes to stating your desires. One quick way to identify the type of work you do want is to invert your complaints: if you dislike micromanagement, you probably prefer more autonomy; if you dislike loud environments, you might want to consider a quieter industry; if you dislike detail work, perhaps you'd be happier working with management-level material, which can be more "big picture" and abstracted.

Finally, as I've noted, you need to be able to find a line of work that interests you and maybe even combines your hobby interests with your talents. It's been said elsewhere that if you love what you do, you'll never "work" a day in your life. That phrase is somewhat incomplete. It's not that you won't ever work; you will, but it won't feel like work because you enjoy what you do.

What You Can Do to Help Your Inside Game
There are (or will be) times when things are not going particularly well in your career.

What do you do when you're facing unemployment? Coping with joblessness isn't just a matter of keeping your resume up to date. Like playing golf or running a marathon, job-hunting is as much an inside game as an external activity. You need to keep yourself moving. What follows is some (hopefully) useful advice I gave myself when I was struggling to find work several years ago. If it's good enough for me, it's good enough to share.

Show Up

The first thing you've got to do is get up at a regular time Monday through Friday. Shower, get dressed, brush your teeth, and see to your personal grooming. Show up like you're a working person because you are. Your job is to look for work.

Avoid Negativity

This goes for the people around you as well as your self-talk (what you say to yourself). Life is too short and unemployment stressful enough without Negative Nellie (or Ned) telling you you're un-wanted, you're no good, or you'll never work again. I don't mean turn into Pollyanna and think everything will always turn out for the best (a lady friend accused me of having rose-colored bifocals), but unem-ployment sucks, and you don't need to have people around you or in your own head telling you bad things all the time.

Be Specific about What You Want

If you're fortunate enough to have a two-income household or to have a "rainy day" fund you can live on for a bit, you can be more specific and concrete about what type of job you want and can take more time to find it. Along with that, consider the whole package: work content, pay, benefits, location, work environment, and all that wacky culture stuff I talk about on my blog. Look for jobs online that fit your magic words, and apply there first. Your cover letters will be better because your enthusiasm for the work will be real.

Be Realistic About the Job-Hunt Process

Usually the only ones who will respond immediately are the comput-ers that collect your resume online. If you're looking for long-term work, the holidays are a bad time to search because a lot of HR de-partments go on vacation. You might be the ideal candidate for a par-ticular job, but it can take weeks or months for your resume to work its way through the system, which is why it's important to put your network to good use (see my next point).

Take Advantage of Your Network

Technical writers get to talk to a lot of different people in the course of our work because we have to learn a lot about many topics. Let people know you're looking for work, and be specific about the type of work you want so people don't send you well-meaning but unproductive ads for jobs you'd never take. The polite thing is not to ask your friends or acquaintances for a job; instead, ask them if they know of a job in their company or circle of experience. Perhaps ask for an introduction or a recommendation or at least a referral. Your network can get you in the door; the rest is up to you.

Keep Writing

National Novel Writing Month provided an excellent opportunity for me to get a first draft of a novel written. Getting it published is still a task for a future date. Not a novelist? Write poetry. Or a journal. Or a specific description of your ideal next job (see above). Keep "sharpening the saw," as Steven Covey liked to say. Use your journal to vent the ugly thoughts in your head so when you speak to others you can be your best self. Just as you don't need Negative Ned dragging you down when you're looking for work, you don't want to be morose or angry in an interview.

Pay Your Bills

If you lack the luxury of a second income or rainy-day fund, march to the unemployment office, sign up, start collecting checks, and then make a promise to yourself to get off relief as soon as you can. Note: if you start collecting unemployment checks, your local or national government will want to see proof that you're applying for jobs for which you are qualified; some will even send you links to jobs in your field—the government doesn't want you to be unemployed forever, either. Also, if you don't have a lot of time or money to waste looking for your "dream job," take what work is available to pay the bills. It might not be ideal, but it keeps you on a solid footing and more importantly it keeps you working. Also, some jobs—especially government jobs—will do credit checks on you. Fair or not, a poor credit rating can affect your chances for employment.

Use the Time to Grow

"Oh, great. You're going to tell me this is a chance to get in touch with my inner feelings?" Yes, that's exactly what I'm going to tell you. Unemployment can be a very humbling (even humiliating) experience, especially if you are someone who defines him- or herself by your work, and you need to take care of yourself. Take some time to figure out what went wrong with your previous employment situation and identify ways you can avoid that situation in the future. Find a new, low-cost hobby or interest and start writing or blogging about it. Stay in touch with your family members and friends—the ones who won't drag you down, of course. Someone told me recently that every time she was unemployed she had an opportunity for self-improvement and growth. I'm not quite so philosophical as that, but it's something to aspire to when I grow up. Still, if you're down and out, taking some concrete steps to build yourself up can only improve your situation.

Interviewing

Interviewing for a job is a bit like going on a first date, with all the worries, self-consciousness, and nerves that go with it. In this case, you're not looking for a romantic partner, but a place to work—ideally doing work you enjoy around people you like. Still, you first have to get through that first interview (date) for both you and your potential employer to see if you will be a good fit for each other. Yes, there's a bit of acting involved, but there are ways for you to still be your best self. What follows are some of the "mind games" I've played with myself during interviews.

Act Like You Don't Need the Job

A lot of acting involves behaving like someone else or as someone with circumstances radically different from your own. So yes, that's what I'm recommending: acting, NOT lying. Much like lying on your resume, that's a great way to ensure that you don't get hired or that you get fired quickly once the lie is discovered. You need to put yourself in the mindset of a person who is calm, contented, enthusiastic, optimistic, and confident.

You know what sort of person acts that way? Someone who doesn't need the job.

Much like dating in the social world, "Needy is not a turn-on." You might make the interviewer feel a little bad that you're out of work, but odds are, so are many of the other people applying for the job. Therefore, saying, "I really need this job (or work)!" is not going to help your case. It is also likely to hurt you in salary negotiations because the employer will think they can lowball you because you need the money. It's better to act as if you are currently employed and to negotiate with your known value in mind.

Believe That You Already Have the Job

By this, I don't mean you should show up with an attitude, start calling everyone by their first names right away, or acting like the boss. Rather than behave as someone who needs to demonstrate your qualifications, assume that your interviewer already knows them. Act like someone who is ready to jump in and do the work. One way to ensure this mindset is to ask about practical matters such as, "What does an average day on the job look like?" or "Who would I be working with (or for)?" In any case, you should go in with some detailed, pragmatic questions in mind. You're not showing up for an inquisition, you're there to have a conversation, and you can feel more confident just by having something of your own to say. A frightened person might be too afraid to ask questions.

Another way to have this sort of confidence is to investigate what you can about the employer or customer and identify an area where you might be of the most help. Or, if you can't find anything, you might ask, "What are your biggest challenges with X project or work?" Either way, you can offer a little free advice on how to make the product or process better. Or, if that sounds too arrogant or like "mansplaining," you can ask, "Have you tried [whatever advice you'd suggest]?"

The goal is to go in there with the confidence of someone who knows what she or he is doing and then to prove it.

Look and Feel Your Best

This usually goes without saying, but you should dress nicely for the interview. What does "nicely" mean? Well, you can start with the "Dressing for Success" section in Chapter 8, for suggestions, with an eye toward "business attire." Also, assuming you've been dressing yourself for 20+ years, you should have a good idea of what clothes make you look good or feel smarter, classier, or more intelligent when you're wearing them. Wear the good stuff. Maybe treat yourself to a good meal after the interview afterward (if you can afford it). Look on the interview as an opportunity to shine and to show your potential

241

employer or customer your best self. Often the best way to help you feel better is to look the part.

Be Enthusiastic

It's entirely possible that the job you're interviewing is not something you want to do all your life–it's just a job to keep body and soul together. There's no shame in that. It might be a job not too many others want or like, either. That doesn't mean you can't sound or be enthusiastic about the work. After all, a steady paycheck might be a definite mood enhancer if you get the job, so you can channel the morale boost from the potential paycheck into your interview mood.

Also, if you're a life-long learner—and if you're a technical writer, it's pretty much an occupational hazard—you can always learn something new, even in a job that you wouldn't normally do. That's more or less how I approached writing for an information technology department. I wasn't gung-ho about the position and I had no idea what I was writing half the time. To compensate, I decided to learn about the technology so I could explain things more clearly, which was why I was there after all. I enjoyed the research and my employers appreciated my diligence. If you like learning, you can be enthusiastic about expressing that.

Mind you, it can be difficult to be enthusiastic if you're asked about long gaps in your employment history, but that, too, can be met with enthusiasm. Rather than squirming uncomfortably and trying to offer complicated explanations, that's an opportunity to demonstrate a positive attitude. "Yes, I know. It's been difficult to find a job for someone with my skills lately, but I know if this opportunity doesn't work out that another will present itself soon."

Be Friendly and Polite

Related to enthusiasm is friendliness. You might be an introvert, like me. That doesn't mean you can't be cordial in your dealings with your potential employer or their staff. Don't just turn on the charm for the interviewer; use please and thank-you when interacting with anyone and everyone you contact at the company or organization, from the CEO to the interviewer, receptionist, or janitor. And while I try to ensure that I at least send an email to my interviewer(s) within 24 hours of talking with them to say thank-you for their time, I've read that a handwritten card shows that extra bit of effort. Even if you don't get the job, it will be remembered and appreciated.

Bottom Line

Again, there is a huge difference between acting and lying. You should not lie about any particular regarding your work history, experience, or skill set. What you might have to do, however, is fib to yourself about how confident you're feeling and your ability to get and do the job. The short version of my advice regarding maintaining your confidence is simply, "Fake it until you make it."

Why Didn't I Get the Job I Wanted?

It happens more often than we would like to admit: we do our best to look good to a potential employer and then, for some reason not always disclosed to us, we don't get the work or job. "Was it something I said?" the reflective technical communicator might ask, "or am I just not good enough?" Before you go beating yourself up over things you don't know or can't control, I'd like to offer a few suggestions for why you did not get a job that looked like a "perfect" fit for you.

Reasons You Cannot Control

The employer had someone else in mind. I know, employers are not supposed to have a job set up for one particular person, but sometimes it happens. They have a particular skill set, background, or experience base in mind and, what do you know? All those factors just happen to match up with a candidate whom they already know. It's not fair, but it's also not personal, meaning they're not excluding only you, they're also excluding anyone else besides you who applied but didn't match their expectations.

They changed their mind. Sometimes a company will have a job requisition open, they'll go through the hiring process, and then someone in the organization asks, "Why are we hiring a new person? We've already got X in another department doing that." Or maybe the budget to pay for that particular head count dried up due to challenges elsewhere. Or perhaps the person you were going to replace decides to take a better offer and stay.

Someone else had better credentials or experience. You might or might not know who your competition is, but sometimes a candidate comes out of left field (say, from way out of town) whose background, experience, or credentials just wow the hiring manager. In which case you might hear something like, "We were very impressed with you, and you made it to our final round, but in the end we chose someone else whose experience directly related to X." You might hear from that employer again if another opening appears, so don't slam that door shut.

Reasons You Can Control

Your experience or credentials did not match what they wanted. The best thing you can do when job-hunting is to use the rifle approach rather than a shotgun. Apologies to any gun haters out there, but the analogy is apt: are you looking to scatter your resume in every direction like shotgun pellets and hope you hit something, or would you prefer to aim for a specific target that best suits your abilities? My advice is to take the rifle approach: do the research, target the best potential employers, jobs, and matches for your preferred type of work, and apply to them first. That means eliminating jobs that are promising but for which you don't have the right experience or skills.

You did something awful at the interview. It could be any number of things: poor attire, rudeness toward the administrative staff, inappropriate questions or statements during the interview. Maybe there are jobs out there where absolutely none of the above matter. If so, and you're prone to the above behaviors, best of luck to you—you've found your people. Otherwise, it's better to err on the side of politeness.

Best advice here would be: if you know you have an interview that day, be prepared:

- Dress appropriately.
- Be on your best behavior: avoid harsh language, inappropriate comments or behavior, or "personal space" violations.
- Have your portfolio and business card available.
- Listen.
- Answer questions in an upbeat, honest fashion.
- Ask questions of your own.

Something ugly turned up in your background check. You can't do anything about your past, but you can do your best to keep your present in shape by obeying the laws of the land, avoiding people who do not obey the laws, and paying your bills. If something does come back, don't lie. Explain the situation with a minimum of defensiveness, explain the consequences, and what you have done since then to make restitution, pay for your crime, or change your behavior.

Something ugly turned up in your social media activity. I've covered this topic before (see Chapter 8), but it bears repeating: employers can and will judge you on the stuff you post on social media—blogs, Twitter, Facebook, Instagram, etc.—so if your public image on the internet is on the wild, partying, or offensively worded side, you might find yourself bypassed or at least asked about what you do in your free time. If you don't share what you do at parties or on your vacations in public social media, you don't have to worry about that, do you? Other things to watch out for: insulting or complaining about employers, customers, or coworkers online. That's a bad habit that's worth unlearning.

Bottom Line
Focus on what you can influence or control. The rest is up to the potential employer. It's a busy world out there.

Job Searching at Mid-Career
When you're fresh out of college, job searching is easy, inexpensive, and visionary. You have most of your life ahead of you, you're not really sure where you'll end up, and any changes you make can be done with very little pain or effort because you have yet to establish yourself in any particular place or field.

Why It's Difficult As You Get Older
It gets a little tougher in your forties.

I hit a rough patch at 40 when the NASA program I was supporting was canceled. Having spent my thirties trying to get into the space business, I then faced the very real possibility of having to give it up. Where could I go next? What should I do? On that particular occasion, I was fortunate to have a manager who went out of her way to

245

ensure that as many of us as possible stayed employed at NASA, albeit in areas outside human spaceflight. So: crisis (eventually) averted. Without that "save," most likely I would have changed industries and maintained my location, but there were other options.

Here's why career changes are harder in mid-career:

- You've probably gotten used to a specific income level and a lifestyle to go with it.
- You've developed a specific set of skills—some of which might be transferrable to another job or industry, but many of which won't be.
- You might have a lot of your personal self-worth invested in a specific career.
- You've got a reputation, clients, and group of friends that derive from what you did before. A new industry means starting "at the bottom," getting to know a whole new group of people, and facing some very humbling learning experiences as you have to start all over in a new line of work.
- You have more responsibilities to handle: spouse or significant other, home, car, small humans, pets, and all the expenses that come with them.

Change is stressful. Your significant other has his or her own career or lifestyle to worry about—how does your change affect them? Will you have to cut back on your expenses? Get a smaller home? Move? Sell the car? Sell the kids? (Kidding.) How much savings do you have built up?

This isn't to say you couldn't have these problems as a younger person. You can and do. However, the older you get, the more responsibilities, people, and stuff you have to take care of, the more complicated and painful a massive change can be. And let's be honest here: you've gotten used to living a certain way for a number of years and you just might not be as flexible in your thinking; change can be more difficult.

What to Do First

This is going to sound a tad touchy-feely, but bear with me. Priority one is to treat the loss of your chosen job or career as a loss, equivalent even to a death, and deaths require a grieving process. You have to acknowledge that pain and take care of yourself or you won't be able to get beyond whatever ugly little thoughts are running like a barbarian horde through your brain. There are good reasons why being fired or retiring from work are among the top ten **most stressful** life events, some of which I mentioned previously.

Many companies provide access to an Employee Assistance Program (EAP) to help individuals cope with unemployment. This can cover everything from emotional counseling to job search assistance to seeking financial or other assistance such as substance abuse counseling. Take advantage of those options if they're available to you.

Once you get your head straight and grieve the loss, you can start making decisions about your future.

Brainstorming Your Future

The transition from your previous career to the next one will depend a lot on your specific life circumstances, so I won't even begin to suggest that what worked for me will work for you. Still, the questions you ask should be similar and will go a long way toward helping you answer the "what do I do now?" question:

- What's your current financial situation? This includes things like how much savings do you have, how many bills do you have to pay, and what can you do to cut expenses now until you're settled into the next thing?
- If necessary, who can you borrow money from to tide you over?
- How long can you operate without income?
- Have you contacted your state's **unemployment office**?
- Is your resume up to date? As a technical writer, do you have a portfolio of products you can show to prospective employers or customers?
- What are your transferrable skills? Which industries or customers might need people with those **skills**?
- What are things you've wanted to try but haven't because you were established in your previous **career**?
- Where do you want to go—professionally, geographically, and personally?

I encountered another career hiccup in my mid-forties when my employer faced cutbacks due to a government shutdown. Instead of seeking another job, I decided to take a leap of faith, move back to Florida, and try freelance writing. To make this happen, I needed to suck it up and spend some time living with my parents and then housesitting for a couple friends for the bulk of a year. That little-to-no-rent period gave me the breathing space to find paying gigs while most of my stuff went into storage. If I'd had a spouse, kids, or other related responsibilities, I would've taken a much different path.

The last piece of advice I'd offer to the midlife career changer is not to be too hard on yourself for making decisions that work for you and yours. For instance, you might find you have to move away from your current neighborhood or city to find the career you want. Or you might have to withdraw from specific activities to reduce expenses or concentrate on your new career. Social safety nets, severance pay, and unemployment benefits aside, you are on your own when it comes to taking care of yourself and managing the next steps in your career. You have to do what works for you.

In Defense of Being Older

"I am not going to make age an issue in this campaign. I am not going to exploit for political purposes my opponent's youth and inexperience."
—Ronald Reagan (age 73), 1984

I read a lot in various tech blogs about how the young—for me, that's Millennials and younger—have an advantage over anyone older because they're more tech-savvy. You know what? They're right. My mom and dad use their computers for email and checking the news, that's about it. My dad refuses to buy a smart phone. I myself have mental blocks about InDesign, Siri, humanoid robots, and several online chat or social media applications.

Points conceded.

However, unlike Mr. Reagan, I can and will take advantage of younger people's youth and inexperience. I need every advantage I can get. The single most important advantage an older person has is simply more time on this Earth to do more things. Electronically, younger people might have larger electronic networks than me and no doubt can call on the "hive mind" of the internet to answer any question they see fit. I can do the same hive-mind research. However, I can put electrons plus my in-person experiences and connections to work to get faster results than electrons alone.

In this case, the older person's advantages are more relationships and face-to-face experiences working with other professionals in one's chosen field. Yes, someone younger might be able to email Eminent Subject Matter Expert X with a request and they might or might not get a response. My advantage might be something as minor as having worked with or met the Eminent Subject Matter Expert and hanging out with them at several industry-related events. Example: when I first started writing articles about space in 2006, I had zero connections; today I can call upon multiple professionals whom I've worked with in some capacity to get the information (or quotations) I need to round out the article.

The longer you've been around, the more people you've had the opportunity to meet; and if you've met or worked with someone, you might have more credibility than someone who's just a LinkedIn connection.

Not all of this is a given, nor is it entirely rational. Human beings are interesting folk, and depending on your reputation, sometimes face-to-face experience isn't the best advantage (corollary of being older—you've had more time to make more enemies).

However, I think it's a mistake to discount the inputs of someone older than you. Respect for the wisdom of age is not always a common practice in the tech sector culture, where young minds and fresh ideas predominate. However, an experienced professional's relationships have something that a younger person's might not: leverage. One of my employers, Zero Point Frontiers, drew upon the wisdom of a couple of Apollo-era veterans to develop their aerospace engineering products. These gentlemen ("graybeards" in NASA parlance) knew what had been done before, how the system worked within specific organizations, and who to call to get an answer or decision quickly because they had the stature to get people to take their calls and listen to them. That's a combination of abilities and experience that's hard to duplicate or beat.

So here are my final thoughts on age in the workplace: if you get the opportunity to pick the brain of or be mentored by a senior professional in your field, take it. Will they have wrongheaded, incomplete, or backward ideas about this or that technology? Possibly, though if you explain its use in practical terms they'll get it soon enough. Might you disagree with them about politics? Certainly, but you're there to work, not vote, right? What that eminent older person might offer you, though, are the insights and connections to improve your own standing and network. Those are lessons well worth learning.

Setting Up Your Resume

I know: you're a writer. You don't need help with writing or editing your resume. If you feel that's the case, skip this section. However, if you think your resume could use some refreshing, bear with me for a bit. You might be a genius in proofreading or setting up technical documents, but how good are you at marketing yourself? What follows are some tips I've lived by since I started working as a professional writer.

As with your portfolio, your resume is a marketing document. Often it is the first impression you give a future employer, so it should receive your utmost attention.

First, the resume has a few basics that should be followed:

- Your name should be at the top, along with some basic contact information (email address at minimum, but also a phone number and street address if you're so inclined).
- You need to talk about your experience in a compelling or pointed way.
- It must be neat and legible (no fancy or cutesy fonts).
- It must be truthful.
- Unless you've been in your field for many, many years, in general it should be no longer than two pages, but I've bypassed this guideline myself on occasion.

The resume, for you proposal writers, is a past performance document. It demonstrates to your prospective employer that you can do the job you're applying to do. There are a couple of different ways you can organize your work history, but generally your experiences, life-career stage, or desired job will dictate the form. For instance, if you're fresh out of college and don't have a lot of work experience, you focus on your degree and any projects you've done while attending school. If you're in your early or mid-career, you can move your degree toward the rear and focus on your job experience. If you've been working for quite a while, or if you're applying for a job for which you don't have a lot of direct experience, you might want to shift to a skills-based resume, which emphasizes your capabilities and accomplishments rather than the amount of time you've been in the workforce.

For years I've included Summary or Objective statements at the top of my resumes, but apparently these are going away. The goal now is to weave your accomplishments into the descriptions of your job experience. Accomplishments are important because they show what new effort or outcome you have brought to the jobs you have done. Examples include: sales made, money or time saved, output produced, or awards won. Lacking numbers, you should focus on unique activities that you accomplished in your role.

- Large documents or projects you completed that made or saved your organization a lot of money.
- Documents or systems you have established that didn't exist before you worked in that position (for example, developed a metrics report, established an in-house newsletter).
- Systemic or process improvements you designed.
- New programs you helped implement.
- Work you did in the midst of a crisis (e.g., hurricane, government shutdown, layoff).

The point is to show why someone should hire you, not someone else. You should be talking about what you've achieved, not just describe your job duties.

From there, everything is negotiable. A chronological arrangement of your job history will show what you have done and when. A skill-based resume is what it sounds like: it summarizes the types of skills you have while simply listing the places you've worked.

I've put my list of publications into a separate document, formatted like my resume. The full resume plus the publications would constitute what academics call a Curriculum Vitae (Latin for "the course of

251

one's life," also called a C.V.). You can have everything together as one document if you like. I've had occasions, though, where the boss wanted my resume but didn't need to know every little thing I'd written, so you might want to ask what's needed first.

Other tips:

- Keep your verbs active.
- Emphasize how you work rather than summarize your job duties.
- Use nothing smaller than a ten-point font.
- Again, avoid cutesy or hard-to-read fonts (Comic Sans is often the prime culprit).
- Depending on the job you're posting for, make certain you are using the "magic words" your future employer expects to see so that you're a good fit. That means showing your experience includes the activities or skills listed in the job posting.
- Don't BS or flat-out lie about your qualifications or experience. If your experience is close to what the employer wants, explain it as such (and remember that employers will check your qualifications).

Beyond that, I wish you luck. I refresh my resume every six months or so to remind myself of what I've been doing to add value and because the job market is uncertain. You're marketing yourself, so make sure you shine!

Setting Up Your Portfolio

Your portfolio is perhaps the third or fourth tool you have to make an impression on a prospective employer, after your resume, cover letter, and initial interview. It is the product you show an employer if they haven't seen any of your work samples or they want to see more.

Small confession here: it took me years to get my portfolio into the neat, tidy order I'm about to share. For much of my career, I put things in there in reverse chronological order and put the resume on top. Well, live and learn. I've picked up a few things. The following are suggestions, not rules. If you have ideas that work for you, I'd love to hear them.

I use a conventional three-ring binder with a pocket at the front end and locks on the binder to reduce the likelihood of pages coming loose.

I still keep the resume up-front. I've also created a separate "Publications" document. That way I can keep my work experience content down to two pages and share publication information only if asked.

Another thing I decided to do with the portfolio is not to share everything I've done from every part of my career. I've trimmed the collection down to five categories of work with the four or five best samples of each. These categories are divided by tabs.

The categories of work I've done are:

- Business and Technical Writing
- Web Content
- Training
- Policy and Advocacy Writing
- Marketing and Promotions

Obviously your work will be organized differently. If you're relatively new to the field, you probably don't need the tabs. However, it is good to include a variety of products. Or, if you've stuck with one type of work—say, journalism—then it's good to show the breadth of your work across multiple topics or publications. Until I had more work products to show, I included school projects in my portfolio.

One set of products I included was the marketing material developed for the International Space Development Program (ISDC) conference I ran because the marketing approach was mine. Did I create the artwork? No, that was my very talented designer friend Tina. However, it was my requirement to display the ISDC "brand" far and wide (another marketing lesson I learned from Disney). Tina's fine logo was plastered on stickers, patches, letterhead, t-shirts, coffee mugs, and signage throughout the conference.

Some other tips when assembling your portfolio:

- Buy a new binder if you're just starting out, or if you've not refreshed your portfolio in a while.

- Take advantage of Avery pre-printed labels or labels you can program when setting up your category tabs. This was necessary for me because my handwriting is just this side of awful.
- Use the same type of sheet protectors throughout the portfolio.
- Proofread any work that's in your portfolio, especially your resume. If there are typos or errors in publications that were beyond your control, be prepared to explain them.
- If you have had work published in print publications, copy or trim it so it fits neatly inside the sheet protector.
- If you have one or more documents that have a "landscape" orientation, be consistent in how you insert them into the sheet protectors (e.g., bottom facing the binding).

Obviously your work doesn't just speak for itself. You should take care to pick your best products and be able to explain why they're in there. Like the ISDC branding example, I could explain to someone, "This is an example of how I ensured my brand was expressed across multiple products." As with your resume, you want to be able to demonstrate products that allowed you or your organization to improve.

Five Tips to Make Networking Work for You
I can't be an introvert all the time, and when it comes to doing my job, I'm surprisingly sociable. This is important because talking to people is how you build the relationships that grow your scope of knowledge. And yes, your network can help you with your career, too.

One reason networking gets a bad rap (and I was very anti-networking well into my twenties) is that it can feel artificial or unearned: "Oh, you got that job because you know Mr. So-and-So." Well, yeah, maybe, but it's not (entirely) like that.

How I Go About Networking
You're under no obligation to do things this way, but perhaps it will help you to think better and differently about making networking work for you.

My primary motivations for building a network are to obtain the knowledge and build the relationships I need to do my job, which is writing products for my customers. That means politely asking around to find out who knows what. Sometimes that person is a front-line employee, sometimes the only person with the information is in the corner office of the administration floor and I have to make an appointment for five minutes of their time. A key to functioning, especially in a large organization or industry, is not necessarily to know everything—though that can happen over time—but to know who does know everything about a particular topic.

Speaking of politeness, regardless of the situation, I make sure to introduce myself in a pleasant manner; explain what I need to know and why; obtain and clarify the answer; and then thank the person providing me the information. If they call or email me, I make sure I respond in a timely manner. I don't just do this when I want something, but every time. These moments of politeness matter because I expect to work with these individuals again. Pleasantness and follow-through have helped me through occasional moments where I "drop the ball." Other people are more likely to be forgiving if they like me and believe I'll recover a situation diligently.

Helping others make connections is another important part of my networking process. It's not just a matter of reaching out to people who have information I need, but sometimes putting those people in touch with each other. Say I know someone who's really smart about "citizen science."[34] I remember that information when I meet someone else who's looking for volunteers to help collect data for a science or engineering project. I don't go out in search of citizen science projects, necessarily, but what I will do is introduce person A to person B if I think that person B knows something that person A needs: "Oh, you need volunteer data collectors? You should talk with Darlene." Et cetera.

If there's a recurring theme to my networking, it's this: I work with my network to help myself (or them) solve problems. I try to learn who knows what and what their interests are so I can call upon those abilities and interests and put the right people on them when the time comes. (I can hear a little voice in my head protesting, "You're just using people!" To which I would politely respond, "I suppose so, but in a work situation, others are welcome to 'use' my knowledge and abilities, too.") Going back to the politeness and follow-up thing, if you're diligent about those practices, you find that people are more

---

[34] See https://scistarter.org/about.

willing to work with you when you ask for help or a favor if you're willing and able to help them solve problems as well.

Notice that up to this point I haven't said one thing about using connections to get a job or a promotion. That comes later (sometimes years later), only after I've demonstrated diligence, politeness, connecting network members to each other, and mutual problem solving on the job.

Personally, I don't enjoy asking for money or a job on my own behalf. However, I am not shy about asking for work. People aren't stupid—they know if you're looking for work it's because you need the pay—but it's sometimes more socially acceptable to ask for and focus on the work. I am passionate about the space business. If I start talking about the work, I'll immediately start diving into the details of what's involved: do you need a report? How long do you expect it to be? Who's the audience? What's your preferred outcome? Do you have a graphic designer? These questions help demonstrate I know what I'm doing and that I'm interested in solving the individual's problem. Sometimes a person I'm talking to is looking for a skill that, quite frankly, I don't have. In that case, I refer them to a peer or company I know that does have those skills. Again, the network helps. If they want to hire me, the money discussion can come after that.

Really, networking can be done on autopilot if you think of it as helping others rather than as work or a chore. You might even have been doing this type of networking without knowing it. It's a matter of being nice to people and being a good worker. That way, in the event someone you know really can help you find work, your reputation will speak for itself.

Networking with Resumes

I once gave a talk on resume writing in which I inverted the thinking on the subject. I suggested that a resume is one of the last pieces of paper you hand over to a potential employer.

Why?

Because it's been my experience that more jobs are acquired through your network than your cold-called resume.

I think the reason I hated networking in my twenties was because of the cynical way it was presented to me: "It's not what you know, it's who you know." That made it sound like the only way you get ahead in life is by making friends with people who have power and influence, and that the only way to make those powerful, influential friends is to suck up to rich people or managers and to use them to get what you want.

Okay, sure, I suppose that's one way to go about it. That was not my style, however. Also, if you're not subtle about the behavior, those rich and powerful people will catch on to what you're doing very quickly.

But really, networking is about a lot more than that. When you're searching for a job, your network equals pretty much everyone you know—preferably those you know well in a professional capacity and who think well of you—and everyone who might know somebody who wants to hire someone with your particular set of skills. When you're trying to find the next job, you need to communicate with the people you know and who know you. You need to be talking about what specific type of work you're seeking.

Why should your resume be the last document you present? It goes something like this...

In a networking situation, someone you know identifies an opportunity for you and provides an introduction to a hiring manager. They open the door for you, having said nice things about you (they do have nice things to say about you, right? Meaning you're a good worker or a pleasant person?). You start the conversation with the employer, which leads to a formal interview. They like you and decide to hire you. The resume then becomes a reminder to them should they need to conduct further interviews or a piece of paper for the HR files. If you've handled everything well up to that point, the resume is almost beside the point.

Your network has opened the door. The rest—from interviewing to actual job performance—is up to you.

Networking Online

At the suggestion of a reader and fellow technical communication consultant Larry Kunz,[35] I thought I'd elaborate a bit on the use of networking to find full-time employment or customers.

In addition to spending a lot of time on the job, many American office workers—and others!—spend a great deal of time online. For instance, the average internet user spends nearly two hours a day interacting in online social networks. Multiply that out and it's approximately 628 hours or 26 days a year swapping jokes, sharing blogs, or posting pictures of cats.

That's a heck of a lot of time. Are you doing anything productive with it? If not, you should.

On the Positive Side...

Professional online networks, from LinkedIn forums to topical blogs and industry news sites, are places where you can contribute to the public conversations (or arguments) regarding your profession or industry. Do you have a unique perspective or insight that can cause one side or another to reconsider their position? You can, over the course of multiple conversations, be considered a respected "voice of authority" on a particular topic or range of topics. And if you don't have any deep thoughts, you can always ask smart questions. You might even find yourself motivated enough to write a blog.

This process of putting your bright thoughts out there helps build your "brand," a.k.a. what people think of you when they hear your name. Odds are, if someone is considering hiring you, they're going to do a little online research to see what they'll find. Wouldn't you like that to be something brilliant?

On the Negative Side...

It's entirely possible you don't spend your free time visiting blogs related to your day job. Perfectly understandable, you might be burned out after a long day of banking, human resources, or whatever. But even if you don't "hang out" where your potential customers or employers do, a lot of your comments are still online, and they can get a good feel for how you behave based on what they see.

---

[35] He writes Leading Technical Writing, a great blog, which can be found at https://larrykunz.wordpress.com

The bottom line is that current and potential employers and customers surf the web, too. And if you're posting online, nothing is private. The only way to avoid people seeing anything is to avoid the internet altogether, and even then other people will still post words and pictures over which you have no control. Good luck with that.

You might not be able to do anything about what other people post about you (though you can do things like untag yourself from photos your friends posted on Facebook). You can do something about the sorts of things you post. That goes a long way toward helping with your "first impression" in the game of online networking.

Philosophers of the Workplace

The future will need technical writers because, among other things, we can act as "philosophers of the internet age."

Before I settled on **Heroic Technical Writing** as the name for the blog and this book, I considered Philosophical Technical Writing due to my interest in the subject, and I see tech writing as a philosophical discipline. It's my goal to be observant of the philosophical context behind the content I write.

Technical communication skills can be applied to activities such as event management, among other lines of work. My experience with **Science Cheerleader** was a case in point. While SciCheer can now boast of more than 300 current and former NFL or NBA cheerleaders with STEM degrees or careers, the organization is still in the growing phase.

For much of 2010 to 2017, it was Darlene Cavalier and me doing everything from marketing and outreach to event and database management. Because the organization and budget started out small, we made up much of our infrastructure as we went along. As a result, I accidentally used or learned a lot of what HR people would call "transferable skills."

Information Design

One key technical communication skill I was able to apply at Science Cheerleader[36] is information organization: anything from creating forms to setting up our original "database" of contacts in Microsoft

---

[36] I retired from the Science Cheerleaders in 2018 once Darlene and I had put in place the tools needed to operate without our continual input.

Excel form. When it came time to bring in a programmer to build an actual database, I got first dibs on describing how it should function and what should be included in it, mostly based on my experiences with the needs of the organization.

Along the way, I also worked on interview templates, event agendas, forms, and blog posts. In each of these cases, the trick was to put information into a useful and usable format so that it could be acted upon later. Usability was important because as we grew, we were building a network of regional coordinators to facilitate and expand upon what we put in place. Therefore, the documents I created and saved needed to be organized, accessible, and easy to modify.

In my more technology-focused writing jobs, I've put together spreadsheets or graphs for anything from tracking competitor products to engineering requirements to sharing performance data. The important common skill used in all of these is putting data into a format that makes sense to the reader.

Writing in Different "Voices"

When I support engineers in my day job, it might not surprise you to learn that I "speak" with a different voice than when I was addressing Science Cheerleaders or their website audience. Engineering writing tends to be more direct and less emotional (unless I'm doing marketing copy, which is a whole different thing).

Cheerleading writing is, well, perky for one thing. Upbeat is another good word. Darlene and I both worked for Disney, so that vibe and attitude carried over to ScienceCheerleader.com and our interactions with the cheerleaders. The tone is upbeat, action-oriented, positive, and supportive ("You can do this! It'll be great!"). This attitude is especially important because the Science Cheerleaders are volunteers when they show up at science-themed events and the like.

The audience for the SciCheer website is primarily girls ages ten and up who are cheerleading and who might or might not have an interest in pursuing a STEM-oriented career. Again, the tone is upbeat and positive, with an eye toward inspiring interest ("This is cool!"). Secondary audiences include the parents of cheerleaders and female scientists who want to see what we're up to.

Understanding What Is Said and How

I learn a great deal about my clients based on the words they use to describe themselves and their work. For example:

- A federal agency will be careful to emphasize its competence, judicious use of taxpayer resources, and careful operating within the law.
- An entrepreneurial company will emphasize newness, excitement, lean-and-mean operations, and flexibility.
- A larger, more established corporation, in addition to whatever its primary culture is, will be more prone to use words that emphasize solidity, trustworthiness, and quality.
- A nonprofit will focus on the importance of its cause, its dedication, and its accomplishments.

Whatever words are used—verbally or in text—constitute the ideals of the organization.

Philosophy as a Career

Technical communication embodies most or all of the philosophical disciplines. Organizing information, in philosophical terms, might be seen as the business form of logic and epistemology, i.e., understanding how to frame and integrate knowledge. Writing in different voices can be seen as a mix of epistemology, ethics, aesthetics, politics, and even metaphysics, as you're shaping words to convey and advance particular ideas about how the world works.

In all these ways, I'd argue, technical communicators serve as practicing philosophers. It is our job to integrate the content (logos), integrity (ethos), and emotions (pathos) of the organization we represent. And if you're supporting all three in a worthy cause, you can enjoy the pleasure of having your work coincide with your beliefs. That's a pretty good way to live.

What Should Students Do to Become a Tech Writer in the Space Business?

You can by reviewing the posts on the "Writing for NASA" page of my blog[37] which covers all my posts on the subject. In this book,

---

[37] https://heroictechwriting.com/writing-for-nasa/

there's also a separate appendix on advice targeted specifically to the would-be space writer.

- More Thoughts for English Majors Who Want to Work for NASA[38]
- Online Mentoring[39]
- What is a "Space Writer," Anyway?[40]

My first post-Disney job was proposal writing for a defense contractor inside the Beltway. That work, plus my volunteer work with the National Space Society gave me the background I needed when I finally applied to a job at Marshall Space Flight Center. If you like space and want to stay in the Washington, DC, area, many of the large aerospace companies have branches nearby, and there's Goddard Space Flight Center in Maryland. Also, there's always NASA Headquarters!

For overall career advancement, I'm probably being a traitor to my fellow English majors, but I'd focus on STEM and take writing as a minor, maybe...definitely take a course in technical writing! I don't speak STEM as well as I should sometimes, and so I find myself having to get smart on a lot of different subjects every time I get a new assignment. Also, it's been my observation that engineers and scientists get paid better than writers, so there's always that. If you've got the talent, interest, and patience to do the math (my big weakness), you'd be foolish to waste that ability. The writing will serve you well in your work communications and you can always write well-informed science fiction or science fact content in your free time.

In addition to the LinkedIn profile, you can see what I'm up to lately by reviewing my Resume page. In the space field, I have a steady journalism gig writing for Spaceflight Insider and I'm also doing some internal communications for Goddard Space Flight Center. My volunteer work has included Science Cheerleader, SciStarter, The Mars Foundation, the Space Frontier Foundation, and the New Worlds Institute.

---

[38] https://heroictechwriting.com/2015/07/16/more-thoughts-for-english-majors-who-want-to-work-at-nasa/
[39] https://heroictechwriting.com/2014/05/02/online-mentoring/
[40] https://heroictechwriting.com/2016/09/01/what-should-you-learn-to-work-in-the-space-business/

My two cents. Best of luck to you!

How Do I Transition from Teaching to Technical Writing?

I'm surprised how many people get tech writing jobs without deliberately trying for it. Don't let a lack of a dedicated degree inhibit you. I got an M.A. because I needed to prove that an English Lit. major could write about aerospace. If you already speak science, you're ahead of me in that respect. You might want to review what sorts of science-related (or process-related) writing you've done up to now that you can show as part of a **portfolio**. Do you blog about science-related topics? That's another way to start **proving** that you can be a technical writer—show 'em your stuff. If you can write, have a portfolio, and a science degree in hand, you're ready to start applying for jobs.

Some jobs might suit you better than others. I don't like doing software documentation, for example. Fortunately, there are a lot of other options out there. For instance, I've written training materials for Nissan in Tennessee, business proposals for a couple of engineering firms, and space-related articles for SpaceflightInsider.com. I'm more of an engineering geek than a science geek, so much of my work is on the engineering side. Most of my work has come through the network of people I worked with when I was a corporate guy (Disney, Department of Defense, NASA). A couple of customers have found me on their own, but my bill-paying work has come from people who already know me as a professional technical writer.

As a starting point, you can reach out through your network to see if anyone you know in the science community needs technical writing work done. Note that I didn't say "a technical writing job." It's a little less daunting if you try to get work as a freelancer—you can just do spot jobs to gain experience on the way toward full-time employment.

If there's a NASA center near you, you can always start by doing a search for full-time "writer" jobs on USAJobs.gov. If you're seeking federal government (civil service) jobs, that's a good site to start. Another place to poke around might be the National Academies (http://www.nasonline.org/about-nas/careers/). A great site for private-sector job searching is Indeed.com.

You might also look into grant writing for science-based organizations and academic institutions. Good grant writers are in short supply and always in demand. If you aren't familiar with grant writing, I think I get some sort of bonus for referring you to **The Grantsmanship Center**, which provides a rather good (though not cheap—around $900) five-day class in grant writing. That will give you the basics, and I found the class useful despite being a ten-year business proposal writer.

All of the above would also apply to editor jobs, though for specialized searches, you might try science-related publications (for example, I think The Planetary Society has a good magazine, **The Planetary Report**—fair warning, though: I have no idea if they're hiring or what they pay).

If you're gung-ho to write for the plant biology field and stick to what you know, you might look for companies that deal with agriculture (your opinion of GMOs might vary) or conservation-related organizations. As far as editing scientific papers, again you might be looking at academic or government science institutions.

One other area you might try is STEM education. I go to a lot of STEM-related events, and I'm constantly amazed at the number of organizations out there to try to get kids interested in science, technology, engineering, and math. Someone has to write their content– why not let it be you?

The last bit of advice I would give is to try to focus on the jobs that fit your background best and that you really want to do. This will allow you to tailor your resume and portfolio to match their needs.

Strategic Planning for the Freelance Technical Writer
I admit I've been winging it on this freelancing thing, for the most part. And by "winging it," I mean that to obtain work, I've tried a variety of things without a concrete plan or work has found me. Generally I've worked with people or industries I know. That's a reasonable and practical way to pursue work, but what if that's not enough? That's when I decided to knuckle down and develop a strategic plan for myself under the assumption that my current network and lines of business will not work forever.

I shared my planning template with a friend and figured, what the heck, my readers might have some use for it, too. I was inspired to write this, in part, after reading Sally Hogshead's How to Fascinate web page,[41] which provides insights on how others see you. I highly encourage you to visit that site as well. Use the following suggested sections as you see fit.

Big Picture

My SWOT: Marketing and business development people like the SWOT (Strengths, Weaknesses, Opportunities, and Threats) quad chart. It's a good starting point for assessing where you or your organization is, business-wise.

For this table, you need to look honestly at how you approach the marketplace with your particular set of skills. Strengths and weaknesses are pretty straightforward. Opportunities are places or industries where you might apply your strengths and skills. Threats are people, other businesses, or situations that might get in the way of you getting the career you want.

Strengths	Weaknesses
1.	1.
2.	2.
3.	3.
Opportunities	Threats
1.	1.
2.	2.
3.	3.

I add value by... List the top three to five things you're good at or *why* you are good at what you do. This is your personal "value proposition," the reason others will hire you over someone else.

I provide the following services... What specific tasks do you perform at your current job? If those tasks are irrelevant to your "dream job," what sorts of things can you do that you would like to get paid

---

[41] www.howtofascinate.com

for? Even better: go wild and conjure up a list of things you'd do for free just because they're fun.

I work best with... This is where you think about your ideal work environment:

- Location (Close to home? Suburbs? City?)
- Company or team size (Big company? Small business? Do you work best alone or with a group?)
- Work content (In what type of industry are you and "your kind of people" working?)
- Operational culture (Are you a neckties-and-dresses kind of person or khakis and gym shoes? How do people behave in your ideal workplace? What does the work location look like? What does your work space look like?)
- People (Highly educated? High energy? "People" people? What do they have in common? What makes them different?)

I will find my ideal job or clients by... If you know where you want to go, then all you need to do is figure out where People Who Want to Hire You will be.

I will obtain a steady (or sufficient) income by pursuing the following strategies/tactics... This was a blurb I added for myself because I'm freelancing. It's the action side of the previous question: "Okay, I know who I want to work for and where I can find them; here's how I'll go about getting their attention."

My elevator pitch will be... This is the very short version of "Why should someone hire me?" Assume you've got to make an impression with someone you want to work with and you meet them in an elevator. You can't freeze up, you have to know what you'll say. Here's mine:

> "I'm a writer that medium to large engineering firms call if they need a lot of new, complex information synthesized quickly and clearly. I'm interested in helping communicate consistently internally and externally across multiple products."

Resources. Website links that provide a starting point for the types of careers, companies, or work you want to pursue.

Is this a full-fledged, business-ready strategic plan? Maybe not, but it's a lot better than winging it, right?

Taking Advantage of Your Opportunities (Entrepreneurship)

Every job is an opportunity. I must have heard this or something like this from my immigrant grandmother and her daughter thousands of times while growing up. The thing is, they were right, and it applies as much to the world of work as it did to household chores.

My mother's favorite question after I'd finished a chore was, "Is that the best you can do?" That's as good a place to start as anywhere. If you're doing your best (with a clear understanding of your customer's or employer's needs or expectations), your work will stand out and be recognized.

Another thing to consider when doing a job is whether you're doing the bare minimum to get by or whether you're going beyond the mere job description. Anything above-and-beyond is adding value to what otherwise might be a thankless, painful, or unpleasant task. Are you doing something better, faster, cheaper, safer, or with more courtesy than others in the same position? When employers are looking for "go-getters," that's the sort of behavior they usually mean.

One other way to increase your value in a position is to grow the job. What this usually means is identifying areas where your skill set could be put to use in new departments, for new customers, or on new tasks that (again) were not in the original job description. This habit of growing your job is especially useful in positions where the employer or customer is not entirely certain what your role is supposed to encompass in the first place.

For example, I was hired as a proposal writer at a medium-size defense contractor in the DC area. They'd never had a tech writer before and weren't entirely certain what to do with me when there weren't proposals to write. My solution during the "down times" was to start walking the hallways or poking through the company website to identify ways to employ my skills usefully. I would start talking to the individual engineering departments to see if they needed any editorial help with their various tasks. In that way, I ended up writing brochures for security systems and technical requirements for military-grade water and petroleum pumps. When proposals started coming in again, my boss found that we needed to hire an additional writer because the

267

company's technical writing demands had increased, and that demand had increased because I went in search of ways to make myself more useful.

So there you have it: if sweet-talking the boss or being on the company cheer squad don't strike you as fun ways to get recognition, you can always try something crazy like improving how you do your job and expanding the scope of what you do. That behavior, in turn, can lead to other opportunities elsewhere that you hadn't anticipated. It's worth a thought, anyway.

What Should You Charge for Your Hourly Rate?

This will either be extremely useful or no help at all. My apologies in advance.

A friend of a friend wanted to know how I go about setting my hourly rate. That I can do. I will not be sharing my own rate here because it varies from client to client and that's not your business unless you plan to hire me. That said, I'll try to lay down some guidelines that might be of use.

Base Your Rate on What You've Made in the Past

In my case, I've had 30 years in the workforce—half of them spent getting paid to write—before I went off on my own. As a result, I knew what full-time employers were willing to pay me. I was also used to budgeting my lifestyle for that rate, so I could use it as a starting point.

Add a Percentage for Benefits

As a contractor/1099 worker, you don't get vacation or health insurance included in your pay. You're not an employee, so you get no benefits. You have to supply those for yourself. And given how much healthcare premiums are going up, you need to make sure you're including money in your rate to cover that. You also might want to retire at some point. Or take a vacation. Those are things you might need to factor into your numbers. The guideline I've used since I started freelancing is my hourly rate as a full-time employee plus 30–35 percent.

Do the Research

Okay, but suppose you're new to this freelancing thing or you're fresh out of college and don't have a salary history upon which to base your rates. In that case, a good place to learn about how to set your rate is by using Salary.com or some other site that allows you to find out what the salary ranges are for your particular role, industry, and experience. Salary.com's primary criteria are job title (e.g., Tech Writer I vs. Tech Writer III), experience or education, and market/city. All of those will be factors in the bell curve of salary ranges. Ideally you want to be in the middle of the curve for your level of experience so that you still have room to grow.

Another good way to figure out what to charge is to look for full-time jobs doing what you want to do on your own and see what an employer is willing to pay for that position.

Be Flexible

My rates fluctuate by client because different customers have different needs, budgets, and expectations. I tend to charge less for nonprofit or small business customers, for example, than I do for commercial or government clients. The latter usually can afford to pay more so you'd be foolish not to pursue those rates. Some employers will negotiate when I suggest a rate. Another thing to consider is that different markets will pay different rates. For example, my standard rate for Huntsville, Alabama, where tech writers are in relatively high demand, is often too high for Orlando, Florida, and too low for Washington, DC. In fact, most of my bill-paying clients are out of state. In any case, again, do your homework.

One thing about government rates: I have a single rate for government customers (NASA, DoD, whomever) because the General Services Administration (GSA)—basically the U.S. Government's in-house procurement department—contracts with business for specific products and services and expects to pay a competitive, consistent rate for a particular type and quality of service. My GSA-style rate was set when I started working for Zero Point Frontiers, and I've more or less stuck with that since then (I did give myself a small "raise" after six years as a freelancer and no one complained).

Be Willing to Negotiate

Whenever I get into a hiring situation and someone is serious about hiring me, eventually they want to know my "number." I've heard it said that whoever gives a number first "loses" the negotiation. I'm not canny enough to play those kind of games, but if you are, you might try asking something like, "I can provide you X level of service and get your product done Y percent better, faster, cheaper with more sprinkles. How much is that worth to you?" and see if you can get them to blink first. One thing I have done is offered up my high-end rate to see if they flinch. If they do, I will probably have to come down on my price. If they take it without question, I end up learning the hard way that I lowballed myself.

Know Your Worth

It doesn't happen very often, but occasionally I'm asked to do work that, quite frankly, will not pay my bills or is a patently lowball offer. Try asking a plumber with 20 years of experience to come over and fix your drain on a Sunday night for $10 per hour. Said plumber will either hang up on you, laugh at you, or both. Tech writers have a useful and necessary skill as well. It is more challenging and requires more skill than a burger-flipper, and they're demanding $15 per hour. Assuming you have the skills to be a technical writer, you can at least look at that as a price too low.

At the same time, there's no need to go overboard. Like I said, if someone flinches at your price, you're either going to have to come down on your rate or walk away if you don't think the employer or customer's offer is worth it. In the end, assuming you can do a good job of putting words together, you should be able to charge, like any other business, whatever the market will bear.

Brand Building

I've had talks with friends about helping me build the "Bart Leahy brand," however I choose to define it. One thing you can do to improve your brand is to share content online that demonstrates your expertise in a particular field. Since 2011, I've focused on demonstrating my competence as a technical writer. That's groovy, but it doesn't necessarily help me demonstrate my worth to my preferred target customers.

My preferred target customers are space people.

To address that gap, I started writing a series of blog entries about the business of human space exploration and made a special tab on my blog (Writing for NASA) that provided links to all of these entries so people interested in seeing what I have to say about the business can tell I know what I'm doing.

The point of all this, of course, is to establish my credentials as some-one who "speaks space." If you have a particular field of expertise, you might want to consider a blog about your industry as well. The point isn't to share proprietary secrets or show that you're the smartest person in the room—after nine years in the space business, I know I am not—but to show that you have knowledge worth sharing.

Let the internet work for you!

Why Do You Need a Marketing Plan?

While it's important to have a strategic business plan as a way to get established as a going concern, it's also im-portant to have a market-ing plan. There are several of them out there, and quite frankly I just looked up "mar-keting plan template" in my  search engine. The model I chose came from Forbes magazine.[42] Here are the primary differences between a business plan and a mar-keting plan:

- A business plan helps you identify what your business does, who your customers are, and how you fit within the market-place.
- A marketing plan helps you identify how you'll make your business known in the marketplace so your self-selected cus-tomers can find you.

Creating a marketing plan is a great exercise for helping you identify the specific, concrete marketing activities you need to do to get your message "out there."

However, using the Forbes model as an example, a marketing plan has seemed insufficient. Somewhere in your business plan and mar-keting plan, you need to know what you're going to say about your services when reaching out to your customers (see also "Creative

---

[42] It's called "Marketing Plan Template: Exactly What to Include," Forbes, Sep-tember 30, 2013, https://www.forbes.com/sites/davelavinsky/2013/09/30/market-ing-plan-template-exactly-what-to-include/#1e71cbea3503.

Briefs" in Chapter 5). In the Forbes marketing plan, Section 3 is titled Unique Selling Proposition. That's as good a place as any to answer some of the following questions:

- What are your unique value propositions?
- Why should customers in your specific market want to hire you?
- How do you talk about your products/services?
- What language will you use in your various marketing outlets (web, business cards, brochures) to fascinate your audience?

The trick is to avoid using a ready-fire-aim methodology, where you start developing marketing materials, elevator pitches, and contact lists without first asking, "Wait, what do I plan to say?" You'd be surprised how often it happens. Take the time to know your answers.

Part VI – Protecting Yourself

Chapter 10: Taking Care of You, Inc.

Whether you're an employee or an independent contractor, you're still a business entity unto yourself, and you need to take care of that entity physically, mentally or emotionally, and financially. I'll focus on things like taking care of your physical and mental health, handling stress on the job, and even planning for retirement. If you don't do these things for yourself, who will?

Health Tips for the Tech Writer

In one of his Peanuts cartoons, Charles M. Schulz has Charlie Brown say, "My mind and my body hate each other." It's a typically Charlie Brown-ish moment, and as a brain-focused non-athlete for most of my life, I related to it for a long time. The problem with this mind-body "argument" is that it really isn't helpful. You don't "have" a body, you are a body, and if you don't take care of your body that mind you use to crank out glorious prose won't be much use to anyone.

All of this came into sharp focus for me in 2014, when I helped my friend Dede (D2) write a class on lifestyle management for obesity patients at Florida Hospital. Without going into exceptional detail, the important overall message of the class was that four major factors play into your physical health: nutrition, exercise, sleep, and stress. If you aren't paying attention to all of them, you're going to end up with an unhealthy body, which leads to an unhealthy mind. D2 and I tried to tie the classes together by cross-feeding the impacts of one factor on the others. For example, if you're under stress, you're probably not sleeping well; lack of sleep can reduce your desire for exercise, and can create metabolic changes that cause you to crave unhealthy foods. The negative feedback loops can start from any one of those four factors.

To use an engineering metaphor, your body is a system, or really a system-of-systems. Something that you're doing (or that's being done to you) in one part of your body will eventually affect the others. As a result of some behaviors such as overloading on soda, smoking, eating a lot of junk food, or not exercising, you can experience several problems that weight gain makes worse, such as diabetes, heart disease, back problems, and even depression.

Again, without reciting the full 13-week class, I'd just like to offer some general thoughts on the four areas of the class that I applied to my own life—perhaps you'll find them useful as you maintain your own system-of-systems.

Nutrition

The best things you can do for your diet are to mind your portion sizes and to reduce your intake of restaurant-prepared and processed foods at home. American restaurants, in particular, have become infamous for expanding their portion sizes beyond all sense of reality. The thing with pro-  cessed foods (most of the shelf-stable things you find "in a box") is that they have a lot of preservatives and not a lot of nutrition in them. You need to focus on eating "natural" foods. And by that I mean vegetables, not processed vegetables; actual chicken, fish, or dairy, not substitutes; and whole grain foods instead of highly processed products like white bread. Focus on the foods on the perimeter of your grocery store—the bakery, produce, meat department—rather than a lot of the long-shelf-life stuff in the aisles.

Exercise

Seriously, do some sort of physical activity that gets you moving. I walk a lot because I've got bad knees, a dislike for gymnasiums, and a lack of grace when it comes to team sports or even riding a bicycle. (Oh, yes: you also need to exercise in conjunction with  eating less and better food, and so forth. Otherwise, you're not going to accomplish a whole lot.) If walking doesn't work for you, try yoga. Or Pilates. Or you can wash your hands of Pilates and try something else. But the most important thing is to get moving—like 30 minutes a day. Once you've started that habit, you can move into more aggressive activities like weightlifting or "cardio" (which is a code word for jumping around and **sweating at speed** for a good stretch). I've also gone to my local YMCA, where they have trainers to help you set goals, suggest exercises that might work for you, and help you set fitness goals.

Sleep

This one surprised me, but in 2014 I started losing energy by mid-afternoon and seriously needed a nap—anything from 20 to 45 minutes or more. A few things were happening, as it turns out, but one of them was sleep apnea, which was brought on by being over-weight and stressed out. Lack

of sleep was also affecting my mood. My shift to better eating and more exercise helped with the weight, and the oh-so-sexy CPAP (Continuous Positive Airway Pressure) machine helped me breathe better while I sleep. Result: no more energy crashes, not as many long naps, and a better mood. Far be it for me to argue with my own body.

Stress

You know better than any-
one what causes stress in
your life. Maybe your work
situation causes you stress,
maybe it's finances or personal matters. In addition to
not being fun, stress, too, can
cause you to gain weight
through a variety of metabolic changes that take too
long to explain here. Whatever situations are causing
you stress, you need to take
action to fix them or recover
from them. In addition to
bringing yourself up from
things that are dragging you
down, it helps to do things
that uplift you and make you

feel relaxed and happy, preferably something that doesn't involve
food or drink. If massage doesn't work for you, maybe a hobby, reading, praying/meditating, or just hanging out with friends or family
(unless they're the ones causing you stress!). Me, I pick up my Annual
Pass and go walking around Walt Disney World. To each your own.

I won't tell you that after taking action on all of the above I am now
an Adonis with six-pack abs (as I told my trainer at the Y, "I'd settle
for a couple of cans"). Quite frankly I think it's an accomplishment
that I no longer finish exercising feeling or looking like I'm going to
die. I've cut out some major junk from my diet (no more Diet Dr.
Pepper or hot wings, alas); made a determined habit of exercising;
found constructive ways to clear stress from my mind; and managed
to get through most of my days without the need to crash for a nap.

And, again, I think the "systems approach" to health is important because it helps me take a balanced approach. It's not just a matter of
going to the gym every day and working out like a crazy man to "fix"
everything. It's a slow, steady, permanent lifestyle change that encompasses what I eat, what I do with my body, how I rest, and how I

relax. In short, it's about taking care of the whole person, mind and body.

Walking Away from the Desk

This is a subset of the health discussion, focused specifically on stress, which is an occupational hazard for many people. The work piles up, deadlines loom, and every new fact or message becomes a potential cause for increased stress or panic. It's not fun.

It might seem obvious that the last thing you should do when a lot of work is screaming for your attention is to take a break. However, that's precisely what I'm suggesting you do. There are still folks out there who smoke cigarettes and take a smoke break. My father was a smoker for more than 50 years, and I know that a lot of times the cigarette helped him calm down. (Never mind the other health risks— I recognized the behavior.) Given that reality, I decided it was perfectly acceptable for me to take a "nonsmoking break," a habit I started when I worked for a smoking boss 20 years ago.

It doesn't have to be 30 minutes away from your desk (your boss might notice that), but five to ten minutes can often be enough. Use the restroom if you have to—that sort of pressure will add to your stress—but then take an extra five minutes and walk down the hall. Visit another floor, step outside, or talk to a friend at the water cooler or on the phone.

The important thing is to get away from your desk for a few minutes. Your brain won't stop processing what's going on, but what will happen is that you're able to get some perspective without the pile of paper or the long list of emails on the screen clamoring for your attention. I gave up feeling guilty about this sort of thing soon after I started it. Just getting the time away from the desk gave me enough of a pause to reset my internal energy and focus on what I needed to do. Another good thing to do during this sort of quick break is to stretch. Odds are, you've locked your body into a tense position, so your arms, legs, and back need a break as well.

The break can be used to talk to a coworker or boss about what you're doing—maybe to commiserate, or maybe just to help you sort out priorities when everything seems like "priority one." And, again, the time away from the work pile enables you to stop focusing on individual trees, take in the forest, and identify what you need to do next.

278

So, again, if you find yourself "chained" to your desk with a heavy workload, pause and walk away. Your body and mind will thank you.

Health Insurance for the Freelance Writer

No one likes to talk about insurance, any more than they like to talk about their ailments. However, both of them are pretty much inevitable at some point. Fair warning: a political comment or two might sneak into this discussion. This is almost inevitable because the U.S. Government has inserted itself into the insurance business. I will keep my criticisms as factual and mild-mannered as I can.

I'll try to answer some basic, no-duh questions, but let me caveat this as strongly as I can: I am not an insurance professional. I am not responsible for any advice taken from this content. If you have serious questions about your insurance, you should talk with your provider.

Why Do We Have Insurance, Anyway?

Why not cut out the middleman (or woman) and just pay doctors directly? The bottom line is that medical doctors' services are highly specialized; the risks if they are wrong are high; and if we run into a serious health problem—anything from massive injury to a life-threatening disease—we as individuals often can't afford to pay for the whole tab. And the bigger the problem, the more expensive the treatment. There are some laws on the books that kind of make insurance necessary (see below). In short: yes, you need health insurance in the event you encounter expensive or catastrophic health issues. I would question the need for health insurance for routine visits, much like I would not expect my car insurer to cover my oil changes, but hey, that's me.

How Does Insurance Work?

Health insurance is a series of bets placed by a company using the premiums of its customers that you or your loved ones won't get sick. If you do get sick, the money pooled from thousands of people, each paying hundreds of dollars per month, is used to help you pay for your doctor bills, medications, bandages, or psychiatric visits. If premiums exceed payouts, the insurance company makes a profit; if payouts due to illness (or accidents or hurricanes) exceed premiums, the insurance company tends to increase premiums on their customers with the highest risk or most expensive plans.

How Do I Get Health Insurance for Myself if I'm a Freelancer?

At the time of this writing, the Affordable Care Act (ACA, a.k.a. Obamacare) is still the law of the land. This was a U.S. Government attempt to ensure that more people would have access to healthcare. In practice, it means the large insurance companies are required to provide subsidized health insurance plans for low-income individuals and families. If you don't qualify for a subsidy (because you make too much money), then odds are you'll be paying more for your monthly premiums as an individual than you would as an employee of a company, where employer-subsidized health benefits are a standard part of a benefits package.[43] Again, as of this writing, you can shop online at Healthcare.gov to see what plans are available in your state, then buy the plan through that site or go to the insurance company whose plan it is and purchase it directly through them.[44] If you decide to live without health insurance, there is a piece of the ACA called the "individual mandate," which basically says that everyone must have insurance or they will be fined. That fine is usually paid out of your income taxes.[45]

You might hope for a pure free-market healthcare industry or a single-payer system to replace what the U.S. has now, but for the moment this is what it is, not what you might like it to be. Sorry.

Setting the Conditions for Workplace Happiness

I read an **article** about "how to be happy at work." One of the points that caught my attention was that some people set very high and specific standards for what will make and keep them happy. If you're a high-powered perfectionist or someone who prefers lots of challenges in your job (I have moments of both, but not all the time), you are restricting the number of times or overall amount of time you can be happy during the day.

---

[43] Editorial note because I cannot stop myself: My insurance premiums have gone up over 100 percent since I started freelancing and ACA has been implemented. I am not a fan, but friends who make less than me sing the praises of the subsidized plans, so it's a matter of perspective, I suppose. Lack of healthcare access is one of the biggest problems and headaches for the freelance contributor. If you find you can't afford to go it alone, find a full-time job with benefits.

[44] I do this because Healthcare.gov had technical issues when it first rolled out.

[45] "No health insurance? See if you'll owe a fee." Healthcare.gov https://www.healthcare.gov/fees/fee-for-not-being-covered/.

Given that, perhaps it's worth stepping back and thinking about why you do what you do. Are you overdoing it? Are you putting too much emphasis on your job? Are you focusing on the right things? This is more or less the thought process I went through after I read the article; then I took the author's suggestion and came up with a list of things I could do during any given day to make sure I'm happy. This list is mine, your interests might differ.

1. Learn something new.
2. Talk (not text, not email) with a close, personal friend or family member.
3. Listen to music.
4. Create something new...fiction, poem, essay, spreadsheet, whatever.
5. Do something good for you.
6. Do something fun for you.
7. Do something constructive in your living space—cleaning, organizing, adding or subtracting something.
8. Think about or expose yourself to something profound.
9. Laugh.
10. Do something good for someone else.

How to Cope with Writer's Block

I've been quite fortunate in my writing career in that I've rarely had writer's block on a paying assignment. Usually, the worst problem I've had while collecting a paycheck has been getting stuck on a **sentence**, and then I get back to it in an hour or so. Writing for myself (say, a novel or this book) has been another matter.

When in Doubt, Ask

On those rare occasions where I needed help getting started, such as when I'm writing a blog or journalism, I suck it up, go back to my customer or manager, and ask, "What do you want me to do with this?" It's not fun to admit that I don't know what's going on, but I'm paid to write, and if I can't come up with anything useful, sometimes I at least need a starting point.

Do Some Reading

I like the fact that reading is part of what I get paid to do, whether it's a book, report, or website. Reading is one of my primary avocations when I'm not working anyway, so getting paid to do it is sort of a bonus. Anyhow, if I'm scouting around for ideas for what to say about my topic, the easiest thing to do is pick up a book or go to a website and start reading about it.

What usually happens as I read is that I get a general notion about what's happening, and then I start asking questions: Why does the process work that way? What happens if X occurs? In short, my writing is formed by what interests me about the topic. I ask my questions, and then I go digging around to see what the answers are. That becomes my "angle" if I'm writing a story.

What Do You Really Think?
Sometimes I have very strong opinions about a topic. That provides me with the energy I need to get the ball rolling. However, if I realize I have a bias, I force myself to work extra hard at writing factually. I also make certain I include a factual, honest interpretation of any opposing viewpoints. The fact that I subtly stack the deck on one side or the other is an issue for my editor: sometimes they let it slide, sometimes they ask, "Have you considered X?" or "You forgot to include Y." Then I go back and add the appropriate level of detail or balance.

Get a Second Opinion
I might not care one bit about a topic. However, I might know someone who does, and I can ask them. "Why is this interesting?" "Why does this matter?" Or even, "What do you think about this?" Once I have an angle, even if it's someone else's angle, I can get rolling. Again, I might not care one way or the other, but it's easier to frame a story with a viewpoint behind it than to share a bland recitation of the facts.

Think about the Structure of What's Going On
Sometimes the very **nature** of a topic—what's happening, how it happens, what it's describing—will determine the type of story or document I need to write. Am I writing about a process? Start with the beginning and move toward the end. Am I describing an object or place? Describe the parts, from largest to smallest (or smallest to largest) or from most to least important, or vice versa. Again, as I noted in Chapter 1, the nature of the thing to be discussed often shapes how I think about it and thus how I write about it.

Read the News

There are times when I'm at a loss for what to write about. That happens on the blog occasionally, though you probably wouldn't know it because I've managed to conjure up so many opinions and bits of advice since 2011. Still, there are days when inspiration doesn't strike. In cases like that, I need to look outside myself and out into the world beyond. Depressing as the news can be, if I'm at a loss for things to write about, I can usually sift through the events of the day and find a technical writing angle to it.

Don't Be Afraid to Play with Ideas

I love writing first drafts. It's like being the first person to make a path through an uncharted wilderness or shaping a lump of clay into a form less messy. The first draft—my first impression—might be completely wrong, but that's okay. I'll try again until the content makes sense to me. It might require writing down a bunch of different impressions or approaches until I find one that makes sense. Once the content is in an order that makes sense to me, the rest is usually just tweaking.

Shifting Gears When Working on Multiple Projects

Whether you're a freelance writer with multiple customers or a staff writer with multiple projects, you might occasionally feel your mental gears grinding as you shift from one project to another. I have a few suggestions for keeping your brain from wearing out.

As I was contemplating this topic, the first thing that came to my mind was (surprise, surprise) a Star Trek episode. In "A Piece of the Action," Captain Kirk, Mr. Spock, and their illustrious crew find themselves on an alien world that has been culturally contaminated by an earlier star-
ship, which left behind a book about the gangs of Chicago in the 1920s. As Kirk and Spock beam down and hijinks ensue, they get into the spirit of things by making off with an antique automobile. The journey doesn't go smoothly, as a 23rd-century starship captain and

his Vulcan first officer jump and lurch through the streets, grinding gears as they go.

That's how it can feel trying to shift from one task to a completely different one with little warning or preparation.

Grinding the Mental Gears

The clutch in any gasoline engine allows you to disengage from your current speed and shift gears to apply the engine's power at whatever speed (gear) you need it to perform. If you try to shift directly from one speed to another on a manual transmission vehicle without engaging the clutch, you'll hear a rather unpleasant crunching sound.

While my description of the mechanical process is undoubtedly leaving out some things (I speak rocket propulsion, not automotive), it's not so different from how your brain can get when rapidly shifting between multiple topics or priorities.

Example: you're hip-deep into writing a conference paper when you're suddenly pulled away from your desk to attend a meeting to take the minutes; oh, and as part of that meeting, you're assigned new work developing a piece of outreach collateral and a speech, each of which is due that week. Oh, yes: and the manager wants the minutes from the meeting back to her as soon as possible. You have just gone from doing one thing to four, and your brain is likely to be a bit overwhelmed.

Putting Yourself in Gear

You return to your desk, where you've got that conference paper document still open on your computer, you've got the minutes from the meeting you just attended to type up now, and you've got two other assignments to think about and prioritize. **What do you do first?**

Disengage the Clutch

The first, best thing you can do, to return to our automotive analogy, is to disengage the clutch. By that I mean that you need to pause, take a breath, and run through your list of newly scrambled priorities before you start doing the next thing. This might mean creating a list of your tasks on paper or in your computer, ranking them by priority, and then determining how much effort each of them is going to require. If everything is a priority, nothing is a priority.

Remember Where You Left Off

If you find that you need to drop the thing you were doing previously and pick up the other three tasks, go back briefly and look at where you left that first assignment. Leave some notes to yourself on where you were in your process so you can get yourself back up to speed when you come back to the task later. Maybe finish the sentence or paragraph you were working on before closing and saving the document.

Keep Your Mind on One Thing at a Time

Once you've gotten your priorities straightened out and the last task in shape, you can (again) pause, shift gears, and move your brain to the first priority on your list to work on. You might be conjuring up ideas for the other items "in the background" while you're doing the one task—that's fine, let your subconscious work on things for a bit—but try to do one thing at a time. I don't know about you, but I can only handle so many tasks at once before I lose track somewhere.

The most important thing you can do for your stress level is to take that pause, disengage the clutch, and give your mental motor a chance to rev up or down for the next task. Like your car, your brain won't wear out as quickly.

Working in "The Little Room"

If you ever take a job doing proposal writing, eventually you will spend some time in The Little
Room. Okay, maybe it's not that little, but there are a few pretty common features of a proposal "war room" regardless of the company or subject matter.

- White boards, bulletin boards, or blank walls for sticking things to the wall, including drafts of the proposal, brainstorming easel-pad sheets, schedules, and other critical data.
- Conference table(s) and chairs.

- Power strips for laptops.
- Legal pads for note taking or scribbling out thoughts, diagrams, or drafts.
- No windows.
- A soda and possibly a snack machine down the hall.

- A technical writer or two flanked by one or more managers or SMEs, who are talking and editing in real time.
- An air of tension because inevitably you are on a deadline.

Given these constraints, it's important to think about the things they don't teach you about in college:

You Need to Maintain Your Energy, Mental and Physical
Sometimes you can get dragged into The Little Room unexpectedly. Are you feeding yourself? Staying well hydrated on a regular basis? These actions are important any day you work, but they become especially critical during moments of high stress, when you'll be expected to respond to multiple demands, multiple changes, and often multiple conversations going on around you—all on a deadline.

You Need to Take Breaks Occasionally
This could be to rest your eyes or relieve your bladder or bowels, but you certainly need the breaks, and if you don't take the breaks, it will eventually interfere with your ability to think and type well.

You Need to Put Your Life on Hold
Okay, this is my choice, not yours. You might have a spouse, significant other, children, pets, friends, or other obligations. You either need to work with them or around them temporarily until your time in The Little Room is complete. I've heard of companies that set up cots in The Little Room until the work is done. I've never gotten to that point, but I have spent some time in the single-digit hours of the morning making last-minute revisions before the doc was scheduled to go to the printer. If you're a full-time proposal writer, how the heck do you find time for a social life, anyway? Okay, I'm kidding, but only

partially…if you have issues with being put into The Little Room even for one day, perhaps the proposal writer's life is not for you.

You Need to Maintain Your Situational Awareness

This includes things like remembering what your deadline is, keeping track of which parts of the proposal still need to be completed, and knowing when you absolutely, positively have to stop typing and submit the document or give it to the graphics person(s) for final layout and printing.

You Need to Have Patience and a Sense of Humor

Stress does funny things to people. Me? My Irish color turns a brighter shade of red, and I talk a little faster. If things get really ugly, I get very quiet and lose my sense of humor entirely. It's not always pretty, and I'm not particularly proud of all that, but if I don't recognize the signs that I'm stressing out, at least my coworkers do. If I start looking particularly stressed, I usually get asked, "Do you need a break?" If someone asks you that, say yes and take the break.

You Need to Remember That Your Time in The Little Room Is Temporary

Management might make crazy demands during proposals, but once the proposal is out the door, they're usually kind enough to give you a break of some sort. I've never worked at a place where I finished a proposal and then was thrown into another Little Room immediately. Even if your job title is proposal writer and you're the only one on staff, you can usually be guaranteed eight hours' rest after a major effort is completed.

So if you want to be (or end up being) a proposal writer, you should be aware of The Little Room, and keep yourself prepared for that day when you spend a lot of "quality time" with your coworkers. It's not just a job, it's an adventure.

Proposal Survival Tips Revisited

Proposal writing is not a sport for the faint-hearted or disorganized writer. For one thing, many times you can get locked into the aforementioned **Little Room** and forced to expend more energy than you normally would interacting with people more often than you would otherwise. This is especially challenging for introverts (I haven't met a lot of extroverted writers, but I'm sure you're out there). Given the amount of work and stress that can go into proposal writing, I thought I'd add a few more "survival tips" for handling proposal season.

Get Things Done Early

One thing that helped my proposal-writing process at Zero Point Frontiers was writing white papers, marketing materials, and other background content on the topic before an RFP ever hit the street. This pre-writing is especially important when you have a new process or widget to sell. If you already know how your process or widget works, you don't have to spend time and mental energy inventing it at the same time that you're trying to respond with a compliant proposal.

Slow Down

This sounds counterintuitive, so let me explain what I mean. Obviously you've got a lot of text to crank out, and you need it done by the deadline. That causes you to speed up your thinking and typing velocity. However, the devil is in the details when it comes to proposal writing. You can miss things easily. You need to take some time to slow down and make certain you have answered the mail, i.e., written a compliant proposal that responds appropriately to the questions the customer wants answered.

Here's another one I've been guilty of due to too much "quick thinking": being discourteous. If we're in a rush, it's very tempting to issue short, clipped orders or responses coworkers don't always appreciate (and which they remember later). Slow down and remember to always take time to say "please" and "thank you" when making requests for information. Also, remember to slow down long enough to explain the how or why behind a request. Just because you're in "proposal heck" doesn't mean everybody else is, and they might not have been living with the content or situation as long as you have.

Obey the Forms

During my single semester of teaching, I made content (following directions) 50 percent of my students' grades because quite frankly that's mostly how I am graded as a professional technical writer. If I don't include everything I'm supposed to in a proposal, that proposal gets bounced before it's even read. If I include things the customer does not want, I can face the noncompliant bucket for a different reason.

Frank Herbert, author of the Dune series, used a phrase in his science fictional world that determined formalized rules for factions fighting each other. This "Great Convention" began every rule with the words, "The forms must be obeyed." In government-speak, this actually means two things: (1) follow the written directions on a proposal, and (2) follow the social or protocol rules when conducting business with your government customers. Some social rules are silly but taken seriously. For instance, I was in one meeting where I was ejected from my chair because a civil servant informed me that chair was "their" seat in the meeting room. Other rules can get you, your company, or the government customer into serious legal trouble. This would be things like trying to get "inside information" from a civil servant on the review board during a proposal blackout period. When in doubt about a course of action, talk to your immediate supervisor or go as far as your company's legal counsel before firing from the hip.

Clarify Roles and Responsibilities Up-Front
This isn't just about who will do what on the work being proposed (the org chart), but something more immediate, like who is responsible for delivering which parts of the proposal while writing it. In a small company, this can be pretty straightforward: it might be you and a couple of other people at most. However, sometimes it's better to create a spreadsheet, list all of the proposal's required boxes, and then assign a name and due date to each of them. I'm also fond of color-coding them as work is completed: green for done, yellow for in-work, red for removed (or "in danger of not being done," use whatever system works for you).

Leave Enough Time for Production at the End
Again, your process could differ, but a good proposal manager has to know exactly when a proposal is due and "back up" into the date to determine when all the content needs to be completed. The content due date is not the same as the proposal due date, which might surprise some people, but is a harsh reality. Regardless of the size of the proposal, time must be allocated for the following minimum reviews:

- Content: Is everything there that's supposed to be there?
- Editorial review: Is everything written correctly?

- Format review: Is everything appearing on the page correctly (font types and sizes, margins, captions, page numbers, headings, headers and footers, logos, graphics)?
- Other proposals, depending on their length and complexity, might require additional reviews or activities:
  - Legal or contractual: Have all of the **certifications and representations** been completed correctly and the proper signatures been obtained? If there is proprietary or sensitive content in the proposal, has it been scrubbed for inclusion, i.e., are you allowed to say that?
  - Graphic design and layout: This becomes especially important if you have a graphics-intensive proposal that requires specialized images to be created (tables, charts, concept art, photos, or drawings). Ideally, include your graphics person or department in the process early so they can start preparing visual content in parallel with writing activities. I know, graphics people: it never happens. But a day's notice is better than dropping it on the artist's desk an hour before it's due.
  - Printing, Production, and Delivery: Despite passing the **Paperwork Reduction Act**[46] in 2000, the U.S. Government occasionally requires companies to deliver multiple hard copies of a proposal, submitted in three-ring binders. Sometimes they even require single-sided printing only! Other proposals require submissions via email, compact disk, or website. Ideally, you're not uploading at the last minute, but if you are (it happens), make sure your email server is working and that you have a draft email ready and proofread so that all you have to do when the final document is ready is attach it and hit send—BEFORE the deadline time. (Oh yeah, and make sure you're sending at the correct time, especially if you're in a different time zone from the receiving office!)

Set Clear Expectations for Subcontractors

Large, multi-party proposals add another layer of complexity to the effort because now you're trying to collect and integrate information from multiple parts of your own organization (over which you have

---

[46] If you're interested: U.S. Code Part 44, §§ 3501–3521.

some authority) and other companies (over which you have practically none). This content might range from technical descriptions of their part of the proposed work to resumes, key personnel bios, past performance narratives, or facility descriptions. As you put together your proposal team, it's better to spell out up-front what you need from subs—length, format, level of detail, images, and other items—so that you aren't facing a self-inflicted hairball as the deadline approaches.

Celebrate the Submission

Notice I didn't say celebrate the victory. There's no guarantee you'll win. When I first started doing proposal writing for pay in 2003, I was told the average win rate on proposals for the Department of Defense was around 50 percent. Proposal writing requires a thick skin. The best time to celebrate is when most of the team is in the neighborhood—at the time of delivery. Thank everyone for their help and patience (even if they didn't offer much of either). Give yourself a little downtime at the end of that day and allow yourself to relax just enough to appreciate the satisfaction of a job completed and well done. If it wasn't well done, well, at least it's done, right?

The deadline-driven nature of proposal writing means that it has a definite rhythm and pressure to it. You either learn to live with it or find a less stressful line of technical writing. However, I can't think of any writing that doesn't have a deadline unless you're writing strictly for fun—at which point how do you know when you're done? I don't mind proposal writing in general, but I'm glad I have the opportunity to do other types of work as well: marketing, brainstorming, engineering documents, strategic planning, and all the rest. And here's the wicked little secret if you're an English major and need a job: good proposal writers are always in demand and the better ones can command excellent, family-feeding salaries. Good luck finding time to write that Great American Novel, though.

Preparing for Retirement

If you're in my college-age target audience, you might not be making much and you probably don't want to think about the R word (Retirement) when your career has barely started yet. However, saving money now is still a good idea. Yet it's about more  than just having cash in the bank. The same low interest rates that make home and car loans more affordable in 2020 also mean your basic savings account or certificate of deposit (CD) is earning around one percent. With the rate of inflation averaging two to three percent, you might as well shove your cash under a mattress for all the good "saving money" will do for you when it comes to retirement. My only firm non-professional's advice on saving and investing for the future is simply this: do it! What follows are some additional points for consideration.

The Magic of Compound Interest

The earlier you start putting your money into a savings account, the longer your money has an opportunity to accumulate. While interest rates are awful right now (see above), banks still offer them as an incentive for you to deposit your money with them. And by deposit I mean opening an interest-bearing account, not placing money in a safe deposit box. The latter is nice but isn't doing anything for you at all. You want your money to work for you, so at the very least you need a savings account of some sort that provides interest—ideally more interest than service charges.

The Speed of Money

In my mind, there are three speeds of money: immediate, near-term, and long-term.

- Immediate money is the money you keep in your checking account to pay bills day to day or week to week.
- Near-term money is your savings account, which covers things like emergencies, slow work periods, large purchases, and vacations. It's still cash and relatively liquid (easily spendable).

- Long-term money is where things get more complicated because there are more options, but that's the money you hold onto until you're ready to stop working…ideally because you want to, not because you have to.

You've got plans for the future, or you wouldn't be going to college, right? What does that future involve: spouse, kids, home, car, travel? All of those cost money. And then there's that whole R-word thing. Eventually you'll need some way to pay the bills when you're not able (or no longer wish) to work. Most of what I'll be sharing in this section will be options for near-term or long-term money in the U.S.

Options

401(k). This is a nice investment option to have, if you can get it (I was in my thirties before I had a job that offered one). A 401(k) is an employer-sponsored investment opportunity that allows you to invest pre-tax money in stocks, mutual funds, gold, or whatever the employer's investment company offers. "Pre-tax" means the money is subtracted from your current paycheck before income taxes are assessed, so you're only taxes on the remaining amount. Taxes are paid a 401(k) once you start withdrawing from the account upon retirement. Employers often offer matching funds up to a certain percentage or dollar amount, meaning whatever you put in, they'll match it up to that amount. Usually there's a range of investment levels you can make, from 1 to 20 percent of your salary, with the employer matching up to X percent (the ones I had usually matched up to 3 percent). The money you put into a 401(k) is invested in a particular type or portfolio of financial instruments, including stocks and bonds for large, medium, small, or international companies, or bonds for municipalities.

401(k)s are useful because you can roll over the amount of money you accumulate from one company's account into another's. However, the exact investments within the account will change if the new employer's 401(k) program is run by a different investment house. What usually happens is that when you get set up in your new employer's 401(k) program, you call up the previous employer's investment house and ask them to close out the account so you can roll it over to the next one. Don't just ask them to close it out and send you a check; otherwise you'll pay a penalty for early withdrawal! You'll incur a big tax penalty (plus some investment house penalties as well) for withdrawing money from or closing the account early, meaning before you turn 65. There are no taxes charged on a rollover. If you had a 401(k) with your previous employer and the new employer doesn't have one, keep the account open—you can continue to contribute to it on your own. The investment house (Merrill Lynch, Edward Jones, or other) is responsible for maintaining the account, not the employer.

Individual Retirement Account (IRA). This is something you can get without an employer sponsoring it. Like a 401(k), the money in the account can be applied to a variety of investment options—stocks, equities, or bonds (more on those later)—and that money is allowed to accumulate until you reach 65 years of age, at which point you have to start withdrawing. Like the 401(k), a traditional IRA is funded with pre-tax dollars and the taxes are paid once you start withdrawing from the account. There's also a Roth IRA, where you put money into the account after taxes so the money is not taxed when you're older. Will taxes be higher or lower when you're 65? Place your bets. Or hedge your bets and open one of each.

Stocks. You can always go to an investment house and purchase stocks individually on your own. Stocks are an opportunity to own a piece of a company. If the company makes a profit, it rewards its investors with dividends. (Note: you will be taxed on these at the end of each year you hold them.) This requires a bit more skill because you have to do the research and guess which stock or stocks will grow in value the most. The trick is to be able to handle a lot of volatility. Some folks do day trading, where they constantly buy and sell stocks on the same day, hoping to make quick profits based on sudden changes in particular stock values. I am not nearly smart enough to do this sort of thing. The one thing I'd advise against is buying only one stock and placing all your faith in that as an investment. The magic word for personal investing is diversification (more on this later).

Mutual Funds. These are large funds that can contain shares in dozens or hundreds of different companies, as well as bonds and other types of investments based on a certain expected rate of return. Mutual funds can be included in an IRA or 401(k) or not. If they aren't part of an IRA or 401(k), you can withdraw money from them without pre-retirement penalties. Like stocks, if you receive dividends or the value of your fund has gone up between purchase and sale—and you'd better hope it does, or you need to change funds—you will have to pay taxes on the sale.

Bonds. There are multiple flavors of bonds, but many of them are the government equivalent of stocks: you're contributing money to a nation, state, or municipality to pay for its operations in return for (usually) a set amount of return. Bonds are considered more stable or reliable investments than stocks because they're backed by a government and you expect to get paid. The higher the rating on the bond (AAA being the best), the more reliable the investment. Of course if they're stable in value, that means they're not growing that much, either.

Other Options. There are something like 100,000 different investment funds out there, focusing on everything from precious metals (platinum, gold, silver) to mutual funds specializing in stocks that meet specific political criteria (e.g., environmentally friendly). If you're seriously interested in what's out there, start reading The Wall Street Journal, Forbes, or CNN Money—and talk to an investment professional. Fair warning: your head might start spinning.

General Advice
Commit to Saving. Start investing for your near-term and long-term savings as soon as it's feasible, and then consider the long-term money untouchable until you really need it or until you're old enough to retire. My preferred near-term cash savings (the "rainy day fund") is equivalent to six or more months' salary. Thanks to part-time work I managed to make my six-month rainy day fund last nine before it finally ran out. The trick—especially for freelancers—is to sock away as much "rainy day" money as you can when you're working to handle stretches when you are not working.

When I can make it work, I try to shoot for saving ten percent of my income for retirement. You might have laughed at that, especially if you're not making much as it is. Note, again, that these are my preferences—your personal situation and capabilities will vary.

Talk to a Professional. I've been as vague as possible here because the only advice I want to offer here is that you should invest for your retirement. How you invest should be up to you. Investment houses have agents who are paid to help people meet their financial goals, usually with an eye toward the long term. Go out and do the research yourself, by all means. You should have some idea of what you're getting yourself into; but there's no shame in talking to a professional investment or financial advisor. And if you're in your thirties or forties (or even fifties!) and still don't have "a plan," it's worth talking to someone about getting one together. As a freelancer I now lack access to an employer-based investment house, so I sought them elsewhere (one nonprofit I found through my church and one for-profit house that was presenting at a neighborhood street fair).

Know Your Risk Posture. This is a big thing for financial advisors to know: how much risk are you willing to accept if the potential reward is also high? Are you willing to lose $X,000 potentially if the eventual gain is 3X the original value? This will affect the types of investments they'll steer you toward acquiring. The young and fearless usually can afford to go for more "aggressive" investments, such as funds that specialize in international markets that might not be as stable or reliable as the U.S. Then again, you might like or want stable growth. You know how much volatility you will put up with, and if the constant peaks and valleys of the stock market make you nervous, well...you know your attitude toward risk, don't you?

Diversify! A financial analyst will tell you this, too. There are different types of investments to meet differing needs: income growth; steady, reliable income; short-term holdings; and long-term holdings. The different options can be used to support near-term or long-term needs. Different investment options offer advantages depending on how much money you have to play with, how close to retirement you are, what the tax burdens are likely to be, and how volatile the markets are. Generally, the closer you get to retirement, the more reliable or stable your investments should be because now you need to depend on that money to pay the bills instead of earning money from a job.

Take Care of Your Family. Most of this content was written with the single person in mind, but the options become more important if you have a spouse or kids. I didn't mention life insurance up to now, but that's worth considering as income replacement for your family if you don't make it to retirement. Also, do you plan to send your kids to college? That will require more liquid, non-retirement assets that you can cash out without a major tax penalty. There are savings accounts called 529 plans, which provide tax benefits to the investor saving money for their child(ren)'s education.[47] Another thing to consider to prevent the state or your relatives from fighting over your assets after your demise is to set up a will or trust with specific instructions about what to do with your money and how to pay for everything.

Another item related to wills that people don't like to think about is a "DNR" or "Do Not Resuscitate" order, which is a signed legal statement that tells doctors taking care of you in a medical emergency not to take extraordinary measure to bring you back from the brink of death. Others will have a statement that asks doctors to take whatever steps necessary to keep you alive, including putting you into a coma until a way can be found to bring you back to regular living. The down side of the DNR is that you might die sooner than you planned; the down side of the latter approach is that long-term medical care for someone in a coma can be expensive and open-ended if the doctors don't know how to bring you out of it.

Wills can even state your wishes—assuming they're financially feasible—for what you want done with your body after your demise: cremation, burial, or other. Morbid? Maybe. However, I had a 20-something friend I worked with at Disney years ago who didn't have a will. Her parents and her late husband's parents fought over where the husband and wife should be buried after the two of them died simultaneously in a car accident. The two ended up buried in different parts of the country. If this matters to you, then address it in your will.

A will is much more important for people who have others (even pets) depending on them. For what it's worth, I set up my will at age 49. Give it some thought, but don't wait too long!

Believe in the Long-Term Health and Growth of the U.S. Economy. This is a piece of advice I picked up from The Millionaire Barber: Everyone's Commonsense Guide to Becoming Financially Independent.[48] Since I was born, there have been five or six big economic

---

[47] Selling stocks or bonds will make you subject to capital gains taxes if the value of those assets increased between the time you invested them and the time you sold/withdrew them.

[48] Written by David Chilton, now in its third edition.

recessions[49] that negatively impacted investments at the time. Recoveries still happen, too. There's an axiom in the investment world that you "buy low, sell high." If you're able to think long-term and you believe the economy can and will recover, you keep buying stocks, funds, or whatever during a recession under the assumption that the current crisis will not last forever. In some ways, we're still reeling from the 2008 housing bubble crash, but the stock market has been at all-time highs. New businesses keep forming but so do government regulations and bureaucracies. Whom do you believe? Investing for the long term still means seeking out assets you believe will have the same or better value in the future because people want and need them. I cannot speak for economies elsewhere, but that sort of optimism keeps the size of the U.S. economy valued at something like $14 trillion. And until the point where I retire, I plan to keep buying. So should you.

---

[49] Okay, maybe six or seven with the COVID-19 shutdown.

Epilogue – Are You Ready to Be a Heroic Technical Writer?

Think you're ready to be a technical writer? If you've read this far, I'm assuming you're at least interested enough to see what other wisdom I might offer in the last few pages. And so, yes, here I will take some time to talk about wisdom and the deeper thoughts that made me get into this line of work, including the philosophical aspects of technical writing and what the future has in store for future technical communicators.

Skill Sets for Freelance Writing

As part of my ongoing quest to meet my readers' expectations (and, as an extra bonus, get content for this book), this section is based on a reader suggestion. Thanks to a reader in Ireland, I'll be covering "What sort of skills you should develop for working alone." This seems like a good thing to cover as the book winds down, so let's dive in!

Working on your own requires a combination of skill sets, behaviors, and attitudes. The skills are more practical items that you might or might not do as an employee for a company or organization. The behaviors and attitudes you either have to cultivate or learn to accept as part of your daily life.

Skills

- **Customer service:** This amounts to meeting your customers' business needs, which includes producing content that matches their needs, format, vision, tone, style, and intentions; delivering content on time and as close to error-free as you can humanly manage; and establishing a sense of good feeling and trust when others work with you.
- **Technical proficiency:** This one seems so obvious, I almost didn't mention it, but you should be (and keep working at being) good at what you do, whether it's writing, editing, researching, formatting, graphic designing, or programming.
- **Calendar management:** Track all of your appointments and, if necessary, due dates to avoid conflicts or missing deadlines.

- **Budgeting:** Know how much you need, how much you have, and how much you're spending, and ideally keep yourself in the positive column.
- **Negotiating:** Have the confidence in your abilities and quality to dispute demands that you lower your rates too much, sacrifice your time unnecessarily, or submit to absurd impositions on how you do your work. Know when to accept a deal and when to walk away.
- **Invoicing:** Track your working hours in a timesheet, spreadsheet, time tracking system, or other mechanism carefully, account for what you've been doing for the customer, and bill honestly and fairly.
- **Networking:** Get and stay in touch with previous, current, and potential customers or friends of potential customers.
- **Marketing:** Create a website, get and carry business cards, have an "elevator speech" ready to explain what sorts of problems you can solve, identify and research your target market.

Behaviors and Attitudes

- **Love what you do:** Work becomes something that can end up doing way more than 40 hours a week, so you'd better like what you do. That'll keep you going on days when other things are going awry.
- **Willingness to accept risk and responsibility:** Understand that you're responsible for your own quality, schedule, pricing, service, and financial solvency; accept responsibility and apologize if you make an error; work expeditiously to rectify that error.
- **Self-starting and determination:** You need to be able to identify what work there is to be done; do it in a sensible order without someone supervising or nagging you; and do it even when you're tired, annoyed, or not certain how.
- **Reputation management, part 1:** Do your best work, protect customer information, follow up on customer instructions or requests, and keep your promises.
- **Reputation management, part 2:** Don't do stupid things that will cause you to lose business. Examples include doing poor-quality work; insulting or otherwise being rude to people you do business with; sharing proprietary information with people

who don't have a need to know it; lying, cheating, or otherwise behaving unethically; complaining about or badmouthing customers on social media (or in person, for that matter); or acting unprofessionally in public (which, again, includes social media).

- **Optimism:** Believe that you can learn what needs to be learned and do what needs to be done to advance your career and keep the bills paid.
- **Politeness and manners:** This is related to reputation management, but really means saying things like "please" and "thank you"; not interrupting conversations without apologizing; paying attention to what someone is saying; apologizing if you have to interrupt a conversation to read a message or take a phone call.
- **Proper communication etiquette:** Be available when you say you're going to be available, answer the phone within three rings, have a businesslike voice mail greeting, answer the phone politely, thank your customer for the call, apologize if you are busy, provide a time when you are available to talk, and then follow up.
- **Develop a support network:** While you might work on your own, you shouldn't be completely isolated, so be certain to have family, friends, partners, and other supporters around to whom you can turn for advice, (occasional) financial help, success celebrations, or the occasional shoulder to cry upon.

The world awaits. Go get 'em, tiger!

Universal Skills

My audience member in Ireland also asked about "Skills or attitudes which transcend trends and time but which can be useful for success in this field." As noted previously, on the skill side, we have practical matters, such as:

- Customer service
- Technical proficiency
- Calendar management
- Budgeting
- Negotiating
- Invoicing

- Networking
- Marketing

Under behaviors and attitudes, the list runs something like this:

- Love what you do
- Willingness to accept risk and responsibility
- Self-starting and determination
- Reputation management (doing good work, refraining from self-sabotage)
- Optimism
- Politeness and manners
- Proper communication etiquette
- Develop a support network

Given all that, are there skills, behaviors, or attitudes that transcend the employee/freelancer divide? Certainly! Regardless of where you go, an effective technical communicator needs to be able to work well on his or her own and with teams. That requires a mix of soft skills, which I covered in Chapter 6. There are also some personal attributes that translate well across multiple environments such as adaptability, a willingness to learn, putting in the time to avoid bad writing, and learning the tools needed to do the job.

In short, because the writer is often such a singular contributor—or, sadly, considered easily dispensable because, after all, "everyone can write, right?"—it's worth taking the time to be the type of worker and person others want working with or for them. Are you pleasant? Productive? Helpful? Flexible? You will, of course, have your own way of doing things and demonstrating these attributes. You're there to produce words that get the job done. How easily those words can be produced often depends on how well you work with others. And quite frankly, that sort of behavior transcends the workplace.

Be a good person. That's the best "universal" advice I can offer.

Do You Need to Be a *Heroic* Technical Writer?

In 2015, I served as a remote (via Skype) guest speaker for an Iowa State University tech writing class to talk about ethics. The discussion also covered a range of other issues, from answering complaint letters to understanding Wikileaks and Edward

Snowden. Ethics inevitably veers into politics because frequently our ethical problems result from how people in power treat those with less of it.

One of the unspoken subtexts I seemed to hear from the students was, "How often do you run into ethically challenging situations in a technical communication environment?" Another way of asking this might be, "How much call is there to be a heroic technical writer?"

The honest answer is: it depends.

Why Do We Need Ethics?

Ethics—guidelines for how humans should behave toward each other to obtain an equitable result—are there for situations when the answer is not obvious. Obvious situations are usually those where you have the freedom to act when asked to contribute to material that you know is designed to harm other people or where you are asked to commit, facilitate, or ignore a crime. Or, alternatively, there are few ethical problems if you are asked to write something truthful about a product or service that is designed to benefit others.

Ethical considerations come up in situations when knowing what to do is not so obvious. The class and I spent a bit of time discussing Edward Snowden's disclosure about the United States' NSA (National Security Agency) surveillance and Wikileaks' sharing of sensitive diplomatic information. People of good and ill intent have provided cogent arguments about whether their actions were ethical or not. My take on Wikileaks (I think the student's question was about Snowden, so I'm correcting what I said here; my bad) is that while shining bright lights on how your country conducts its diplomacy might be a good thing to some, in other cases revealing the information can and did put other people in real **danger, to the point of getting them killed**. So in situations like those, where whole nations are involved in the equation, some thought should be given to the potential negative consequences of revealing the information—or how it is revealed.

That said, the occasions where you're likely to face a world-changing ethical issue are rare. Not impossible, but rare.

Working Ethically in Everyday Situations

My attitude toward issues less grave than national security is still to handle situations as honestly, openly, and clearly as you can within the system you are given. That means keeping the secrets you signed agreements saying you would keep. It also means clearly calling someone on their bad behavior or escalating the issue if they do not provide a good answer or cease and desist. If escalation does not resolve a problem, then move it up the chain of command. If the chain of command won't help and no internal ethics committee exists to address a problem, then you take it outside the company, taking with you all the documentation demonstrating that you made good-faith efforts to resolve the problem in-house.

Here are some of the typical situations that will call for ethical evaluation:

- Keeping or divulging **secrets**
- Obeying or disobeying the rules or authorities
- Taking or refraining from an action that poses potential harm to others

I've had situations where a manager wanted to know what was going on with one of my projects. The project team was, in fact, having heated discussions about some engineering issues, but they wanted the content of the discussions kept within the team. Acknowledging a problem without sharing the content would be an ethical way to handle the situation as long as there was nothing critical happening that could affect the organization in a negative fashion.

Alternatives to Ethical Behavior

It is possible to have an ethical stance that says, "I'm in it only for myself." You might think that you can do whatever you can get away with because you're one small person in a very large, profitable corporation. Your "ethics" in this situation would mean that you value advancing your own career or protecting your own reputation over any other consideration. You can proceed this way, but don't expect to be particularly trusted or well-liked. There are social (karma) costs to thinking this way. If you are perceived to be a devious character, you might find it hard to get or maintain employment. To paraphrase Ayn Rand, you can avoid ethics, but you can't avoid the consequences of lacking ethics.

And really, if you face an ethical dilemma that you feel is beyond your ability to judge clearly, ask the opinions of reputable people you trust—keeping the details to a minimum—or find a lawyer. It's a tricky world. You should do the right thing to the greatest extent possible but not (especially if you yourself are not complicit in any wrongdoing) at the expense of putting yourself into jeopardy. I'm not certain there are life-or-death situations out there in the technical writing field, but if you encounter one, it's still worth trying to do the right thing.

Being a Heroic Technical Writer: What It Really Means
When I first started the Heroic Technical Writing blog, a friend asked me, "Are you wearing a cape while writing?!?" No, not quite.

However, I do take a heroic attitude toward my work. For an excellent articulation of what "the heroic" means in practical or literary terms, I recommend reading Ayn Rand's The Romantic Manifesto, her nonfiction treatise on aesthetics. (Mind you, I'm not a full-blown Rand supporter, but this book really had an impact on me.) My mental shorthand for Rand's romantic take on heroes is simply this: a hero believes that his cause is just and worth fighting for. A hero sees challenges and believes himself brave, strong, intelligent, or capable enough to overcome them.

To tie this back to heroic technical writing, why do we read about or watch movies about heroes? Because we want to see people succeed and we want to think that, if Hero X can do something great or difficult, then so can we. In my day job, that means helping a scientific or technical team communicate a proposal, a success story, or a program so the progress of civilization can continue. If that seems a little hokey or on the egghead side of the thought scale, I'm cool with that. I happen to believe in space exploration as a good in and of itself. I am not an astronaut, engineer, or scientist, but I want the effort to succeed.

As a "heroic" writer, that means giving them my best prose to help those more technically gifted achieve their goals. It means I want to learn what's going on in this world, technically and managerially. It means I will ask a "stupid" or uncomfortable or difficult question if I have a doubt about a course of action because I believe in integrity and want all data in the open. Being a hero means doing a good job, but it means more than that. It means trying to write things I've never written before. It means if my efforts don't succeed, I try again until I get it right. It means pushing myself to keep doing better. And it means working hard for a cause I believe in.

Lastly, as a heroic person, I want to believe that my choices matter, that I am responsible for the actions I perform, and that those actions can result in my outcomes being achieved as well as I can. Those actions could mean writing a proposal, standing up for a friend, achieving my personal and professional goals. I believe this technical-writing life is worth living and that I have it within my power to take the actions necessary to make that happen. That, to me, is heroic living.

It's a good way to live, but no, I don't get to wear a cape.

Appendix

Special Topic: Learning the Space Business

Originally, this book had a much narrower scope and a different title. It was going to be "An English Major at NASA." The goal of that original document was to help people like me get a job in the space business. However, in the end, I decided to broaden the scope of the project to be of service to all aspiring tech writers. Then it got even broader, and I wanted to help students and young professionals operate well in the working world, regardless of career, resulting in the book you've just read.

That said, I still get the most questions from my blog readers on "How do I get your job?" To help those of you interested, I present this appendix. For additional information on this topic, you might want to refer to the "Writing for NASA" page on my blog: https://heroictechwriting.com/writing-for-nasa/.

Between 1997 and 2006, when I was merely a citizen space advocate rather than a space professional, I read a ton of books on the subject. As was my habit, I focused on hardware for getting human beings off of Earth and onto other places in the solar system, both what had already been done as well as what some were envisioning. I was also reading what I could about the politics of space exploration: how it was justified, how it was sustained, and who was doing what.

This reading served several purposes:

- It helped me get familiar with my subject matter in a more-than-science-fictional manner.
- It provided me with a grounding in the underlying sciences that affected the reality of what was being done.
- It allowed me to understand—as far as a guy without serious math or engineering skills—how the technology worked.
- It helped me understand what the "big ideas," the major players, and the primary issues or controversies in the industry were.
- It ensured that I would enter the workplace with a broad historical understanding of the topic, not just the tactical information needed to do a specific job.

Another useful thing all the reading did was help me identify potential topics to write about and—more importantly—possible places or programs for which I could work!

Having worked a number of space-related jobs starting in 2006, in autumn of 2017 I set myself the task of providing my readers an overview of the space business. The following sections are the result of that work.

What Should You Learn to Work in the Space Business?

Before I delve into the industry itself, it's worth taking a moment to contemplate what science and technology disciplines the space industry includes.

Physics

There's no getting around physics in the space business. It includes, as its name implies, the physical behavior of pretty much everything in the universe, including mechanics (how things move), thermodynamics (how objects create or lose heat), electromagnetism (how everything from radio frequencies to x-rays to magnetic fields work), acoustics (how sound waves function), and optics (how light behaves). It also encompasses things like astronomy (the formation, behavior, and death of stars), cosmology (how the universe was formed and operates today), and quantum mechanics (the behavior of the basic materials that make up the universe—like the things that make up atoms).

Physics touches everything, so having at least a working knowledge of the language is a good start toward working with the other sciences. It is quantitative (requiring arithmetic, algebra, trigonometry, calculus, and other forms of calculation) and often sets the standards for purity or rigor in other sciences.

Aerospace Engineering

This targeted form of engineering encompasses a variety of disciplines, including the flight of aircraft (aeronautics), launch vehicles (rockets), and spacecraft (crewed and uncrewed). "Aero" is what I'd call an integrated form of engineering,[50] as it relies on several other

---

[50] For an excellent reference on the systems view of spacecraft engineering, I highly recommend Space Vehicle Design by former NASA Administrator Mike Griffin.

types of other engineering fields as well. Aerospace engineers design hardware that has to account for getting off the ground (thrust and lift) and getting to a specific destination (control) through a hazardous environment and landing in one piece. If the object is an aircraft, it might or might not have people on board, in which case you have to include the ability to sustain a crew and land safely into the design. If the object is a satellite with no crew aboard, the satellite has to stay in a stable orbit for a specific amount of time. If the object is a missile, the payload or warhead has to be intact until it reaches the target and then detonate as designed (no getting around it, rockets began as missiles first).

While aerospace engineers are designing vehicles that do all this, they have to account for the density and motion of the atmosphere (weather); heating (from the sun and friction from the air); environments and vibrations (the former being interactions with the atmosphere and the latter being the physical responses created by the vehicle's own propulsion hardware); propulsion (propellers, jets, ramjets, solid rocket motors, rocket engines); dynamic controls (avionics); system monitoring and controls (computers); and life support. And all of those disciplines are complicated by operations in space, where atmosphere can range from nonexistent with intense radiation to thick, crushing, and poisonous.

Planetary Science (a.k.a. Planetology)

This is another integrated discipline, which encompasses how planets—including our own—are formed and operate as integrated systems. Here on Earth, humans have been studying how our world works for as long as we've been around: trying to understand everything from weather to earthquakes to volcanoes and hurricanes. Mixed in with all those studies are things like physics, chemistry, geology, hydrology, and in Earth's case biology. Now, thanks to our planetary orbiters and landers, we're doing the same types of studies throughout the solar system on everything from Jupiter and Mars to moons and asteroids.

Why do we study these things? Some of it is survival-based: we study weather, plate tectonics, and volcanoes to better understand how our world works and how to survive on it. On other worlds, we're trying to find out how they're different, why they're different, and how what they do affects life here. It's a bit self-centered, to be certain, but for the moment human beings are more or less alone in the universe, so we're trying to figure out where we came from and how to keep going.

Astrophysics/Cosmology

This is our attempt to understand where we (and everything else) came from on a universal scale. Beyond our own sun and solar system is the Milky Way–a spiral of stars a hundred thousand light-years across and comprising anything from 100 billion to 300 billion other stars (depending on what you read). And beyond the Milky Way is our local group of galaxies, a trillion other galaxies, combined with quasars, black holes, and other astronomical phenomena we're only beginning to discover. It's a big universe out there, so big you can get a little dizzy trying to imagine how massive it truly is. Still, as humans, we ask questions: what's in it? What is it all made of? What is it doing? Does any of it pose a danger to us? And while it's not really an astrophysical question, we can still use our observations of the nonliving universe to determine if the conditions for life exist elsewhere in space.

Life Support Systems

While we're busy making our own world challenging to live in down here, we're also trying to figure out how to set up artificial habitats that would enable us to survive long-term out beyond this planet. Humanity's longest-lasting experiment in that regard has been the International Space Station, which has been occupied continuously since the year 2000. Still, it's difficult to call that a permanent outpost, as there have been (at this writing) over 60 different crews living and working up there at any given time. The longest any single person has lived in space at one stretch is 437 days. What does it take to keep people alive and healthy in space or on another planet longer than that? We're still learning. We know the basics we need to survive here: water, air, food, clothing, and shelter. To those items we've learned to add exercise (at least if someone living in microgravity wants to walk around without ill effects when they return to Earth) and mental health.

All of this is very different from having people settle in space permanently on a space station, on the Moon, or on Mars. To do that, we will have to send people there to find out. Living on other worlds will challenge and expand what it means to be human. Lessons learned "out there" change how we determine who we are and what's necessary for life back here on Earth. Even more challenging lessons lie ahead if we ever hope to make human habitats beyond Earth self-sufficient and independent. All of these activities are adventures in technology as well as human endurance, psychology, sociology, and yes, eventually politics.

Why Study All This?

The nifty part about studying or working in space is that they amount to a philosophical activity. It forces us to confront a largely unknown universe, determine how we fit into it, or how we might make ourselves able to live in it. Extending the abode of life beyond Earth permanently is beyond our current abilities, but it is an effort (in my estimation) worth pursuing. Given a few billion years, our sun is supposed to expand into a red giant, so we'll need to be somewhere else eventually or stay home and roast. Okay, so maybe that isn't a problem for the 2020s...but developing defenses against the giant rocks flying around our solar system could become an issue at any time.

The study of space, how to travel into and through it, and how to survive there long term are some of the challenges that human space ventures will tackle in the coming decades and centuries. As a technical communicator, the best thing you can do if you want to be a part of it is to get yourself acquainted with as much of the various studies as you think you can handle and then dive deeply into the topics that really interest you. The odds are good that you can find writing that needs to be done and can get paid to keep the journey going forward.

So You Want My Job?

As more thoughts came to me about advice for English majors who want to work as a space writer, I realized that it takes a lot of effort just to get smart about the space business—the technology, business, and politics of it all.

Below is a list of the various resources I've absorbed over the years to "get smart" about writing in general and writing for the space business specifically. It's a mix of books on writing, space fiction, space opinion, science, and other bits. One last sub-list comprises the journalistic or blog resources I consult to keep up on current news in the business. These sources should not be considered comprehensive, but merely a good introduction to some of the primary issues, political points of view, and even paradigms space people use as part of their shared cultural shorthand. And if you don't have a lot of time to read, I've flagged which resource on each list I'd recommend you read first if you only have time for one.

I hope this information is useful to you. The bottom line, as I discovered through a long and slow learning process, is that if you want to work in any line of work, you have to demonstrate you're passionate about it and that you have taken the time to learn about it. It's probably wrong that I enjoy my job as much as I do, but hey, there are worse things I could be writing, right?

Stuff to Read

On Writing

Writing Science Fiction and Fantasy by Analog and Isaac Asimov's Science Fiction Magazine

From Dawn to Decadence: 500 Years of Western Cultural Life, 1500 to the Present by Jacques Barzun

Zen in the Art of Writing by Ray Bradbury

The Artist's Way by Julia Cameron

How to Write Fantasy and Science Fiction by Orson Scott Card

World-Building by Stephen L. Gillett

On Writing by Stephen King

Time Travel: A Writer's Guide to the Real Science of Plausible Time Travel by Paul Nahin

The Romantic Manifesto by Ayn Rand

Aliens and Alien Societies by Stanley Schmidt and Ben Bova

Style: 10 Lessons in Clarity and Grace by Robert Williams[51]

On Space (Nonfiction)

Stages to Saturn: A Technological History of the Apollo/Saturn Launch Vehicles by Roger Bilstein

The Lunar Base Handbook edited by Peter Eckart

Architecture for Astronauts: An Activity-Based Approach by Sandra Hauplik-Meusberger

Homesteading Space: The Skylab Story by David Hitt, Owen Garriott, and Joe Kerwin

---

[51] If you read only one book on this list, it should be this one.

Mining the Sky by John L. Lewis[52]
The Starflight Handbook: A Pioneer's Guide to Interstellar
Travel by Eugene Mallove and Gregory Matloff
Paradise Regained by Gregory Matloff, C Bangs, and Les Johnson
The High Frontier: Human Colonies in Space by Gerard K. O'Neill
Packing for Mars: The Curious Science of Life in the Void by Mary
Roach
Space Politics and Policy: An Evolutionary Perspective by Eligar
Sadeh
Blogging the Moon by Paul Spudis
The Case for Mars by Robert Zubrin
Entering Space: Creating a Spacefaring Civilization by Robert
Zubrin

On Space (Fiction)
Welcome to Moonbase by Ben Bova
2001: A Space Odyssey by Arthur C. Clarke
2010: Odyssey Two by Arthur C. Clarke
The Fountains of Paradise by Arthur C. Clarke
Rendezvous with Rama by Arthur C. Clarke
Medea: Harlan's World edited by Harlan Ellison
The Forever War by Joe Haldeman
The Man Who Sold the Moon/Orphans of the Sky by Robert A.
Heinlein
The Past Through Tomorrow by Robert A. Heinlein
Going Interstellar edited by Les Johnson and Jack McDevitt
Ringworld by Larry Niven
Green Mars by Kim Stanley Robinson
Red Mars by Kim Stanley Robinson[53]
The Right Stuff by Tom Wolfe

---

[52] There are a lot of amazing books on this list, but again, if you have time to read only one, I'd make it Mining the Sky because it envisions a civilization and economy that encompasses the entire solar system and so is great for a "big picture" view of the future.
[53] Red Mars has a solid mix of technology, characterization, "sense of wonder," and overall literary quality, even if I disagree with it half the time.

How to Live on Mars: A Trusty Guidebook to Surviving and Thriving on the Red Planet by Robert Zubrin

On Science/Technology
Books:
The Discoverers by Daniel Boorstin
Abundance: The Future is Better Than You Think by Peter Diamandis
A Brief History of Time by Stephen Hawking
Science Matters: Achieving Scientific Literacy by Robert M. Hazen and James Trefil[54]
Out of This World: The New Field of Space Architecture edited by A. Scott Howe and Brent Sherwood
Hyperspace: A Scientific Odyssey Through Parallel Universes, Time Warps, and the 10th Dimension by Michio Kaku
The Singularity is Near: When Humans Transcend Biology by Ray Kurzweil
Future Shock by Alvin Toffler
N-Space by Larry Niven
Playgrounds of the Mind by Larry Niven
Cosmos by Carl Sagan

Videos/CDs/Classes:
Engineering an Empire: The Complete Series[55]
Joy of Science
Understanding the World's Greatest Structures: Science and Innovation from Antiquity to Modernity

Current Periodicals/Blogs
Aviation Week and Space Technology
Space.com

---

[54] This book is the must-read choice for this list because it covers the broad landscape of science in general.
[55] My favorite on this list by a long margin, if only to watch Peter Weller talk about history.

Spaceflight Insider[56]
Space News
The Space Review
TMRO.tv

---

[56] While this site has changed owners, I appreciate its intent, which is to share happenings in space with a non-expert audience (full disclosure: I wrote for them for a couple of years).

Acronyms

What, you thought you'd get away from a tech writing book without seeing an acronym list? Not so fast. Note that not all of these are defined in the text because I figured that most of them are common enough (e.g., CEO) not to require explanation. However, in the interests of thoroughness, they are included here.

a.k.a.	Also Known As
ACA	Affordable Care Act
ADDIE	Analysis, Design, Development, Implementation, and Evaluation
AI	Artificial Intelligence
AIAA	American Institute of Aeronautics and Astronautics
ASAP	As Soon As Possible
B.A.	Bachelor of Arts (degree)
B.S.	Bachelor of Science degree
B2B	Business to Business
bc:	Blind Copy
BD	Business Development
BS	Bovine Scatology
C.V.	Curriculum Vitae
CAD	Computer-Aided Design
cc:	Carbon Copy
CD	Certificate of Deposit
CD	Compact Disc
CE	Chief Engineer
CEO	Chief Executive Officer
CGI	Computer Generated Imagery
COFR	Certification of Flight Readiness
CONOPS	Concept of Operations
CPAF	Cost Plus Award Fee
CPAP	Continuous Positive Airway Pressure
CPFF	Cost Plus Fixed Fee
CPIF	Cost Plus Incentive Fee
CRM	Customer Relationship Management
CUI	Controlled Unclassified Information
DC	District of Columbia
DNR	Do Not Resuscitate
DoD	Department of Defense
DVD	Digital Versatile Disk

DVR	Digital Video Recorder
EAL	Eastern Airlines
EAP	Employee Assistance Program
FAR	Federal Acquisition Regulations
FBI	Federal Bureau of Investigation
FBO	FedBizOpps, Federal Business Opportunities
FFP	Firm Fixed Price
FL	Florida
GCR	Galactic Cosmic Ray
GMO	Genetically Modified Organism
GSA	General Services Administration
HBCU	Historically Black Colleges and Universities
HQ	Headquarters
HR	Human Resources
HTML	Hypertext Markup Language
ID/IQ	Indefinite Delivery/Indefinite Quantity
IEEE	Institute of Electric and Electronic Engineers
iOS	Apple's operating system language
IRA	Individual Retirement Account
IRAD	Internal Research and Development
ISD	Instructional Systems Design
ISDC	International Space Development Program
IT	Information Technology
ITAR	International Traffic in Arms Regulations
J&A	Justification and Approval
JANNAF	Joint Army-Navy-NASA-Air Force (conference)
JOFOC	Justification for Other than Full and Open Competition
M&IE	Miscellaneous and Incidental Expenses
M.A.	Master of Arts (degree)
MB	Megabyte(s)
MOOC	Massive Open Online Course
MPAA	Motion Picture Association of America
MS	Microsoft
MSFC	Marshall Space Flight Center
N/A	Not Available
NAICS	North American Industry Classification System
NASA	National Aeronautics and Space Administration
NASCAR	National Association for Stock Car Auto Racing
NBA	National Basketball Association
NDA	Nondisclosure Agreement
NFL	National Football League

NIAC	NASA Institute for Advanced Concepts
NSA	National Security Agency
NSFW	Not Safe for Work
ODC	Other Direct Cost
OOH	Occupational Outlook Handbook
OSTP	Office of Science & Technology Policy
P.P.S.	Post-Postscript
P.S.	Postscript
PBAN	Polybutadiene Acrylonitrile
PC	Personal Computer
Ph.D.	Doctorate of Philosophy (degree)
PM	Project Manager
PPT	PowerPoint
PUG	Payload User Guide
Q&A	Question and Answer
RFI	Request for Information
RFP	Request for Proposal
RSRB	Reusable Solid Rocket Booster
RSS	Really Simple Syndication
RTFM	Read the Frickin' Manual (other, less polite versions of this acronym exist)
SBA	Small Business Administration
SBIR	Small Business Innovation Research
SEMP	Systems Engineering Management Plan
SEO	Search Engine Optimization
SF	Science Fiction or Speculative Fiction
SLS	Space Launch System
SMART	Specific, Measurable, Achievable, Relevant, and Timely
SME	Subject Matter Expert
SOP	Standard Operating Procedure
STC	Society for Technical Communication
STE	Special Test Equipment
STEM	Science, Technology, Engineering, and Math
STTR	Small Business Technology Transfer
SVO	Subject-Verb-Object
SWOT	Strengths, Weaknesses, Opportunities, Threats
T&M	Time and Materials
TIM	Technical Interchange Meeting
TRL	Technology Readiness Level
TV	Television
U.S.	United States

UCF	University of Central Florida
UK	United Kingdom
URL	Uniform Resource Locator
USA	United States of America
USB	Universal Serial Bus
VPN	Virtual Private Network
WIIFM	What's In It For Me
XHTML	Extended Hypertext Markup Language
XML	Extensible Markup Language
YMCA	Young Mens Christian Association
ZIP	Zone Improvement Plan

Printed in Great Britain
by Amazon